Center Stage

A Curriculum for the Performing Arts

Kindergarten / Grade One
Grade Two
Grade Three

Center Stage Contributing Writer:

Fleda Evans
Drama Educator
California State University, San Jose

Center Stage Consultants:

Paul Blumenthal
Special Education Consultant
School District of Philadelphia

Leora Chwalow
Early Childhood Consultant
Solomon Schechter Day School
Bala-Cynwyd, Pennsylvania

Polly Erion
Drama Specialist
Mill Valley, California

Crystal Tilton Olson, Ed.D.
Director of Curriculum and Instructional Services,
Sacramento, California, County Office of Education;
Award, California's Outstanding Art Supervisor

Center Stage Reviewers:

Jackie Erceg
Art Specialist
Tracy School District
Tracy, California

Barbara Ivy
Primary Teacher
Denton, Texas

Center Stage

A Curriculum for the Performing Arts

Wayne D. Cook

Contributing Writer
Fleda Evans

Kindergarten / Grade One
Grade Two
Grade Three

Dale Seymour Publications

Managing Editor: Diane Silver
Product Manager: Bev Dana
Project Editor: Lois Fowkes
Production/Manufacturing Manager: Janet Yearian
Production/Manufacturing Coordinator: Barbara Atmore
Design Manager: Jeff Kelly
Cover design: Rachel Gage
Illustrations: Rachel Gage
Text design: Jeff Kelly

Acknowledgments: page 57: "Who Has Seen the Wind," by Christina Georgina Rossetti, is from *Sing-Song,* Macmillan Publishing Company, 1924; page 108: "Swift Things Are Beautiful," from *Away Goes Sally* by Elizabeth Coatsworth, is reprinted with permission of Macmillan Publishing Company, copyright 1934 by Macmillan Publishing Company, renewed 1962 by Elizabeth Coatsworth Beston.

Story scripts for "The Stonecutter," "The Bremen Town Musicians," "The Deer and the Tortoise," and "The Poor Turkey Girl" are from *Story Chest: Treasured Tales from Many Lands,* by Steve Osborn; Addison-Wesley Publishing Company, 1992. The story script "The Rainbow Goblins" is from *The Rainbow Goblins* by Ul De Rico. Copyright © 1978 Thames and Hudson. Reprinted by permission of Thames and Hudson.

Grades K–3
Order number DS31155
ISBN 0-86651-574-7

3 4 5 6 7 8 9 10–ML–00 99 98

This Book is Printed
on Recycled Paper

Contents

About the Author

Wayne Darby Cook had his first professional theatre experience while serving in the military, at which time he decided to pursue a career in the theatre. Mr. Cook received his B.A. in Theatre from Point Park College in Pittsburgh, Pennsylvania, and subsequently studied drama with Brian Way at the Theatre Centre in London. It was at the Centre that he was awakened to the potential power of creative dramatics, and directed his efforts to working with students and teachers.

Mr. Cook has been a drama instructor at the Theatre Centre in London; California State University, Long Beach and Penn State University; and drama consultant for the Pennsylvania Department of Education. He has worked with students of all ages, from preschoolers to teachers in training. Mr. Cook has worked with inner-city students, students at risk, and prison inmates. He has written drama curriculum for the Glendale and Chula Vista school districts in California, the California Visual and Performing Arts State Framework, and the Academy of Visual and Performing Arts at UCLA.

Mr. Cook was creator and host of a weekly television program for young adults and has had numerous television, film, and stage roles. He continues to act professionally, and performs in a one-man show, dramatizing the poetry of Langston Hughes.

Mr. Cook is currently the Program Administrator for the Artists in Schools program of the California Arts Council in Sacramento.

Dear Teachers . . .

It is my passionate belief that the arts, and in particular drama/theatre, change people's lives! I've seen it happen! I've seen it with preschoolers discovering the world around them and the wonderful world inside them. I've seen it with elementary school children who become involved in class for the first time, or who speak for the first time with confidence and respond positively rather than negatively to school.

I've seen it with the so-called delinquent teenager who through drama discovers a talent and interest, and therefore a sense of self-worth never before experienced. I've seen it with prison inmates while working as an artist in our correctional facilities. Some of these inmates will never leave the system, yet they develop a new awareness of themselves and begin to take responsibility for their lives. Some of them have told me that if they had had the opportunity to experience the arts in their younger lives, they might have made different choices and might have avoided the correctional system altogether.

I find the trends in education—the ways of attempting to find out how and what to teach children—fascinating. My experience as an actor and drama specialist working within the educational community has been varied, to say the least. I can remember earlier in my career working for the Pennsylvania Department of Education as a drama consultant. My task was to travel around the state presenting workshops on the power of drama techniques and how drama could be used in the classroom. The approach at that time was not so much teaching drama as a discrete discipline, but rather using drama to teach other subjects.

I can remember standing in front of a group of administrators and teachers at workshops and challenging everyone there with the statement that drama could do just about anything in the classroom. No subject was off limits; I could use drama in science, social studies, math, and language arts.

To test my assertion, teachers presented problems in specific subject areas. On the spot, I described a drama experience that could achieve the stated learning goal, or at least enhance the skills necessary for knowing and under-standing the particular subject area.

What I didn't understand at that time was that the way I was using drama to teach other subject areas is the very essence of what drama is all about, and in fact is one of the reasons I am in this art form. Drama incorporates problem solving, creativity, and the ability to use old information in new ways. New perspectives are discovered, and in the discovery process, holistic thinking is increased. These are indeed the skills employed by artists in this art form.

Drama and education are inseparable. All of the skills that drama/theatre techniques utilize are inherent in human knowledge and experience. When I work with classroom teachers, I now begin with what teachers already know naturally about drama. They are already skilled in instructing 30 or more children at once. They can stimulate 30 minds; they can present an interesting environment in which to grow; they can give children the skills to make connections to their identities as individuals; and they present information in a way that helps children understand the correlation between mere information and the ways in which this information will affect their lives.

Drama experiences do not exist apart from other experiences, nor are they experiences that only a few gifted children have. Drama is what we, as adults and children, involve ourselves in every single day of our lives. Drama is the journey, not the destination. Drama/theatre offers you the world in your classroom, an opportunity for both you and your students to solve real problems and challenges. This curriculum can be the beginning of your exploration into that world.

Start to evaluate the drama that you already do in your classroom. I'm sure you will realize that the technique you use to heighten perception about a concept is indeed a skill that is part of drama/theatre. Only you can begin to make such connections in the classroom, and you can use this curriculum as your guide.

An important resource to this curriculum is the artist living in your community. Local artists provide a link between community and school—a way to motivate and inspire children and adults alike in the processes of drama/theatre. With a true collaboration between the educational and artistic communities, you will succeed in preparing literate, sensitive, and creative problem solvers to effectively lead all of us into and beyond the year 2000.

I applaud the work that you have already done in the education of our youth, and I hope that *Center Stage* will inspire you to include drama in that education. As you involve your students in these activities and have questions, look to that playful part of your own heart and soul for answers. The search can be as interesting and delightful as knowing the direct path we must go.

Within each of us there is a song, a rhythm, a speech or a movement that has roots from which to grow and expand. Children love to move; they love to imagine; they love to pretend to be different people, animals, or objects. What they need is someone to provide a safe environment for that growth to occur. Drama/theatre is a wonderful way for children to experience their worlds, both real and imagined. The challenge is yours.

Sincerely,

Wayne D. Cook

Preface

Drama curriculum is not about creating professional actors, although the experience may spark those who have the calling. A drama curriculum is about life, about preparing students to think responsibly and creatively, which in turn will affect their quality of life. Drama gives students the opportunity to experiment with life from many perspectives, to challenge old assumptions and beliefs, and to look at a problem through many eyes. Drama gives students the confidence to reach out, and it prepares them to make better decisions.

Each student brings his or her own life's experiences to the creative dramatics process. Drama connects students to their environment, to each other as human beings, and to themselves. Drama excites. It motivates! It teaches the joy of learning and the joy in discovery. It teaches ways to solve problems which can be enlightening and liberating as each individual contributes to the solution.

The art discipline of drama/theatre includes a wide range of activities and experiences geared toward developing the individual skills of the child. It also provides opportunities for the acquisition of knowledge that represents the heritage of drama/theatre, both past and present.

Drama/theatre is an art form. The unique value of the theatre experience is that it involves students as active rather than passive learners. Through experiences in drama/theatre, the students will be able to:

- Experience success and the joy of discovery.
- Develop the "self." Students will learn to discover, express, and accept themselves.
- Learn to communicate effectively.
- Solve problems inventively in both real and imagined situations.
- Learn from society, past and present, drawing from the rich contributions of multicultural groups that make up the American heritage.
- Use critical and creative skills.
- Understand drama/theatre as an art form.
- Approach other art forms with insight.

The most important single factor in the use of drama in the classroom is the teacher. For drama/theatre to flourish in basic education, the teacher must believe that creative dramatics works, and must consciously create the time and provide the resources for drama/theatre activities to happen in the classroom.

Introduction

PROGRAM DESCRIPTION

Center Stage is a complete, discipline-based drama/theatre curriculum in two books, one for grades K–3, the other for grades 4–6. The materials contained here cover the primary grades, and consist of lessons for three grade levels (K–1, 2, 3) with story scripts, resources, and other information for the teacher. Each grade level contains 30 lessons, which build sequentially within and across the grade levels to provide a continuum of activities and experiences that foster individual growth and development. *Center Stage* also provides strategies to include the arts in other content areas and practical suggestions about time, resources, commitment, and class management styles.

PROBLEM SOLVING

In every lesson of *Center Stage* students work on problem solving, either individually or cooperatively. Many lessons within *Center Stage* involve observing, communicating, comparing, and categorizing not only to better understand dramatic concepts, but also to understand oneself and one's relation to the world.

Part of the problem-solving process is the dramatization itself. A good director of a play expects his or her actors to experiment with their roles. Even though the form or structure of the play remains basically the same, the actors bring something new and different to each rehearsal. By experimenting with characterizations, moods, vocal delivery, and ways of moving, the actor brings life to the playwright's words and intentions.

It is the same for students involved in creative dramatics; although the content and structure of a session need to be established, students find solutions through the freedom of using their creative energies within specific boundaries.

CREATIVE DRAMATICS

The particular form of drama/theatre activity used throughout *Center Stage* is creative dramatics. Creative dramatics is drama for the players, not the audience. A student begins with what he or she knows, and using imagination, experiments with that knowledge to create something new and to gain more knowledge. Through creative dramatics, *Center Stage* gives students this opportunity to experiment. Creative dramatics can be extended to formal play performance, but the emphasis in this curriculum is on the development of the individual—the process rather than the product. The culmination of a creative dramatics activity in *Center Stage* is a sharing of a story, poem, or movement, allowing students to realize the results of the problem-solving process in which they were involved.

INTEGRATING DRAMA WITH OTHER CONTENT AREAS

Education has moved towards a more holistic approach to the child. Many educators no longer concentrate on each content area separately, but focus on the total curriculum, realizing that all parts must fit together as a balanced whole. They also teach to the differences in children, using the cognitive and affective curriculum to meet the needs of kinesthetic, visual, and auditory learners.

In both science and the arts, students use critical thinking skills to observe, compare, order, and categorize the sights, sounds, and movements in the world around them. Certain scientific topics, such as light, sound, and perception, are particularly appropriate areas to integrate with the arts.

Both the social studies and the drama curriculums place much emphasis upon the ideas, values, and beliefs of many people from many lands who have contributed to a vast body of knowledge. Students should recognize that literature and art reflect the inner life of a culture. To support this learning, *Center Stage* introduces stories, fables, and fairy tales that incorporate conflict and raise value issues that are both interesting and age-appropriate.

Drama and language arts are obviously interrelated. Oral language skills are integral to the process of drama. Children learn to move, to understand relations of movement to non-verbal communication, and then to speak. A continuous sequence of skill development in language arts is the body and soul of drama/theatre. Students' experiences in role-playing, leadership, and decision making—for example, when they plan classroom publications cooperatively, dramatize reactions to a novel, or engage in formal speaking situations—provide models for comparable roles in their lives.

In both mathematics and the arts, students learn how to analyze problems and select strategies. Some strategies that carry over from drama to math include:
- Making a model
- Drawing a picture
- Organizing information in table or chart
- Finding a simpler related problem
- Acting out the situation
- Restating the problem
- Looking for patterns
- Guessing and checking the result
- Working backwards

In both mathematics and drama, it is important that students feel free to take risks, and that they see that there are many ways to arrive at the "right" answer

In *Center Stage,* Connections activities demonstrate how drama activities can enhance another subject. These activities can act as a springboard for th integration of drama into the content areas.

A MULTICULTURAL CURRICULUM

Arts education is a superb vehicle for creating a bridge across cultures to foster mutual understanding and tolerance. Many lessons in *Center Stage* draw upon the wide variety of literature available to students that is representational of the diverse world community in which we live. As the world becomes smaller through technology, the importance of using literature that includes all people in all lands becomes greater. Through drama/theatre, students compare stories from different cultures, put themselves in others' shoes, and begin to understand how all of us in the world community can learn from each other.

In teaching a multicultural curriculum, it is important to go beyond the first step of learning about cultural holidays and historical figures to infusing every area of the curriculum with exploration and comparison of the similarities and differences of the peoples of the world. Lessons in *Center Stage* stress the value of diversity, and introduce historical, critical, and aesthetic issues.

It is also important to recognize and draw upon the strengths of the diversity of cultures within the classroom. Lessons in *Center Stage* are open-ended with the multicultural classroom in mind, precisely so that each teacher can adapt the activities to the wide range of backgrounds in his or her particular class.

ORGANIZA-TION

Each grade level, identified by an on-page tab, begins with an overview of the subjects covered, along with the table of contents. Each lesson, throughout the six grade levels of *Center Stage,* is organized in the following manner: the planning section, which consists of the Component, the Subject, the Objective, Materials, and special notes; the body of the lesson, which is divided into Warm Up, Explore, Develop, and Evaluate sections; and additional information, which contains Connections (to other content areas), specific suggestions for Special Needs children, and Resources.

COMPONENT

Lessons in *Center Stage* are organized by the four components in a discipline-based arts curriculum: Aesthetic Perception, Creative Expression, Historical and Cultural, and Aesthetic Valuing. The purpose of the lessons within each of these four components is as follows:

Aesthetic Perception   These lessons guide students in developing a fuller awareness of the nuances of light, color, sound, movement, and composition. Heightened perception sensitizes the individual to the world and provides a stimulus for imagination and creativity. Aesthetic awareness also enables students to comprehend and respond to the elements of an object or event and to express and appreciate it in greater depth.

Creative Expression   These lessons give students the opportunity to originate, create, perform, and interpret drama/theatre activities. Direct personal involvement is necessary for understanding the structure and language of drama/theatre. Creative expression enables students to know themselves and to appreciate one another's uniqueness.

Historical and Cultural   In these lessons, students develop a broad base for understanding artists, their works, their evolution, and their effects on society in the past and present. Learning the importance of drama/theatre activities to various cultures, past and present, helps students gain appreciation and understanding of these cultures and of their own heritage.

Aesthetic Valuing   These lessons enrich the student's awareness and response to beauty in art. To develop aesthetic values, students study the sensory, intellectual, emotional, and philosophical bases for understanding drama/theatre and increase their ability to make judgments about art works. Students develop criteria for arriving at personal judgments.

SUBJECT

This heading identifies at a glance one of the nine subject areas upon which each lesson is built.

Subject areas in *Center Stage* include:

Sensory and Emotional Awareness   Creative dramatics increases students' visual, aural, tactile, and kinesthetic perception of their environment. This ability to perceive is basic to creative expression and aesthetic appreciation. Lessons concentrate on the use of the five senses, emotions, and sensations—real or imagined.

Rhythm and Movement Movement is the external expression of an internal idea, intention, or feeling. Activities in rhythm and movement develop cooperation and cohesiveness as a group. Movement is an essential element of drama and a basis for all physical communication.

Pantomime Nonverbal communication of an action, an activity, a mood, a feeling, or an idea offers students practice in self-expression, thus developing their ability to communicate through an intricate language of symbolic and individualized gestures.

Oral Communication The voice is an instrument for the expression of meaning and feeling, whether in speech or nonverbal sound. In practicing vocal skills, students also learn receptive, or listening skills.

Storytelling Storytelling is a special form of oral communication, the oral tradition of passing stories on from one generation to another.

Improvisation Improvisation is the creative, cooperative, and spontaneous dramatic response to rapidly changing and unanticipated dramatic stimuli. A creative problem is presented with no preconception of how it will be solved, thereby permitting everything in the environment (animate or inanimate) to serve the experience.

Characterization Exercises in characterization are geared towards the development of real people on stage under imaginary circumstances. The focus is on ways of moving, talking, and feeling that are unique to a particular individual.

Playmaking Lessons in playmaking center around an original story improvisation. The story may be a real-life situation or an imagined one. The improvised story is carefully structured and planned, played, evaluated, and replayed, with no formal audience.

Technical Elements Scenery, lighting, props, costumes, makeup, and sound are all part of drama/theatre. Although many of these technical subjects are not studied in depth, they are important in an overall understanding of drama/theatre.

OBJECTIVE

For each lesson a statement of a specific goal relates directly to the subject area and to the four major components of Aesthetic Perception, Creative Expression, Historical and Cultural, and Aesthetic Valuing. The objectives are sequential in nature and focus on the creation of original dramatic and visual art, the discussion of aesthetics of art, and the investigation and appreciation of the historical and cultural contributions of our multi-ethnic community.

MATERIALS

Each lesson lists supplies and materials that may be needed. These include visual arts materials, informational resources, and community resources. Because many lessons are built around a specific piece of literature, that source is also identified. However, this selection is only a suggestion; other sources may also be effective.

WARM UP

The Warm Up is a three-to-five-minute activity. It can be used as a self-contained lesson—if the purpose is simply to introduce a few dramatic concepts—or it can function as an introduction to a comprehensive creative drama lesson. This format allows effective ways to communicate complicated and abstract ideas to students as well as introducing them to the various skills used in drama/theatre, such as listening and vocalization, concentration, improvisation, and movement. The Warm Up activity is designed to lead the students directly into Explore.

EXPLORE

Explore gives students a chance to try out some of the ideas they have developed during Warm Up. The activity here often involves some creative drama experimentation as well as discussion. Warm Up and Explore together will take about 15 minutes.

DEVELOP

Develop gives students a chance to convey through body movement and language the ideas and concepts presented. Students may work in groups or individually. The entire lesson, from Warm Up through Develop, will run approximately 45 minutes. Develop fully explores the objective listed by giving students the opportunity to try out their own ideas in discussion and dramatization. It is a sustained activity that often involves risk-taking and cooperation, and active participation by all the students.

EVALUATE

Student evaluation *Center Stage* offers questions for student discussion and/or suggestions for an evaluation activity, such as writing or drawing. The evaluation reflects the objective of the lesson and allows students to participate in their own growth.

Teacher observation In general, questions are presented for teachers to consider while students are involved in an activity. These questions also reflect the objective of the lesson and are guidelines to key behaviors that should be observed.

CONNECTIONS

Specific activities are offered that relate the concepts, skills, and techniques used in drama/theatre to the mathematics, science, social studies, language arts, and other arts curriculums.

SPECIAL NEEDS

When appropriate, specific ways to involve students with special needs are suggested. (General guidelines for working with special needs students are discussed further on pages xxi–xxii.)

RESOURCES

Resources provide both classroom materials and references that help involve students in story development. Resources also include particular recordings and videotapes that help create a mood or motivate movement activities. To provide background in drama/theatre and historical perspectives, materials are listed for the teacher's reference, as well.

TEACHING CENTER STAGE

KINDERGARTEN/FIRST GRADE

In the primary level of *Center Stage*, the lessons for kindergarten and first grade are combined under Grade 1. It is intended that the lessons offered at first grade also be taught at kindergarten—with this important difference: because of kindergartners' shorter attention span and less developed capabilities, they will complete only the Warm Up and Explore sections of each lesson, which could run only 15 minutes. At first grade it is expected that students will be able to go on and complete the Develop section—thus expanding the lesson to 45 minutes.

Of course, if a kindergarten class is capable of sustaining attention for a longer period, the teacher should go on to appropriate parts of the Develop section. Repeating these lessons at first grade will only serve to reinforce concepts, and because students will be bringing with them more advanced thinking skills, the discussions and activities themselves will become more sophisticated.

Many of the experiences in the Develop section are designed for individual and group problem solving. Kindergartners may not be ready to work independently or in small groups, so you may want to hold discussions in a whole-class format.

The Evaluate section almost always relates to the total 45-minute lesson, and so will not apply to the shorter kindergarten lesson. The objective for each lesson is fully met only by completing the Develop section. The kindergarten teacher should still assess students' learning through observation, however, and students themselves can evaluate their learning in a brief, informal way, even if the teacher only asks a question or two to provide closure.

LESSONS

Each teacher must approach drama/theatre activities from the place where he or she is most comfortable and confident. With *Center Stage* as a resource, that confidence should grow. The material in this guide serves as a solid basis from which to begin a program of drama in the classroom. As you gain experience, make notes on what is particularly successful for you. Feel free to add to or delete from the lessons according to your own style and your students' abilities.

Some of the later lessons at each grade level involve review and extension of skills taught earlier, so ideally the lessons should not be taught out of order. It is certainly acceptable to present a lesson out of order to meet specific needs, but realize that you may have to introduce or review a dramatic concept for a more complete understanding by your students.

The materials or books listed in a particular lesson are not the only ones that will work. Others with which you are more familiar may be substituted. Use the source listed and the accompanying techniques as a model for involving the students creatively and dramatically through literature.

Before teaching a lesson, go over it in your mind's eye. Try to visualize the amount of time each segment of the lesson will take. Such analysis will help in having a well-paced lesson with interesting and smooth transitions from one activity to another. Avoid delays by having all the materials needed for an activity organized before the lesson. One of the easiest ways to lose the interest of the students is to allow them to stand or sit idly while you gather materials. Be prepared.

Each lesson in *Center Stage* is cumulative—the Warm Up section leads directly into Explore, and Warm Up and Explore provide the impetus for Develop, the activity session. The entire lesson takes approximately 45 minutes. For kindergartners, or teachers who are just beginning to experiment with drama in the classroom, or students with limited attention spans, the lesson may be ended after Warm Up or Explore. Keep focused on the lesson objective, even if you are using this shorter form of the lesson. If you are only teaching Warm Up and Explore, be sure to provide closure by asking students one or two questions to review what they have been discussing.

The culmination of each Develop activity in *Center Stage* is the sharing of a story, poem, or movement. Sharing does not mean that students passively watch others (although they could), but rather that they actively participate in the results of the process with which they were involved. Following the creative session, a few minutes should always be devoted to evaluating what has been accomplished. Bring students back together if they have been working in groups, and ask open-ended questions in a positive, nonthreatening, and constructive manner. By reflecting upon and internalizing the experience, students' sensibilities and perceptions about their experience will be heightened.

Keep your instruction simple, focused, and open-ended, so that students can discover the joy of learning by doing. Their creative thinking skills will be strengthened, and you will have the reward of enthusiasm and intellectual curiosity from your students.

ASSESSMENT

Student Evaluation   Assessment is an important part of arts education. Part of the evaluative process in drama involves sharing the ideas students have worked out. In the beginning stages of drama/theatre, students should be given the choice of whether or not they want to share their story, scene, or improvisation with the entire class. No pressure should be placed upon them to share, since the process rather than the end product, should be emphasized. As students become more confident in what they do, sharing becomes a natural extension of group activity.

With younger students a discussion about the activity is sufficient. However, during discussion, insist that students avoid such statements as: "Group number one was the best," or "I liked Joe's story the best." Focus the discussion on the students' involvement, their ability to work together, and elements of the activity that were successful, or that should be changed next time. Ask such questions as, "What did you like about the ending of the story?" "Was there a particular movement that helped you know what that character was feeling?" or "What new ideas for your own story did you get from seeing this scene acted out?" Possible questions are included in each lesson.

When discussing a student's opinion about a scene or story, always ask, "Why did you like the story or scene? What happened in the story or scene that gave you the feeling that you liked it?"

Have students interact during evaluation. One group may discuss its improvisation, story, or exercise with another group. The discussion should be positive. There is no room for negative evaluation at this stage in the drama process.

Teacher Observation   Educators must be accountable for what students learn. Recently, educators have praised teacher observation as an effective way to assess the learning process in school arts programs.

Through observation, the teacher has the advantage of seeing the growth of each student. The teacher can evaluate whether students are actively involved and whether they use problem-solving skills to create dramatic art. The teacher can evaluate the students' confidence level as they approach the arts, and how students' growth in the arts translates into growth in other subject areas.

Through observation, the teacher can determine the direction an activity should take or how long an activity should continue. For example, if students have a high unfocused energy level when entering the room, beginning with a low-key, focused activity would be in order.

For each lesson of *Center Stage*, questions are provided for the teacher to consider during and after the lesson. If many of the answers to these questions are negative, the presentation of the activity should be reviewed. Perhaps directions were not clear enough. Perhaps an abstract concept was not sufficiently discussed for students to proceed with an activity. Perhaps ground rules were not carefully laid out, or perhaps the activity itself was too long or too advanced for the students. Lessons should be carefully analyzed and revised accordingly, and if necessary, repeated in a modified form.

SPECIAL NEEDS

Center Stage is a curriculum for the mainstream classroom. Recognizing, however, that special needs students are often mainstreamed, many lessons in *Center Stage* include specific suggestions for adapting a particular activity for this audience. Students are given appropriate yet challenging opportunities for creative expression—e.g., learning impaired students experience sequencing, the visually impaired experiment with body movement, and hearing impaired students participate in a rhythm activity through feeling vibrations.

The general suggestions that follow will help you work with the particular special needs students in your classroom.

Mentally Impaired   The less able a mentally impaired student is, the more difficult it is for her or him to understand the abstract. Therefore, adapt activities so that they are as concrete as possible. Repeat directions often, and have the students physically move through the directions to understand them better.

Learning Impaired   Many of the *Center Stage* lessons provide opportunities for success for learning impaired students as they become physically involved in the full range of activities—music, expressive movement, pantomime, and the re-creation of stories. Be prepared to offer help with organization, as well as to rephrase a concept or instruction, show a physical example, or present the concept from a different angle.

Physically Impaired   Encourage the physically impaired to participate as fully as they can in lessons involving movement. Partial movement should be accepted according to each student's abilities. Challenge these pupils to find effective and safe ways to express themselves in movement lessons.

Socially and Emotionally Impaired   With socially and emotionally impaired students, use the emotions of story and play characters to explore and work with the emotions and feelings of students themselves. Sensitivity to others, to animals, and to the environment, as well as good working relationships in a group can also be developed through drama activities.

Hearing Impaired   The hearing impaired use many modes of communication, including sign language, electronic voice amplification, writing, and lip reading. Learn and use the method that is most successful with your students. Many of the activities involving music can be used with these pupils, as they compensate for their hearing loss to some degree by feeling the music's vibrations through their chairs and the floor. However, when necessary and feasible, use visual stimuli in place of auditory stimuli to achieve the stated objective.

Visually Impaired   An important fact to recognize in working with visually impaired individuals is that only a minority are "totally blind." The range of severity of visual impairment is wide: some students can perceive objects, while others may be limited to color perception or light and shadow only.

Adapt the lessons according to the needs of your individual students. Obtain audiotapes, Braille, and large print materials from local agencies and libraries for the visually impaired; have a visually impaired student work with a helpful classmate; substitute tactile (mosaic, sculpture, relief paintings, or maps) and auditory stimuli for visual stimuli.

Many visually impaired individuals lack experience with radical changes of their bodies in space. Most of the movement activities can benefit them in this area.

Having special needs students in a mainstream classroom provides unique opportunities for the mainstreamed students as well as the special needs students for learning from each other and developing respect and social responsibility. Be patient, sensible, and flexible as you adapt the *Center Stage* program to the abilities of your special needs students, and work toward the goal of the fullest participation possible for *all* students.

TEACHING TIPS

CHOOSING DRAMA/THEATRE MATERIALS

As you become more comfortable with the models in this curriculum, you may want to select your own materials for creative dramatics, either to provide variety, or to suit the specific needs of your students. Keep the following suggestions and criteria in mind as you make your selections.

Ideas The simplest way to begin creative dramatics is with a single idea. How an elephant moves, what a wave looks like, what it feels like when one sees a birthday cake are all examples of ideas for creative dramatics. Moving from the dramatization of an idea to the dramatization of a series of ideas to form a story is an easy step.

Stories A story chosen for creative dramatics must be suited to the age and taste of the students. It must challenge them, but not be too difficult to dramatize. It must meet special literary and dramatic standards: The plot must be simple, logical, and full of action with not too many incidents. The characters and their dialogue must seem natural and believable. The story must have emotional appeal, a strong climax, or turning point, and a quick and satisfying ending.

Most stories contain a conflict between good and evil, and students should be led to distinguish between right and wrong. However, refrain from overt moralizing or stating ethical truths. Children want to see cause and effect and judge for themselves, and the influence of the story is far greater if they are allowed to do so.

Historical Events   Historical events can be used for creative dramatics. An imaginary story may be developed around the event if necessary to add strong dramatic appeal, a strong climax, or a quick and satisfying ending.

Poetry   Poetry, when used for creative dramatization, should be simple and clear to the students. Students should be able to understand what the poem is about and to share in the feeling behind the words. The poem should contain words that are rich in sensory and associative meaning, and the subject matter should give new and everyday experiences importance and richer meaning. When a poem is chosen for rhythmic interpretation, it should have a good rhythm and a compatibility of sound and subject. If chosen to develop a mood, a poem should contain ideas that lead students to a deeper understanding of the emotion expressed. If a poem is chosen for its story content, it must meet the requirements of a good story for dramatization.

Music   If music is used with creative dramatics, it should entertain students and hold their interest; it should be musically suitable to their age group; it should stimulate creative activity; and it should provide a satisfactory emotional and educational experience at the students' own level of development.

Although a leader provides the dramatic material, the students, with their own ideas, determine how the material should be developed and dramatized. Every individual has innate creative abilities. If these are encouraged they will grow; if they are suppressed and discouraged, they disappear. A warm and trusting relationship between teacher and students allows students to freely express their ideas and lose their self-consciousness.

RULES AND LIMITS FOR CREATIVE DRAMATICS

Limits and structure can give students a sense of security as they explore creatively within the structure. For activities, develop the limits with genuine concern for students' safety and comfort. When students are new to creative dramatics, set simple, understandable rules. Say, for example:

"The first rule about drama is that we never, ever laugh at one another. We can laugh *with* one another if something is funny, but we never laugh *at* one another.

"The second rule about drama is that whenever I say, 'Freeze,' you must freeze. That means your mouth as well as your body.

"The third rule is that any kind of violence—tripping, pushing, pulling—will stop the drama activity immediately."

Give students room to imagine and create, but if rules are broken, stop the drama experience. Usually students enjoy the drama experience so much that peer pressure on any offenders will cause them to abide by the rules.

GROUPING

Once the concepts are introduced and students have been given guidelines, they can work on their own or in groups to complete a task. The objective of having students work in groups to solve problems should be developing the spirit of cooperation and collaborative skills. These skills must be practiced, however, and such practice often results in loud, sometimes messy, and seemingly disorganized classroom behavior. Nonetheless, resolving disagreement is a worthwhile goal, and the process will become smoother as students find ways to work out differences of opinion.

Drama/theatre activities naturally lend themselves to group work, but each teacher must determine whether his or her class is ready for this responsibility. Activities should be teacher led at first, and directions should always be clear and complete.

To determine whether your class is ready for group work, assign a group lesson, and observe group dynamics. Ask yourself these questions:

- Are individuals or groups actively working on the creative problem to be solved or are they looking or wandering around the room?
- Are they constantly asking for help?
- Can the group choose characters or focus their attention without arguing or bickering?

Usually a group that is ready for this responsibility will quickly assemble and begin the process of discussion, casting, and rehearsing. However, if the class does not seem to be ready, go through the process with one group of students to provide modeling for the others.

BREAKING INTO GROUPS

There are creative and effective ways of grouping and pairing students so that they gain the fullest benefit of the lesson. Consider whether your students should work in pairs, small groups, or as a whole group. When breaking the class into large and small groups, consider the following procedures:

- Count off by fours or fives to create equal groups.
- Count off by pairs: A and B, or one and two.
- Send a boy and girl pair to each of several designated spots in the room.
- Give the class a math problem on dividing the entire class into equal groups of, say, four each.
- Use the alphabetical order of first or last names to create groups.
- Use other categories; for example, children who have younger brothers; children who have specific pets; children who are wearing blue socks or red shirts.
- Allow the class to divide themselves into four or five equal groups. (This process requires a rather mature and experienced class.)

CLASSROOM ENVIRONMENT

Creating a special mood when the students are entering the classroom will heighten their anticipation and interest about what is going to happen. In the classroom setting, the mood can contribute to the success of a lesson. For example, if the lesson focuses on stories that take place in different environments, the teacher might play *Close Encounters of the Third Kind* or another mysterious musical recording; he or she might also close the blinds. Then the teacher could begin the lesson in a whisper, to stimulate students' imaginations about different environments.

Many drama activities can be done in the classroom even while students are in their seats. However, an open space is an ideal location. Either clear a space within your classroom or secure the auditorium or multipurpose room for the creative drama activity. Make sure that whatever space is used is relatively free from obstruction and safe for all students, including those with special needs.

Introduction to Grade One

The sequence of the lessons in Grade 1 is cumulative. Students are brought step by step from awareness of selves—sensory, emotional, and kinesthetic awareness—to communicating those elements to their peers through simple improvisations based on their own imaginations and on selected resource materials.

Lessons at the Grade 1 level offer experiences in:
- an awareness of the senses and their relationship to the creative process;
- a perception of rhythm and movement as the external expression of an inner idea or feeling;
- the use of the voice as an instrument of communication, both in speech and nonverbal sound;
- spontaneous and creative responses to problem-solving situations;
- an awareness of students' own cultural heritage and the heritage of other cultures.

The uniqueness of the lessons in Grade 1 involves the student's discovery of self. As the child explores the senses, body language, and speech patterns, he or she begins to develop a sense of who he or she is in relation to the larger world. The activities in movement, rhythm, and sensory awareness are the cornerstones on which to build other drama/theatre activities.

Especially because these lessons are to be used with both kindergartners and first graders, students will bring to creative dramatics differing degrees of sophistication, and will learn at different rates. However, opportunities for success at many levels abound. Repeating lessons will reinforce students' understanding of the basic concepts.

Contents of Grade One

GRADES K-1

LESSON ONE

Exploring the Sense of Touch

COMPONENT   Aesthetic Perception

SUBJECT   Tactile Awareness

OBJECTIVE   Students increase their sensory aware-
                ness and perception by touching objects
                and defining their qualities.

MATERIALS   A collection of objects of distinctive
                sizes, shapes, and textures, such as a
                rock, an orange, popcorn, a feather, a
                sea shell, a tennis ball, and a rubber
                band (avoid sharp or prickly objects);
                drawing materials

WARM UP   Invite students to close their eyes and touch the surface of the desks or
                tables, their hair, their cheeks. Ask how they can tell the differences in the
                things they feel. Are the shapes different? Do the outsides feel different?
                Are the temperatures the same? What about the size and weight? Ask
                students to describe the things they felt. Encourage a wide variety of
                descriptions, such as "bristly," "soft, like kitten fur," "slippery, like ice."
                Establish a focus by telling students, "We are going to find out how the
                sense of touch is important in our everyday lives." Ask, "What if we
                couldn't feel? For instance, suppose you put your hand on a hot burner
                on the stove. If you didn't have your sense of touch, what would happen?"

EXPLORE   Sit with your students in a circle. Tell students that you are going to pass
                around a number of small objects of different sizes, shapes, and textures
                (see list of materials). Invite students to look at each thing being passed
                around, then close their eyes and feel it. Ask, "Is it hard or soft, round or
                square, smooth or rough, heavy or light?" Give each student a chance to
                hold and examine each object. Encourage students to describe briefly the
                weight, size, shape, and texture of each object. Again, develop oral lan-
                guage skills by encouraging the use of different adjectives to describe the
                objects. Ask students to compare each object with other objects.

DEVELOP   Ask the students to close their eyes and imagine a specific object—for
                example, a kitten, a baseball, a leaf, an ice cube, a fork, a beanbag. Sug-
                gest that students "hold" the imaginary object in their hands, and think of

how it feels in terms of temperature, shape, texture, and weight. Repeat the exercise with a different "object." At this point, ask various students to describe the objects they imagined. (*Note:* Since this is a beginning exercise, perhaps not all the students will respond. Don't pressure students; as confidence grows, so will the response. Give everyone an opportunity to describe the imaginary object. Then let students draw a chosen object.

EVALUATE

Student evaluation: Ask the students which objects were easiest to identify by touch. Was it because of familiarity? If they were unable to identify some of the objects when their eyes were closed, what was the reason? Ask the students if their fingers and hands moved when they touched imaginary objects. See whether students can think of instances in their own lives in which they might encounter both the real and imagined objects. Ask the students how touching an object as well as seeing it helped to describe it better.

Teacher observation: Were the students interested in others' descriptions of the objects? Did the students grow in awareness of the differences in size, shape, texture, weight, and temperature? Did the students' ability to identify objects by touch seem to increase by the conclusion of the lesson? Were the students encouraged to feel free to communicate their discoveries and reactions?

CONNECTIONS

Mathematics: Connecting sensory awareness with three-dimensional geometric shapes such as cubes, cylinders, triangular prisms, cones, and pyramids could be an extension of the initial drama lesson. Let students touch and feel objects placed in a bag or box. Then they can communicate, compare, and categorize the three-dimensional shapes. Two-dimensional geometric shapes (circles, squares, triangles) may also be identified by touch. The shapes may be grouped for counting or for creating geometric patterns.

RESOURCES

Aliki. *My Five Senses.* (rev. ed.) Crowell Junior Books, 1989.

Broekel, Ray. *Your Five Senses.* Children's Press, 1984.

Parramón, J.M. et al. *Five Senses (Touch).* Barron's Educational Series, Inc., First U.S. edition, 1985.

Exploring the Sense of Sight

COMPONENT	Aesthetic Perception
SUBJECT	Sight
OBJECTIVE	Students increase their awareness of the importance of the sense of sight in identifying objects.
MATERIALS	About ten small objects found in the classroom, such as a pencil, piece of chalk, sheet of paper, eraser, marble, crayon

Note: As part of the Develop section of this lesson, you may want to take students on a tour of the school grounds. Prearrange for volunteers (parents, aides, or other adults) to assist in supervising students on the tour.

WARM UP

Suggest that students close their eyes and picture in their minds a specific object, for instance, a new red crayon. Ask a few students to describe it, using the information learned in Lesson 1 (shape, size, texture, weight). Define *color* as a quality that is seen only. Ask the students to define *red*. (Note that the descriptions will be comparisons with other colors, or with other objects of the same color.) Ask what would happen if we could not see to pick up the crayon. How could we know to pick up the right color? If there are visually impaired students in the classroom who would feel comfortable sharing how they cope with such problems, you might ask them to do so.

EXPLORE

Ask students to use their sense of sight to identify two or three objects in the room that have different colors, sizes, shapes, and textures. Encourage them to describe and compare the objects.

DEVELOP

Place four or five different objects on a table in front of the students. Allow them to observe the objects for about 30 seconds. Then cover or remove the objects and ask students to describe them and the positions they were in. For example, ask, "Where was the yellow pencil?" (between the blue marble and the red crayon) Rearrange the objects and repeat the activity two or three times to build observation skills. Give students the task of finding objects in the classroom different from the materials already shown, such as something that is very large, rectangular, and shiny, or something that is round with a rough texture. Ask for volunteers to describe something in the classroom that has not been previously discussed in terms of size, shape, color, and texture.

You may want to arrange for the students to take a walking tour of the school grounds and discover what is there. Ask the parent, aide, or other adult to list the objects the group finds on their tour. Have students list not only things they see, but also things they hear and smell. Give students the task of finding and describing different objects on the tour.

EVALUATE *Student evaluation:* Ask the students how, by looking, they can tell the difference between objects. Can students tell what the characteristics of an object are (size, shape, color, texture)? Ask students to look at a familiar object at home very carefully and describe it to the class the next day.

Teacher observation: Did the students seem to increase their powers of observation by the concluding activity? Were all the students participating? Did the students develop an appreciation for the qualities of an object in terms of size, shape, color, and texture?

CONNECTIONS *Science:* The scientific process depends upon powers of observation. Encourage students to notice and describe characteristics and events that they see in the world around them. For instance, create a weather chart and note characteristics of the daily atmospheric conditions. The class could select certain categories to observe. Such categories might include observable conditions such as the light of the day, whether there are clouds in the sky, and rain or no rain. Conditions related to the change of seasons could be observed and listed. Emphasize the sense of sight by listing on the chart only those conditions that can be seen.

SPECIAL NEEDS Visually impaired students will use their senses of touch, hearing, and smell to identify various objects in the environment. Give students a prescribed amount of time to handle and describe the objects on the table.

RESOURCES Aliki. *My Five Senses.* (rev. ed.) Crowell Junior Books, 1989.

Broekel, Ray. *Your Five Senses.* Children's Press, 1984.

Parramón, J.M. et al. *Five Senses (Sight).* Barron's Educational Series, Inc., First U.S. edition, 1985.

Exploring the Sense of Smell

COMPONENT   Aesthetic Perception

SUBJECT   Smell

OBJECTIVE   Students increase their sensory awareness by identifying different odors.

MATERIALS   Small quantities of items with distinctive
odors, such as dill pickles, garlic, an
orange, flowers, a lemon, honey, vanilla,
soap; a small paper bag for each student;
cotton balls

WARM UP   Define the sense of smell as the ability to receive information through our
noses. Ask for some examples of how we use this sense in our everyday
lives. Ask, "What are some of your favorite smells? What smells do you
try to get away from? How can you use your sense of smell to tell what is
happening?"

EXPLORE   Place items with distinctive odors in bags, one to a bag. If the item is
liquid, put a little of it on a cotton ball and place it in the bag. Have the
students sit in a circle and pass each bag around. Ask each student to
smell the contents of the bag without looking inside. Then ask whether
anyone can identify and describe briefly what is inside. Was the smell one
the students had smelled before? Where? When? What did it remind you
of? Continue this procedure with one or two more items in bags.

DEVELOP   Define an actor as a person who plays a part in a theatrical performance
(in a play, on television, or in motion pictures). Tell students that actors
create the illusion of smelling something when the object is not there to
smell. Example: We see a character in a play smelling the wonderful
fragrance of flowers outside the house. We can see that there are not any real
flowers on the stage, but the actor acts as though the flowers were there.

Tell students that they are going to have a chance to act out an idea without words. Give each student an empty bag and suggest that they imagine
some object in the bag that can be smelled. Give each student an opportunity to act out smelling the object in the bag and to show her or his reaction to it. Let the rest of the group try to guess what the object being
smelled might be.

EVALUATE

Student evaluation: Ask each student to identify what he or she was imagining the smell in the bag to be. Ask, "Where in real life would you encounter that smell?"

Teacher observation: Were the students able to make a transition from the real to the imagined smells? Could they add details to their smell reactions so that the others would understand more than just "good" and "bad" smells?

CONNECTIONS

Language Arts: Let students create several class poems about objects that have distinctive fragrances or aromas: a sprig of cedar, an orange, a rose, or a clove of garlic. A vocabulary bank and/or a webbing or cluster map could be created with input from the students, using words, phrases, or visual images elicited by the particular aroma. The form and length of the poem can be determined by the subject the experience level of the class. Write the group poem in large print on chart paper and display it near the object that stimulated the poem so that students can continue to connect the olfactory experience with the descriptive words of poetry.

SPECIAL NEEDS

Assist students with limited motor skills in handling individual bags to smell.

RESOURCES.

Aliki. *My Five Senses.* (rev. ed.) Crowell Junior Books, 1989.

Broekel, Ray. *Your Five Senses.* Children's Press, 1984.

Parramón, J.M. et al. *Five Senses (Smell).* Barron's Educational Series, First U.S. edition, 1985.

Exploring the Sense of Taste

COMPONENT | Aesthetic Perception

SUBJECT | Taste

OBJECTIVE | Students increase sensory awareness by using the sense of taste to identify various foods.

MATERIALS | Bite-size pieces of foods such as lemon, apple, peas, lettuce, orange, carrot, bell pepper; toothpicks for picking up the foods

Note: Before offering foods to taste, be sure to find out from parents whether any students have food allergies or dietary restrictions.

WARM UP | Ask how many students like peanut butter and jelly sandwiches. Ask one or two students why they do. When the answer, "They taste good," is offered, define taste as the flavor of whatever is put into the mouth. Ask how many students have baby brothers or sisters at home. Invite a few of those students to show how babies taste food that is offered to them. Ask, "What do you think babies are learning when they taste food?" Answers might include likes and dislikes.

EXPLORE | Ask each student for his or her favorite and least favorite foods. Write the students' responses on the board under "Likes" and "Dislikes," and ask students to notice whether the likes and dislikes fall into categories of sweet, sour, bitter, or salty.

DEVELOP | Define *pantomime* as acting without words. Ask students to remember what their favorite foods taste like, and to pantomime eating them. Ask them to remember the taste of their least favorite foods and pantomime eating them. To continue the activity, let the students work in pairs. One member of the pair closes her or his eyes while the other picks up a toothpick with something to taste on it. At a signal, "Taste," the students with their eyes closed are given the foods (very carefully, so that no one gets poked). All eat, keeping their eyes closed. Repeat the activity with the tasters giving the bites so that all the students have an opportunity to explore the sense of taste. The person offering the food records what the taster likes and doesn't like. If necessary, identify any unknown foods for students.

EVALUATE   *Student evaluation:* Ask, "How many had a bite of something you've never tasted before? Could you tell some of the foods more by the feel of them on your tongue rather than by taste? What sense were you using other than taste?" Ask the students to choose a food from the Likes/Dislikes list that they haven't tasted and try it at home.

Teacher observation: Were the students convincing in their pantomimes of tasting? Did they gain insight about taste as an identifier as well as a source of pleasure? Were they challenged to try, and accept, new or unfamiliar flavors?

CONNECTIONS   *Science:* Focus on developing students' skills of observation through their sense of taste. With their eyes closed, let students taste samples of foods that come from plants and try to identify them. Allow one student to record on a chart which plants can be identified by taste. Foods could also be categorized by what parts of the plants they are, such as roots, leaves, or fruits. Analyze the data to determine whether roots, leaves, or fruits were easier to identify by taste. Another investigation could be made at a later time to find out whether students' ability to analyze by taste had improved.

SPECIAL NEEDS   Assist students with motor control difficulties. Otherwise this activity could be completed with any group.

RESOURCES   Aliki. *My Five Senses* (rev. ed.). Crowell Junior Books, 1989.

Broekel, Ray. *Your Five Senses.* Children's Press, 1984.

Parramón, J.M. et al. *Five Senses (Taste)*. Barron's Educational Series, Inc., First U.S. edition, 1985.

Exploring the Sense of Hearing

COMPONENT	Aesthetic Perception
SUBJECT	Hearing
OBJECTIVE	Students increase sensory awareness by identifying sounds in the environment.
MATERIALS	Items already in the classroom, such as erasers, paper, pencils; sound effects recording, either commercial or home-made, if available

Note: Refer to the list of sounds the students heard on their walking tour of the school grounds in Lesson 2, "Exploring the Sense of Sight."

WARM UP

Define sound as that which is heard. Then distinguish between mechanical and natural sound. Mechanical sounds are all those sounds made in the environment by manufactured objects, such as alarm clocks, cars, TV sets, and blenders. Natural sounds are all those sounds made by natural means, such as the wind, voices, thunder, breathing, and dogs barking. Define *hearing* as the ability to receive information through the ears. Ask, "How can being able to hear sounds keep you safe?" Ask for examples of sounds that don't involve the human voice (sirens, a car approaching, or strange footsteps in a house).

EXPLORE

If recordings of both natural and mechanical sound effects are available, use them, and ask the students to identify the sounds. If such recordings are unavailable, use materials in the classroom to make sounds; for example, an eraser hitting the chalkboard, crumpling paper, a pencil tapping on a desk, doors opening and closing. Which sounds are pleasant? Scary? Soft? Loud? Difficult to identify? After students identify the objects that make the sounds, ask, "We know what is causing these sounds, but what else could make such sounds?" For example, a crackling fire could make a sound like that of crumpling paper; someone knocking might sound similar to a pencil tapping.

DEVELOP

Divide the class in half, and have one group make a particular sound. Suggest a number of sounds, such as a clock ticking, a bell ringing, a siren, the wind, or the ocean, so that the group may try imitating each sound using the mouth. As you did in Explore, ask the students in the other group to suggest what other objects could make each sound.

Ask the students to put their hands tightly over their ears. What do they hear? Then have the students uncover their ears, be as quiet as possible, and listen to sounds inside and outside of the classroom. Ask them to decide for themselves whether the sounds are mechanical or natural.

EVALUATE   *Student evaluation:* Ask the students what new sounds they heard. Which were pleasant? Which were scary? Which ones sounded like something different from what they were? If desired, make lists on the chalkboard.

Teacher observation: Did all the students participate in "gathering" sounds? Did they all seem to understand the difference between mechanical and natural sounds?

CONNECTIONS   *Music:* Music is organized sound. Let students discover objects in the classroom that can create an interesting sound. They can then organize a sound composition, a soundscape with a musical form. For example, an ABA form could be created by "playing" one set of sounds (A), then playing contrasting sounds (B), and ending with the sounds that started the composition (A). Create another ABA form by layering the sounds. Start softly with one sound; add more sounds and increase the volume; eliminate some of the sounds and return to the initial soft sound. The composition could be written on chart paper with invented notation to produce a musical score that students could "read" to play their instruments for a re-creation of the soundscape.

SPECIAL NEEDS   For hearing impaired students, use vibrating instruments such as drums or xylophones. The students can feel the varying degrees of sound vibrations that the instruments create by touching them while they are being played.

RESOURCES   *Living Sound Effects*, Vols. 1, 3, 7, 10. Bainbridge Ent. Co.

Miscellaneous Sound Effects, Vol. 10. Total Records.

Parramón, J.M. et al. *Five Senses (Hearing)*. Barron's Educational Series, Inc., First U.S. edition, 1985.

Spier, Peter. *Gobble, Growl, Grunt*. Doubleday, 1971.

Exploring Mood: How Do You Feel?

COMPONENT — Aesthetic Perception

SUBJECT — Emotions

OBJECTIVE — Students identify, respond to, and communicate different emotions in stories.

MATERIALS — The Grimm fairy tale, *Snow-White and the Seven Dwarfs*; the playscript of *Rumpelstiltskin* by Paul Galdone; pictures from books, magazines, and papers that show body stances and gestures

WARMUP

Tell the students that in many stories there are various actions by the characters that may make them laugh, make them cry, or make them angry. Refer to a story read together recently in class. Examine responses to the story by asking such questions as, "Did the story make you happy or sad? Did the story make you angry? Which part of the story made you feel happy or sad or angry? Why?"

EXPLORE

Give a short synopsis of a well-known story, such as *Snow-White and the Seven Dwarfs*. Then read a segment of it, such as the happy ending. Do the students agree that the ending of the story was a happy one? Ask them why. Did the ending make them feel happy as well?

Read a part of a story that highlights a different emotion, such as the sadness of the princess in *Rumpelstiltskin* when the little man comes to take her baby away. Ask students how this part of the story makes them feel. How do their responses differ from their responses to the ending of *Snow-White*?

DEVELOP

Say to the students, "You have just told how you felt about the parts of the stories we read. But there is another way people can show how they are feeling about something. We can use words to *tell* someone how we are feeling, but we can also use our bodies to *show* feelings." In an open space, as a whole group or in small groups, let students show how they would convey various emotions with their bodies. Tell the students that you are going to say some words, and they are to show with their bodies how they would express each feeling. Use such terms as *happy, sad, angry, joyous, disappointed, bored,* and *lonely*. Also ask students for suggestions of emotions to portray, and let the students try them. Ask them to move about (set the rule that they must not touch each other), showing one of the emotions talked about. Tell them to "freeze" (make statues), then have various students guess what emotions the others are portraying.

EVALUATE

Student evaluation: Ask the class to compare the different ways the same emotion was expressed as students made their statues. What did they like about the interpretation of each emotion?

Teacher observation: Were the students able to identify the different emotions? Did students become aware that their bodies show how they feel? Did both outgoing and shy students participate in the activity?

CONNECTIONS

Language Arts: Students need to have good literature read aloud to them on a daily basis. A daily diet of rich language experiences will increase students' listening skills, develop their "ear" for language, and enlarge their vocabulary and ability to comprehend increasingly complex stories and scripts. Students also need to recognize and experience the varied emotions of amusement, sorrow, joy, love, hate, pride, frustration, and fear that they have as a response to those stories. Stories that can be used to elicit feelings are *Feelings,* by Aliki; *First Flight,* by David McPhail; *Where the Wild Things Are,* by Maurice Sendak; *When the New Baby Comes I'm Moving Out,* by Martha Alexander; *Alexander and the Terrible, Horrible, No Good, Very Bad Day,* by Judith Viorst; *Touch! Touch!,* by Riki Levinson; *The Giving Tree,* by Shel Silverstein; *Nana Upstairs and Nana Downstairs,* by Tomie de Paola, *The Napping House,* by Audrey Wood; and *I'm Coming to Get You!,* by Tony Ross.

SPECIAL NEEDS

For hearing-impaired students, use signing experiences with this activity, or provide visual materials to aid students in participating. Special needs children benefit especially from being able to express their emotions. Visually impaired students will have to touch other students during the "statue" portion of the lesson in order to guess which emotions are being portrayed. This part of the activity will be difficult in any case for visually impaired students, who lack visual exposure to body language.

RESOURCES

Alexander, Martha. *When the New Baby Comes I'm Moving Out.* Dial Books for the Young, 1971.

Aliki. *Feelings.* Greenwillow Books, 1984.

Center Stage: Creative Dramatics Supplement. (contains "How Are You Feeling Today?" poster) Available from Dale Seymour Publications.

de Paola, Tomie. *Nana Upstairs and Nana Downstairs.* Putnam Publishing Group, 1973.

Galdone, Paul. *Rumpelstiltskin.* Houghton Mifflin Company, 1985.

Grimm, Jacob and Wilhelm. *Snow-White and the Seven Dwarfs.* Farrar, Straus, & Giroux, Inc., 1987.

Levinson, Riki. *Touch! Touch!* Dutton, 1987.

McPhail, David. *First Flight.* Joy Street Books/Little, Brown & Co., 1987.

Ross, Tony. *I'm Coming to Get You!* Dial Books for Young Readers, 1984.

Sendak, Maurice. *Where the Wild Things Are.* HarperCollins Children's Books, 1988.

Silverstein, Shel, *The Giving Tree.* Harper & Row Publishers, 1964.

Viorst, Judith. *Alexander and the Terrible, Horrible, No Good, Very Bad Day.* Atheneum, 1972.

Wood, Audrey. *The Napping House.* Harcourt Brace Jovanovich, 1984.

Using the Voice and Body to Create Sounds

COMPONENT   Aesthetic Perception

SUBJECT   Sounds

OBJECTIVE   Students identify and then create sounds using the voice and/or movement in a story.

MATERIALS   *Bear Hunt,* by Anthony Browne

WARM UP   Tell the students that you are going to tell (or read) a story that has many noisy actions in it, such as walking over a bridge and wading through water. Ask the students to listen carefully for such sounds suggested by the story. Tell or read *Bear Hunt,* and then ask for volunteers to identify the sounds and to demonstrate how they could be made by using their voices and their hands and feet.

EXPLORE   Let students decide which sound effect they created is most appropriate to each part of the story. Demonstrate and let students practice making each sound. Some sounds may be done in unison, some individually, and so on. Retell the story, with the students adding the sound effects as needed.

DEVELOP   Ask the students how the sound effects might be improved (for example, everyone starting together, making the sounds longer or shorter duration, changing them). Repeat the story, having the students add the improved sound effects. Ask if following the suggestions made an improvement in the telling. If the students want to, and time allows, repeat the story a third time.

EVALUATE   *Student evaluation:* Were the sounds identifiable and appropriate to the story? Did watching and listening to others help students create the sound themselves?

Teacher observation: Were the students able to focus on the story and to create unified sounds at the appropriate times? Were the students able to control visible physical energy in creating the sounds?

CONNECTIONS   *Language Arts:* Introduce students to additional works of literature that could be enhanced by created sounds and improvised action. One such book is *Hattie and the Fox* by Mem Fox. Read the story to the students several times until they are familiar with the predictable text; then let students improvise sound effects for each character. Have most of the class produce the sound effects and tell the story while a selected cast acts it out. Repeat the activity until every child has both acted out a story character and created sound effects.

SPECIAL NEEDS   With physically handicapped students, adjust the ways in which sounds are made using various parts of the body, such as stamping feet and clapping hands, to enable all students to participate in this activity.

RESOURCES   Browne, Anthony. *Bear Hunt.* Doubleday & Company, Inc., 1990.

Fox, Mem. *Hattie and the Fox.* Bradbury Press (Macmillan), 1988.

Exploring Rhythm and Movement

COMPONENT	Aesthetic Perception
SUBJECT	Rhythm/Movement
OBJECTIVE	Students develop flexible and diversified physical movement in response to rhythmic patterns and moods in music.
MATERIALS	Music with strong, marked rhythms; rhythm instruments

WARM UP   Define *rhythm* as a regular, recurring pattern in sound and movement, found in many areas of life. Ask, "Where can we find rhythm in ourselves; what parts of us make rhythm?" (Possible answers: heartbeat, breathing) Ask, "What other places do we find rhythm?" Such answers as music, marching, and clocks ticking might be expected.

EXPLORE   Ask, "What can we do with our bodies to express rhythm?" After students make a few suggestions, let them move about under direction in a cleared area. Have them hop, skip, or jump to music with a marked rhythm. Use rhythm instruments, if desired, instead of music. Vary the movement, changing the activity from time to time (hop to skip, for example).

DEVELOP   Tell the students that through our bodies, we can show emotions, demonstrate actions, or act like another person. Again, using marked rhythmic music, ask the students to walk (hop, skip), showing how the music makes them feel. Ask for one-word responses from the students about how they felt during the music. Repeat the exercise to show some activity, perhaps carrying a flag, pulling a cart, or driving a flock of geese. Do the exercise a third time, now having students pretend to be some other person, such as a grandfather, a mother, a baby, or a friend.

EVALUATE   *Student evaluation:* Ask the students to describe briefly who they were. If time permits, make a list of their suggestions of where rhythm is found in our lives (dancing, ocean waves, seasons, for example).

Teacher observation: Were the students able to move freely and unselfconsciously? Have they grown more perceptive of rhythm and movement? Were students able to demonstrate emotions, activity, and character through movement?

CONNECTIONS *Social Studies:* Most cultures have distinctive music and rhythms for ceremonial or celebrative occasions. Play some recordings of music from various cultures and let students move the way the rhythm suggests, then locate the countries identified by the music on the map or discuss the cultures in terms of historical time. Discuss similarities and differences in the rhythm and movements prompted by the music. Recordings from Native American ceremonies might be used, as well as African rhythms, Chinese New Year music, and Viennese waltzes.

SPECIAL NEEDS Have students with limited motor skills hum to the music and reproduce it in any way they wish (tapping their fingers, nodding their heads, conducting, etc.) They also can contribute to the discussion of movement.

RESOURCES *Burl Ives for Boys & Girls.* MCAC, Universal City, CA.

Flamenco, Cameo Classics. Moss Music Group, N.Y., N.Y., 1989 (tape or CD).

Lawrence, Esther. *Songs of the Jewish People.* T-KUME Records, L.A.

Strauss, R. *First Waltz Sequence.* Moss Music Group, N.Y., N.Y.

Exploring Movement as a Group

COMPONENT	Creative Expression
SUBJECT	Rhythm/Movement
OBJECTIVE	As a group, students engage in purposeful movement that involves problem solving.
MATERIALS	Cassette or record player; any upbeat jazz recording, such as *Crusaders 1,* by the Jazz Crusaders

WARM UP

Have students stand in a cleared area. There should be at least an arms' width between students. Play some expressive music and let the students move in any way they wish, each within her or his own space. Enjoy all the different ways the students are moving.

Comment on the diversity of movement by pointing out that each student's movement belongs to him or her, and may not look like anyone else's in the room. Ask half the students to perform their movements briefly, while the other students watch. Then have the other half perform their own movements. Briefly compare the movement of different individuals.

EXPLORE

Ask one student to demonstrate his or her own movement to the music. Have the other students watch, and after a few bars, begin to imitate the movement. Now everyone should be moving in the same way.

After a few bars of music with everyone following the leader, point to another student, who changes the movement to his or her own. Then have everyone in the group imitate the movement of the new leader. Continue this process until everyone has had a turn being leader.

DEVELOP

Arrange the students in groups of five or six. Challenge each group to agree on one specific way of moving together. Say, "Although there are six individuals in the group, see if your whole group can move the same way to music." Give the students a few moments to decide their group movement. The decisions are theirs, but stress that everyone in each group should be doing the same movement. If time allows, each group can share their movement with the rest of the class; if time is running short, have all the groups perform at the same time.

EVALUATE

Student evaluation: Ask the students what they liked about each movement activity. Ask them which of the movement activities they liked the best, and why. Ask whether there was anything in the small group movement activity that they would change.

Teacher observation: Were students able to work together effectively in determining what group movements to do? Did everyone participate in presenting ideas, or did one person dominate the group?

CONNECTIONS

Social Studies: A goal of the social studies curriculum for young children is to help build a sense of self-worth. This goal is achieved through deepening the appreciation of their own ability to explore, create, solve problems, communicate, and assume individual and group responsibilities.

A democratic society needs both creative, independent leaders and cooperative members of groups. Examples of both can be found in literature. *Stone Soup* by Marcia Brown could serve as a discussion starter for the class. The story of reluctant cooperation among the people of the town could be pantomimed to demonstrate understanding of group processes. The students will discover that leaders like the three soldiers "don't grow on every tree."

RESOURCES

Brown, Marcia. *Stone Soup.* Scribner (Macmillan), 1947.

Jazz Crusaders. *Jazz Crusaders 1.* Chisa Records.

Kellaway, Roger. *Creation.* Van Gelder Studios.

Simon, Paul. *Graceland.* Warner Brothers Records, Inc.

LESSON TEN

Exploring Different Environments Through Movement

COMPONENT Creative Expression

SUBJECT Rhythm/Movement

OBJECTIVE Students create a scene about sensory qualities in an imagined environment.

MATERIALS None required

WARM UP Have the students sit in an open space. Tell them to close their eyes and imagine different locations such as a desert, a forest, a snowy island, a muddy field. Ask the students questions that will help them add detail to their imagined scenes, such as "What is on your snowy island? Is it snowing right this minute? How cold is it? Who else is on this island with you? How difficult is it to walk?"

EXPLORE After students have spent a few minutes imagining different environments, select one specific environment and ask the students to move through that particular place. Say, "We have imagined what it would be like walking through a muddy field; now when I give the signal, let's move about as if we are in that muddy field. Begin moving. You are by yourself in that field. The mud is sticking to your feet. Feel how heavy your feet are becoming as the mud sticks to your shoes. What is happening to your body as you move through that muddy field?"

DEVELOP Use the same process to examine some of the other environments. After each activity, ask the students what happened to their bodies as they moved through the environment. After the students have moved through several environments, divide the class into small groups. Have each group choose an environment. Ask that each group talk briefly about what kind of story could take place there. If, for example, the chosen environment is a snowy island, what could happen there? Children could make a giant snowman or -woman! A group of children could meet a polar bear! Explorers could be looking for gold!

Each group must decide quickly on one topic. Ask the groups to think about each of the five senses as they make up a scene built around the selected topic. They should ask themselves what they can see, hear, smell, touch, and eat on the island. Ask each group to share briefly their information about the chosen environment.

If time allows, have the class act out one or more of the sensory experiences. Example: On the snowy island the students find all kinds of furry animals that they have never seen before. They pick them up and pat them, and talk about what they are and how they could have come to the island.

EVALUATE

Student evaluation: Ask students which environment/location they enjoyed moving through the most. Why? Did they find a wide variety of situations that challenged the five senses?

Teacher observation: How effective were students in conveying different environments? Were they imaginative about what they saw, ate, smelled, heard, and touched?

CONNECTIONS

Science: Select an outdoor site where the class can experience a rich environment to develop their observational skills using their senses—sight, hearing, smell, taste, and touch. If it is not feasible to visit a neighborhood park, walk to a specific place on the school grounds to observe with the senses. Students can feel the texture of the bark of trees, smell plants and fresh air, hear the sounds of birds and moving water, and see buildings, sidewalks, and streets. (Use caution in exploring with taste.) Help students understand that all of the objects perceived by the senses are composed of matter and make up the physical world in that specific environment. Upon returning to the classroom, list by sensory categories what students observed in their outdoor environment.

SPECIAL NEEDS

Utilize the student's strengths in experimenting with various environments. For example, give visually impaired students the opportunity to use their highly developed senses of touch and hearing in describing various environments. All children should be able to participate in this activity in some way.

Exploring Characters Through Movement

COMPONENT	Creative Expression
SUBJECT	Rhythm/Movement
OBJECTIVE	Students use movement and music to be different characters in different environments.
MATERIALS	A variety of expressive and dramatic recordings representing jazz, classical, and folk music, such as *Chariots of Fire*, by Vangelis, *The Rite of Spring*, by Stravinsky, *Graceland*, by Paul Simon, and *Harlequin*, by Dave Grusin and Lee Ritenour; record or cassette player

WARM UP

Ask the students to listen as you play a selection of recorded music. Tell them to close their eyes and imagine that they are moving to the music. Ask whether they are moving quickly or slowly. Ask, "What parts of your body are moving? Are your movements big or small?" Play another selection of music and give students another opportunity to see themselves moving in their imaginations. Ask whether their movements changed when the music changed.

EXPLORE

Call on individual students to describe the ways they saw themselves moving. Repeat one of the selections, and in a cleared area, have the students move as they saw themselves moving.

DEVELOP

Have the students move again, but this time ask them to think about who they could be while moving to the music. Suggest that they might be someone from a story the class has read, or some real sports hero, or a well-known personality. Say, "Decide what character you will be while moving to the music." Then play a few minutes of the selection so that students can select their characters. If the music playing is *The Rite of Spring*, the character chosen might be one given to great changes in emotion; the students' movements might be strong, with much change in direction and shape. Ask, "Who are you—what kind of character are you?" After the students respond, say, "Now that you know *who* you are, *where* are you?"

Get responses. Continue with, "When I put the music on again, think about your character, and where your character is, and move the way your character might move to this music." Allow students several minutes to move to the music.

Compare some of the choices that students made. Encourage them to elaborate on their scenes. Then have them move again with increased perception and understanding of their individual movements.

EVALUATE

Student evaluation: Give students an opportunity to write simple sentences about their characters. (If necessary, students can dictate their sentences to an adult.) Let students draw pictures of their characters.

Teacher observation: Did different styles of music affect the students' movements and ideas? Could students understand that the sounds they heard affected the ways in which they moved and created characters?

CONNECTIONS

Music: Guide small groups of students to create improvised musical sounds to which other students move. Have each of four or five students in a small group select an instrument such as maracas, quiro, claves, hand drum, cymbals, rhythm sticks, xylophone, metallophone, or glockenspiel. Individual students will need to explore possible musical sounds that can be created with their chosen instrument. After a cooperative planning session, let the small group perform their sound piece. As the improvised music is performed, remaining students responsively move in an open space to the music. The activity is repeated until all students have had an opportunity to both create music and move to the improvised sounds.

RESOURCES

Grusin, Dave, and Lee Ritenour. *Harlequin.* Arista Records.

Nash, Grace C. *Creative Approaches to Child Development with Music, Language and Movement.* Alfred Publishing, Inc., 1974.

Simon, Paul. *Graceland.* Warner Brothers Records, Inc.

Vangelis. *Chariots of Fire.* Polygram Records.

Stravinsky. *The Rite of Spring.* Columbia Records.

Using "Statues" to Create a Story

COMPONENT	Aesthetic Perception
SUBJECT	Body Awareness
OBJECTIVE	Students use "living statues" to create a story.
MATERIALS	Assorted crayons and marking pens for drawing

WARM UP Tell the students, "The body can move in many interesting ways. You can move more than your arms in making a shape. What else can you move?" (head, shoulders, and torso) Explain to students that they will move freely about in an open space. (Remind them that they are not to touch each other.) Tell students that you will give a signal (say "freeze" or beat a drum) when students are to stop. They are then to take on an interesting shape with their body that they can hold for a while for everyone to see. Observe the shapes and comment on the variety of statues: "This shape is very small (large, round, straight)," and so on.

EXPLORE Continuing this exercise, ask the students when they are "frozen" to imagine who they are and what they are doing. For example, one student might freeze in a shape that is twisted and low to the ground. Ask the student, "Who are you? What could your character be doing right now?" The student might respond, "I am a strange snake from Mars, and I'm looking for something to eat." Expect varied responses and respect students' choices.

DEVELOP Select one of the ideas suggested by the students and ask them to add details to the idea to make a simple story about the character. Ask, " Is there more to tell about the person or where he is? What has happened to make the character be where he is and do what he is doing? What is the next thing that will happen?" Suggestions might come from the entire class, or solely from the creator of the story.

You might have students just verbally tell more about the story, or you might ask the students to physically act out parts of the story. Following the telling of their ideas, the students may draw pictures of their character, considering where the character is and what else could be in the picture (forest, spaceship, moon, other character, and so on).

EVALUATE   *Student evaluation:* The students may share their pictures and discuss all the different settings in which their stories originate.

Teacher observation: How effective were the children in transferring interpretation of living statues into an actual character's movements? Did students become more aware of their physical shapes and ways to use those shapes in a story?

CONNECTIONS   *Visual Arts:* The experience of "freezing" into statues can be used to connect students to statues by important artists throughout history. Show students reproductions of statues that they may first "scan" (look at long and carefully) for shape and space—positive and negative. Examples for scanning might be Rodin's *The Thinker* and Brancusi's *Bird in Space.* Each statue could be scanned, discussed, and then recreated with the students' own bodies. Let each of them become each of the statues.

Discuss with students statues they have seen in their school or community. Perhaps a field trip could be scheduled to an art museum for the purpose of scanning statues or sculpture pieces. After scanning, it would be appropriate to have the students "freeze" in the shapes of the museum statues.

RESOURCES   Janson, H.W., and Anthony F. Janson. *History of Art for Young People.* (3d ed., revised and expanded). Harry N. Abrams, Inc., 1987. (contains pictures of *The Thinker* and *Bird in Space.*)

Mettler, Barbara. *Creative Dance in Kindergarten.* Mettler Studios, 1976.

Russell, Joan. *Creative Dance in the Primary School.* (3d ed.) Northcase House.

Exploring Movement: Pantomime

COMPONENT	Creative Expression
SUBJECT	Pantomime
OBJECTIVE	Students become aware of the body as a tool for expressing ideas, emotions, and characters, and recognize pantomime as one of the basic elements of drama/ theatre and its vocabulary.
MATERIALS	*Snow-White and the Seven Dwarfs, Jack and the Beanstalk,* or other stories from classroom literature

WARM UP
Define for the students the term *pantomime* as using the body to express an idea, an emotion, or a character—acting out an idea without words. Pantomime tells who we are, what we are doing, and how we feel about it. Point out that pantomime uses no "props"—objects to handle. The body alone expresses. Ask the students to pick up a pencil and put it down again, watching carefully what the arm, hand, and fingers do. Ask them to repeat the action without the pencil.

EXPLORE
Briefly review the five senses (Lessons 1-5). Ask students to stay in their seats while they hear a telephone ring, pick up the receiver, and listen to a friend ask them to go have pizza. Tell them to show without words how they would agree, and then put down the receiver. Ask how they think their faces showed how they felt. Did the rest of their bodies show how they felt? Did they return the telephone receiver to the very same spot where they picked it up?

DEVELOP
Move the students into a cleared area, reminding them to maintain at least an arm's distance between each other. Tell the students that they are each holding a ball in their hands. It has shape and weight. The students are to throw the ball hard with one hand. After a few throws, ask, "Did your arms swing back in preparation to throwing? Did your arms and bodies follow through the action after the ball left your hand?" Stress that pantomime requires a complete action. Repeat the exercise, emphasizing the completeness of the action.

In pairs, have students pantomime two characters who interact, either from classroom reading material or from familiar stories (the wicked witch and Snow-White; Jack and the man who buys the cow for beans from Jack). Briefly tell the part of the story to be pantomimed. (Jack offers the cow for sale. The man has no money, but will give a handful of beans for the cow. The exchange is made, and each is happy.) Point out that pantomiming this scene will show who each person is, what he is doing, and how he feels about it. Repeat the exercise, asking the students to add more detail, such as the man pulling the beans from his pocket and counting them, or Jack taking the beans and carefully putting them in his pocket.

EVALUATE   *Student evaluation:* Ask the students if they were able to begin and follow through the action to completion. Ask them how easy or difficult it was to do all three things at once: perform the action, be someone else, and convey the idea of what is happening.

Teacher observation: Were the students able to understand clearly the three essentials of pantomime? Did they use their bodies effectively, moving freely? Did they grasp that the action must be initiated and followed through to completion? Were they able to add details?

CONNECTIONS   *Language Arts:* Use some "action" pictures from one or two familiar stories. Some of the pictures should involve an object. Have the students discuss what is happening in the picture, what led up to the event, and what might happen in the future. This helps students with sequencing, imagination, and visualization. Have students look at the picture very closely for all the details and then take turns acting the scene out in pantomime. Both the pantomime and the discussion will help increase students' verbal skills.

SPECIAL NEEDS   Seat hearing impaired students where they have good vision of the speaker or interpreter. For visually impaired students, describe pictures in detail, and use oral and tactile clues during the paired part of the activity. Students with limited motor skills can do some activities even if they are confined to a wheelchair.

RESOURCES   Galdone, Paul. *Jack and the Beanstalk,* Clarion (Ticknor & Fields), 1982.

Grimm, Jacob and Wilhelm. *Snow-White and the Seven Dwarfs.* Farrar, Straus, & Giroux, Inc., 1987.

Scarry, Richard, *Richard Scarry's Best Story Book Ever.* Golden Press, 1980.

Recalling Favorite Stories

COMPONENT   Historical and Cultural

SUBJECT   Storytelling Traditions

OBJECTIVE   Students compare stories to discover
similarities and differences.

MATERIALS   Several anthologies of familiar stories,
folk tales, and fairy tales

WARM UP   Share a story from your own childhood with your students. Tell them
which stories were your favorites when you were growing up. Briefly tell
your students why you enjoyed those stories so much. For example, if one of
your favorite stories was *Jack and the Beanstalk,* give them the reasons why
you liked that one particularly. Was it because you were frightened by the
giant? Was it the excitement of climbing up the beanstalk through the
clouds? Was it because a much-loved person told you the story? Did it tell
you something about that person and/or your culture? What childhood
traits did you have that made that story appeal to you?

EXPLORE   Ask the students to name their favorite stories. List their responses on the
board under different headings, such as Fairy Tales, Animal Stories, Stories about Ancestors, and Stories about Present-Day People. Did several
students choose the same story? Question the students as to why they
liked their stories. Ask similar questions to those you asked about your
own personal favorites. Compare the students' stories and reasons for
liking them to yours. Are any of them the same?

DEVELOP   Add a column to the lists on the board for what students learned from their
favorite story. See whether different stories seemed to teach the same lesson.

Read one or two of the stories that students have named, especially those
chosen by several students. Compare those stories with the one you liked
while growing up. Can any comparisons be made in the content? Your
story may be more traditional than students' current favorites, or some
timeless stories may be enjoyed now just as much as in years past. Give
students the understanding that sometimes stories change with the time
and place, but often lessons that the story is intended to teach remain the
same and are repeated in stories over many years.

If time allows, choose one of the stories suggested by the students and have them act out parts of that story. Choose a specific part of the story for them to act out, paying attention to characters, setting, and action in the story.

Encourage students to ask their parents, relatives, or guardians about their favorite stories.

EVALUATE

Student evaluation: In pairs, small groups or as a class, have the students discuss the reasons why stories are enjoyed, and name more stories. What kinds of stories do they dislike? Ask them to write about or draw parts of a story they either like or dislike.

Teacher observation: Did students offer a variety of sources for their stories? Could they describe what it was about the stories that made them favorites? Were students able to compare and contrast lessons learned from different stories?

CONNECTIONS

Social Studies: Help students take their first vicarious steps into times past by inviting a grandparent of one of the students or an older member of the larger school community to come into the classroom and tell a favorite story. Encourage the students to ask questions of the guest storyteller. Let them know that asking questions of an older person is one way of doing research in history. Students can learn that history and cultural values are passed from one generation to another through the telling of stories.

RESOURCES

Bettelheim, Bruno. *The Uses of Enchantment: The Meaning and Importance of Fairy Tales.* Random House, Inc., 1989.

Briggs, Raymond. Virginia Haviland, ed. *The Fairy Tale Treasury.* Dell Publishing Company, 1986.

Galdone, Paul. *Jack and the Beanstalk.* Clarion (Ticknor & Fields), 1982.

Osborn, Steve. *Story Chest: Treasured Tales from Many Lands.* Addison-Wesley Publishing Company, 1992.

Exploring Story Action: What Are You Doing?

COMPONENT	Aesthetic Perception
SUBJECT	The Five W's: *What*
OBJECTIVE	Students learn to recognize the *What* in a story as one of the basic elements of drama/theatre and its vocabulary.
MATERIALS	*Corduroy,* by Don Freeman; *Momotaro: The Peach Boy,* by Linda Shute; Action Cards (3-by-5-inch cards with various tasks written on them; these list the character from the book and something the character did)

WARM UP Tell the students that the *What* in a story for this lesson is the actions that take place in the story—what the characters are actually doing. Ask the students to think about all the different actions they had to do that morning to get to school.

EXPLORE Read a story such as *Momotaro: The Peach Boy,* by Linda Shute, or *Corduroy,* by Don Freeman. Ask the students to identify the *What,* or actions, in the story. What are the characters doing? (How does Obaasan reach the peach? What do Momotaro and the animals do when they meet? How do they get across the water? and so on)

DEVELOP Give selected students cards that you have made with various *What* situations printed on them. These are actions that one of the characters did in the story you read. Say, "Could you pretend that you are outside planting a garden, or placing all the food on a table for a big meal, or riding in the woods on an imaginary bike? Review briefly with the students the definition of *pantomime* (Lesson 13). Remind them that they must convey actions with body movement only. Read the cards for the students if necessary. Have one student at a time, or small groups of students, pantomime the *What* situation found on their cards. Give as many students as possible an opportunity to participate in the activity.

Read the story again, if time allows, asking students to identify the action, or what happens, as the *What* in the story.

EVALUATE

Student evaluation: In small groups or in pairs, have the students compare with one another the different actions or *What* they did to get to school that morning. Ask them to compare those actions to the ones they acted out from the story.

Teacher observation: How effective were the students in identifying the different events in a story? Did the students' ability to recognize the *What* in a story increase by the end of the lesson? Did acting out the story situations increase their understanding?

CONNECTIONS

Social Studies: Help students develop a beginning sense of historical empathy by considering how it might have been to live in other times and places, and how their lives would have been different. By exploring the *What,* or actions in well-selected stories, students will increase their comprehension of works of literature related to the past. Have students pantomime *What* situations selected from books such as *The One-Room School at Squabble Hollow* by Rosemarie Hausherr, *When I Was Nine* by James Stevenson, *Tales of a Korean Grandmother* by Frances Carpenter, and *Christmas on the Prairie* by Joan Anderson.

SPECIAL NEEDS

With some special children you may need to use shorter segments of the stories to develop concentration and sequencing skills. Perhaps some children could benefit from having a partner to help with the activity.

RESOURCES

Anderson, Joan. *Christmas on the Prairie.* Clarion (Ticknor & Fields), 1985.

Carpenter, Frances. *Tales of a Korean Grandmother.* C.E. Tuttle, 1972.

Center Stage: Creative Dramatics Supplement. (contains Five W's poster) Available from Dale Seymour Publications.

Freeman, Don. *Corduroy.* Viking, 1968.

Hausherr, Rosemarie. *The One-Room School at Squabble Hollow.* Four Winds Press (Macmillan), 1988.

Shute, Linda (retold by). *Momotaro: The Peach Boy.* Lothrop, Lee & Shepard Books, 1986.

Spolin, Viola. *Improvisation for the Theater: A Handbook of Teaching and Directing Techniques.* Northwestern University Press, 1983.

Stevenson, James. *When I Was Nine.* Greenwillow Books, 1986.

Creating a Scene from Imagined Objects

COMPONENT   Creative Expression

SUBJECT   Imitation of an Imagined Object

OBJECTIVE   Students create and communicate a scene around various imagined objects.

MATERIALS   List of objects that students will use for their scenes (for example, a swing; a doorknob; trees in the wind; an egg beater; a rocking chair; fire; a fountain; a door)

WARM UP   Let the students move around in a large open space. Tell them they will have one second to make their bodies represent various objects such as trees, snakes, balls, or statues. Say, for example, "You have one second to change into a tree!" Comment on their abilities to change, and continue, "You have one second to change into a car that is parked and not moving!" Encourage original and inventive interpretations. Other objects to represent might be a cloud, a rock, a chair, or a table.

Ask students to think about the objects they are representing. What does each object really look like? What is its shape? How can that shape be created with the body?

EXPLORE   Ask each student to choose an object, make the shape of that object with their bodies, and move the way that object would move. You may have to suggest objects if the selection process takes too much time. Have a list of objects prepared from which the students may choose if they wish. The list might include such objects as those listed under Materials, or any you wish to provide. Ask some of the students (all those whose names begin with *B*, for instance, or all those in a certain area in the room) to demonstrate their objects. Ask the remaining students to guess what the various objects might be.

DEVELOP   Divide the class into small groups of three or four students each. Ask the students in each small group to create an event around the objects they each chose to represent. For example, if three students were a tree, a snake, and a ball, they should make up a scene that would include each of the objects.

Give instructions to the students such as: "First, talk about the place where your scene happens. Then talk about how it begins. What happens next? Remember that you have to include all the different objects in the scene." Do not allow the students to spend too much time talking, but urge them to act out bits of the scene as they go along. After a few moments, ask the students to try acting out their plot so far. If they do not yet have an ending, ask them to plan how it might end.

If time allows, ask the groups to share their complete scenes with the rest of the class.

EVALUATE   *Student evaluation:* Ask students what the most difficult part of planning the scene with their small group was. Did their story include all of their objects, or did they leave one out? How did the scenes begin and end?

Teacher observation: Did the students use the objects in imaginative ways to create their scenes? Could students work together in small groups? Evaluate each group's ability to work independently.

CONNECTIONS   *Language Arts:* Compile a class book from the stories small groups created from imagined objects. If student skills permit, have each group cooperatively write the created story on large chart paper. If students are not able to write the stories independently, each group can dictate its story to an adult or older student. These stories can initially be displayed in the classroom and subsequently bound in a class book. The students will enjoy seeing their stories develop from an oral product of their imaginations to a concrete form of print on paper.

SPECIAL NEEDS   With developmentally disabled children, the leader may have to side-coach. This is a technique used during dramatic activities or rehearsals, in which the leader or director offers suggestions or comments from the side, to heighten and advance the scene or story.

With visually impaired students, refer only to objects that they have experienced in some sensory way. It would not be realistic, for instance, to refer to clouds.

Dramatizing "The Stonecutter"

COMPONENT	Historical and Cultural
SUBJECT	Improvisation
OBJECTIVE	Students act out parts of stories after listening to and reading selected parts of the Japanese folk tale "The Stonecutter."
MATERIALS	None required

WARM UP Review with the students the fact that stories come from every part of the world. Point out that in the United States Americans have come from every country in the world and have brought their stories with them.

Point out on a map or globe the location of Japan and introduce the story of *The Stonecutter*. Ask students what they think a stonecutter does for a living. Then identify for them what he does.

EXPLORE Read the story of "The Stonecutter" from the Appendix of CENTER STAGE. Challenge the students to be aware of all the different characters in the story (*Who*), and all the different settings of the story action (*Where*). Remind students of Lessons 10 and 11, in which they explored environments and characters through movement.

After the class has listened to the folk tale, ask questions such as, "Who is the first character we see and hear about in the story? Where did the spirit live? What made the stonecutter want to be rich?"

DEVELOP Help the students select one part of the story for a scene to dramatize. First, determine the *What* (the action or plot). What happens first in the scene? Next? and so on. Then determine which characters in the story (the *Who* of the story, such as the stonecutter, the spirit of the mountain, the rich man) are needed for the scene.

The next step is to experiment with the dialogue that should be included in the scene. Use an approximation of the dialogue that exists in the story. Ask the students who says what to whom, and what the reply will be. Be sure the students use only the dialogue necessary to the scene.

Quickly establish the setting (the *Where* of the scene). Select students to act out the scene, with the remaining students observing. If time allows, repeat the scene with different performers, allowing for development of character and action.

EVALUATE

Student evaluation: Allow the students to evaluate their effectiveness in listening to the story and using what they heard to create their own characters and dialogue. Ask the students the meaning of the story. What do they think about the stonecutter always wanting to be someone other than what he was? Ask the students, "If you were to play the scene again, what would you change?"

Teacher observation: Were students able to use the story they heard to develop dialogue and actions for the story? Could students identify the *Who,* the *What,* and the *Where* of the story? Did the students have a satisfactory creative/performing experience?

CONNECTIONS

Social Studies: Students are developing a sense of place and an understanding that their community is interconnected with the wider world. Locate Japan on a globe. Let the children touch Japan and also the approximate location of their own community. Establish the understanding that Japan is the setting for the folk tale "The Stonecutter." Show students pictures of children living in Japan. If there are any Japanese or Japanese-American students in the class, ask them to share any information they have. Lead students to discover some unique characteristics of the island country and also some geographic aspects of Japan that are similar to some in their own location. Place resource materials in a learning center where students can continue the exploration of Japanese geography and culture, or develop a bulletin board display from student drawings showing geographic similarities and differences.

RESOURCES

Center Stage: Creative Dramatics Supplement. (contains audiotape of "The Stonecutter" and Five W's poster) Available from Dale Seymour Publications.

Exploring Folktales and Their Morals

COMPONENT   Historical and Cultural

SUBJECT   Folklore

OBJECTIVE   Students identify the moral in a story and learn about the historical role of the storyteller.

MATERIALS   "Androcles and the Lion," from *The Fables of Aesop*, edited by Joseph Jacobs; *Anansi the Spider: A Tale from the Ashanti*, retold by Gerald McDermott

Note: If possible, to conclude this lesson, invite a storyteller to come into the class-room and share his or her art form with the students. (There may be storytellers in the community—a parent, or someone in the school. Check with your school or local librarian for assistance.)

WARM UP   Choose a story you have read recently and ask whether it is trying to teach a lesson. For example, is there a lesson to be learned from *Little Red Riding Hood?* Introduce the word *moral* and its meaning (concerned with or relating to what is right or wrong in human behavior, or the lesson taught by a particular story). Many stories are written to be entertaining, but also to teach us a lesson. Morals from such stories might include: Don't be greedy! Listen to your parents! Work hard! Ask students if they recognize morals in other stories. Have them give examples.

EXPLORE   Read the story "Androcles and the Lion." Ask students what they think the moral of this story is. What happens when someone is kind?

DEVELOP   Tell the students that a storyteller is someone who tells a story in his own words, without reading it. Often the role of a storyteller is to pass on the oral traditions of his or her culture. In Africa the storyteller used to travel from village to village teaching people the difference between right and wrong and good and evil through his stories.

If possible, invite into the classroom an African storyteller from the community, or a storyteller who will tell a story from African culture, such as *Anansi the Spider: A Tale from the Ashanti.* Ask the students to tell the moral of the story. How is it shown? Why are Anansi's six sons named "See Trouble," "Road Builder," "Stone Thrower," "River Drinker," "Game Catcher," and "Cushion"? Involve the students in a discussion with the visiting storyteller about her or his art form.

EVALUATE *Student evaluation:* Have the students compare the differences between reading a story and telling it orally. Which do they prefer?

Teacher observation: How well did the students understand the meaning of the word *moral*? Did the story examples seem to increase their understanding? Did having a visiting storyteller increase students' awareness of how stories are used to pass on cultural values?

CONNECTIONS *Social Studies:* To continue developing students' awareness of past and present cultures, and to explore further the storyteller's role in teaching the moral values of a society, share with students some of the information in the following books. *The Fables of Aesop* can lead to a many-faceted discussion about the slave who taught morals through brief, subtle stories that have been told and retold for hundreds of years. *Doctor Coyote: A Native American Aesop's Fables,* by John Bierhorst traces the passage of the stories from Aesop to Aztec. *The Lion and the Rat* is a fable from France by La Fontaine, illustrated by Brian Wildsmith. *A Story, A Story* by Gail E. Haley will reinforce the role of the storyteller as a purveyor of a society's value system. Labels could be placed on a map to indicate the geographic origin of each fable.

RESOURCES Aesop. *The Fables of Aesop.* Edited by Joseph Jacobs. B. Franklin, 1970.

Bierhorst, John. *Doctor Coyote: A Native American Aesop's Fables.* Macmillan, 1987.

Haley, Gail E. *A Story, A Story.* Atheneum (Macmillan), 1970.

La Fontaine. *The Lion and the Rat.* Oxford University Press (reprinted in paperback), 1986.

McDermott, Gerald. *Anansi the Spider: A Tale from the Ashanti.* Henry Holt & Company, 1972.

Exploring Character: Who Are You?

COMPONENT	Aesthetic Perception
SUBJECT	The Five W's: *Who*
OBJECTIVE	Students create drama by portraying more than one character in a story.
MATERIALS	*The Three Bears,* by Paul Galdone, or another familiar story

WARM UP

Read a story such as *The Three Bears.* Before you begin, tell students to listen carefully so that they can identify all the different characters in the story. At the end of the story, ask the group to name the characters.

EXPLORE

Ask the students to imagine that they are one of the characters in the story. Tell them to think about who they are. Questions to stimulate imagination might include: "What does your character look like? Make a picture of the character in your head. How does your character move? Awkwardly? Gracefully? Quickly or slowly? How does your character talk? Dress?"

Next say, "Now that you have a picture of your character in your head, think about how your character is different from another character in the story. How are the two alike?" Ask students to share some of their ideas with the group.

DEVELOP

In a large open space, have the students move and behave like the character they imagined earlier. This can be done with all the students exploring movement at once, or by asking individual or small groups of students to move while others watch.

Questions to ask and comments to make while the students are moving might include: "Is your character young or old, small or large? How can you show that? Think about your character as you are moving. Show me how your character would walk, run, and move in slow motion. Take a few minutes to plan and then move the way your character would move."

Once the students have investigated all these nuances of their characters, give them an opportunity to try another character in the story. Say, "If you were Daddy Bear, you might try being Baby Bear," and so on. Give all students an opportunity to play different characters in the story. Ask how it felt to play different characters. Ask what it was like to watch one person playing different characters.

EVALUATE

Student evaluation: Have students tell about, write about, or draw the characters they most enjoyed portraying, being as descriptive as possible. (Some students may only list descriptive words.)

Teacher observation: Were the students able to identify with all the characters in the story? Did the students understand that the *Who* in a story pertains to each of the different characters? Were all of the students willing to participate?

CONNECTIONS

Social Studies: Awareness of cultural diversity in both the present and the past can be developed by exploring characters in literature from a variety of cultural, historical, and geographic settings. For example, explore the characters in the Japanese setting of *A Pair of Red Clogs* by Masako Matsuno; the Pueblo Indian setting of *Arrow to the Sun* by Gerald McDermott; or the African setting of *Mufaro's Beautiful Daughters: An African Tale* by John Steptoe. Build understanding of the characters in these selected stories of diverse cultures by asking students to explore as they did in *The Three Bears*.

SPECIAL NEEDS

With physically impaired students you may have to adjust some of the free movement throughout an open space, but all students should be able to experience the thrill of playing one or more characters in a story.

RESOURCES

Briggs, Raymond. Virginia Haviland, ed. *The Fairy Tale Treasury.* Dell Publishing Company, 1986.

Center Stage: Creative Dramatics Supplement. (contains Five W's poster) Available from Dale Seymour Publications.

Galdone, Paul. *The Three Bears.* Clarion (Ticknor & Fields), 1985.

Matsuno, Masako. *A Pair of Red Clogs.* World Publishing Co., 1960.

McDermott, Gerald. *Arrow to the Sun: A Pueblo Indian Tale.* Viking Penguin, 1974.

Steptoe, John. *Mufaro's Beautiful Daughters: An African Tale.* Lothrop, Lee & Shepard Books, 1987.

Exploring Color: The Rainbow

COMPONENT	Aesthetic Valuing
SUBJECT	Sensory Awareness
OBJECTIVE	Students use different colors as motivation to interpret meaning and movement qualities of characters in a story.
MATERIALS	*The Rainbow Goblins,* page 242

WARM UP Ask students to name their favorite colors. List them on the board. Ask, "Where in nature can you find some of these colors?" Students should be able to give such examples as the sky, cherries, sunsets, and grass. Encourage many examples.

EXPLORE Ask the students if they have ever seen a rainbow—the colors of the spectrum which appear when sunlight shines through water droplets. A rainbow is often seen after a brief shower late in the afternoon. List the colors of the rainbow (red, orange, yellow, green, blue, indigo, and violet). Say, "Each one of the colors is very different from the others. Can you imagine what the movement of each color would look like? How would you move like the color blue?"

Assign a color to each student, distributing the seven colors equally. Say, "If your color suddenly came to life, how would it move?" Have students move in an open space as their color of the rainbow. While the students are moving, say, "Think about what the color feels like. Does red move the same way as blue? Why do the colors move differently?"

DEVELOP Divide the class into groups of seven. Assign one color of the rainbow to each student in the group. This can be the same as or different from the student's previous color. This color will be their character in the story, *The Rainbow Goblins,* by Ul De Rico. In this story there are seven goblins, each of whom has his own color of the rainbow. Remind the students of three of the five W's of the story (*Who, What,* and *Where;* or characters, action, and setting). Refer to Lessons 10, 15, and 19. Read the story to the class and ask students to listen to see how their character behaves.

If necessary, read the story again so that students become aware of various locations and actions for which their characters are responsible. Have each group of seven act out an assigned scene in the story as the other groups watch. Comment on the movements and characterizations of the participating students, focusing on the mood of each color.

EVALUATE

Student evaluation: Following the dramatizations of the scenes, ask how effective each group was in portraying the color characters. In their small groups of seven, have the students talk about eating rainbows. What do they taste like? Are they sweet? Are they sour? What relation does the taste have to the color's character?

Teacher observation: How effectively were students able to interpret the colors of the rainbow? Were they creative in their characterizations of the goblins? Were their characters interesting to watch? How successful were the students in connecting and relating colors with movement?

CONNECTIONS

Science: In science students are making observations about the natural world in which they live. If weather conditions provide a rainbow, the class might have the opportunity of observing the colors in a natural setting. A more predictable opportunity could be provided by bringing a crystal prism into the classroom. Hold or hang the crystal prism where the sunlight will diffract the light into a spectrum containing the colors of the rainbow. A discussion could involve information about light and diffraction, but the power of exploring color will probably come from observing a "rainbow" directly.

SPECIAL NEEDS

Many visually impaired individuals are able to see color. With those who are not, assign a sound to each of the colors of the rainbow. As sighted students identify the colors by sight, the visually impaired child would identify each character by a different sound. For instance, a whisper would equal blue, a clap would be red, and so on.

RESOURCES

De Rico, Ul. *The Rainbow Goblins.* Thames Hudson, Inc., 1978. (This book is out of print, but the text is in the Appendix of CENTER STAGE.)

Exploring Design

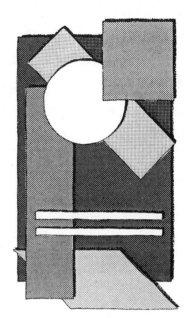

COMPONENT	Aesthetic Perception
SUBJECT	Perception
OBJECTIVE	Students create different designs within an established space using visual art pieces and their bodies.
MATERIALS	Large prints of works by Sophie Taeuber-Arp, David Hockney, and Romare Bearden, or other art with prominent shapes and colors; masking tape; large construction paper shapes, such as squares, rectangles, circles, triangles, and so on, in various colors and sizes

WARM UP Show the students an abstract painting, such as one by Picasso, that incorporates different shapes and colors in its design. Ask the students what they see in the painting. Say, "Look at the different kinds of shapes and colors in the picture. Do you see anything that looks like an animal, person, or some kind of object? Where?" Each student may see something different in the abstract shapes and colors. Encourage individual responses. Ask also whether the shapes come in contact with other shapes in the picture.

EXPLORE Give a student several large paper cutouts of shapes of varying sizes and colors. Ask him or her to arrange the shapes within a limited space. This space could be a large square or other shape marked on the floor with masking tape. Tell the student to arrange the cutouts in any way she or he wishes within the taped space. Discuss the overall design that is created by asking, "Did (name) use all the space, or did (s)he arrange the cutouts in just one part of the space? Do the shapes touch or overlap each other? Do you think (s)he was trying to make the shapes look like a particular object?" Give another student a chance to create a different design in another taped space. Point out, or ask the students, what the similarities and differences are between the two.

DEVELOP Remind the students that the body can make interesting shapes as well. Tell students that they are going to make shapes with their bodies. Divide the class into groups of five or six students each. Assign a different shape to each student within each group. (You may wish to give each student a paper cutout and suggest that she or he make that particular shape.) Ask the students in each group to make their body shapes within a limited space. Using the type of questions and comments in Explore, comment on the design each group creates.

If time allows, have each group plan specific movements that could be done together and that could describe the design they created earlier in the lesson. Ask, "If your shape were to come alive, how would that shape move?" Have students perform their movements for the rest of the class. Comment on each moving design that students create. Show the abstract painting again and ask the students what new shapes and colors and ideas they see in it.

EVALUATE   *Student evaluation:* Make the comment that there is a difference between the static design of paper shapes and the living design made with the students' bodies. Ask, "How were the two experiences different? How did you use your bodies to create shapes?"

Teacher observation: How effective were the students in arranging the shapes in a limited space? Were students more effective working individually or working together? Did you notice any heightened awareness about the content of the painting following this activity?

CONNECTIONS   *Mathematics:* In mathematics students are developing sorting, classifying, and patterning skills. Ask students to sort and classify the design pieces according to shape, size, and color, having them give reasons for their classifications. Extend the work with the shapes to creating patterns, making sure to have enough duplicate shapes for repeated patterns. Patterns can be created by individual students or by small groups. Establish a math activity center where individuals may continue to sort, classify, and create patterns using the various shapes.

SPECIAL NEEDS   Students in wheelchairs can make various shapes by moving their wheelchairs and creating a design on the floor.

For visually impaired students, prior to the lesson, reproduce several major shapes from the chosen painting in paper or fabric of various textures such as sandpaper, corduroy, or felt and attach them to poster board so that it roughly resembles the art. This will give students the tactile experience of the art.

Creating Mood with Pictures and Movement

COMPONENT Aesthetic Valuing

SUBJECT Sensory Awareness

OBJECTIVE Students use physical movement to create different moods and settings used in children's literature.

MATERIALS *Harry and the Terrible Whatzit,* by Dick Gackenbach; *Umbrella,* by Taro Yashima

WARM UP Show the students the illustrations in two storybooks such as *Harry and the Terrible Whatzit* and *Umbrella*. The illustrations for each story are very different because the theme and content of each story are different. Show the students a number of pictures from both books and discuss how the scene drawn and the colors used make them feel—happy, sad, frightened, lonely, and so on. Ask students, "Do you think the illustrator drew the pictures the way he or she did so that you would feel a certain way about the story or the action and characters?" Point out how the setting, or *Where* of the story, affects the mood.

EXPLORE Read each of the stories and compare students' initial responses to the pictures to what they feel after hearing the stories. Did their first impressions from the pictures change after hearing the content of the stories? Do they feel that the pictures are right for each story? For example, when Harry goes into the cellar to find his mother, do the pictures match the mood of what is happening in the story of his finding the two-headed Whatzit?

DEVELOP Select an illustration from one of the stories and show it to the students. Have the students move to an open space and recreate the illustration. If more than one character is required, divide the class into small groups. Then direct the students to move and speak and finish the incident illustrated in the story. Ask, "How can you show us the place where the story happens and the feeling of the scene you are dramatizing? If you moved in a certain way, such as slow, fast, or jerky, would that help show us the kind of place where you are?"

Repeat this process with other illustrations, focusing on the sensory qualities of the story. Before each dramatization, ask, "How are you going to show what you heard (saw, smelled, tasted, or touched) in your scene?"

EVALUATE   *Student evaluation:* Ask how different groups showed sensory experiences in their scenes. Have the students comment on and compare the different moods created by certain movements.

Teacher observation: Could the students transfer impressions about setting and mood to actual movement activities? Did the students become increasingly aware that physical movement could help convey the feeling of being in a specific setting?

CONNECTIONS   *Language Arts:* To develop students' comprehension skills, continue to investigate mood and setting with various pieces of literature. Ask students to describe mood and setting after they hear told or read aloud a book such as *Bringing the Rain to Kapiti Plain* by Verna Aardema; *Juma and the Magic Jinn* by Joy Anderson; *Hawk, I'm Your Brother* by Byrd Baylor; *Even If I Did Something Awful?* by Barbara Shook Hazen; *A Chair for My Mother* by Vera B. Williams; *The House on Maple Street* by Bonnie Pryor; or *Sam, Bangs, and Moonshine* by Evaline Ness. Ask such questions as, "Where is this story happening? How does it make you feel?" Note that there can be more than one setting in a story. Share the illustrations and emphasize connecting vocabulary with sensory experiences.

SPECIAL NEEDS   Visually impaired students may need verbal descriptions or tactile experiences to identify settings that other students are seeing in illustrations and conveying through movement.

RESOURCES   Aardema, Verna. *Bringing the Rain to Kapiti Plain.* Dial Books for Young Readers, 1981.

Anderson, Joy. *Juma and the Magic Jinn.* Lothrop, Lee & Shepard Books, 1986.

Baylor, Byrd. *Hawk, I'm Your Brother.* Macmillan Publishing Company, 1976.

Gackenbach, Dick. *Harry and the Terrible Whatzit.* Clarion (Ticknor & Fields), 1984.

Hazen, Barbara Shook. *Even If I Did Something Awful?* Atheneum, 1981.

Ness, Evaline. *Sam, Bangs, and Moonshine.* Holt, Rinehart and Winston, Inc., 1980.

Pryor, Bonnie. *The House on Maple Street.* Morrow Junior Books, 1987.

Williams, Vera B. *A Chair for My Mother.* Greenwillow Books, 1982.

Yashima, Taro. *Umbrella.* Puffin (Penguin), 1977.

Evaluating Performances

COMPONENT   Aesthetic Valuing

SUBJECT   Evaluation

OBJECTIVE   Students learn the meaning of evaluation and its relationship to the basic
components of a story and to an audience.

MATERIALS   None required

WARM UP   Ask the students to think about an episode from their favorite TV shows,
but not tell what it is just yet. Ask them to think about one thing they
would change about the episode if somehow they could change anything
they wanted. For example, the story might be longer, or more time given
to the children in it.

Introduce the term *evaluation* and its meaning (reflecting on and making
judgments about one's own efforts, as well as the efforts of others). Evaluation is used in theatre to help communicate the play or story better.
Sometimes a playwright even changes parts of a play after seeing how an
audience reacts to it. Say, "Think about a particular episode from your
favorite TV show. Would you like to have added something, changed
something, or left something out that you think would have made the
story better?" Let several students describe episodes and offer brief comments.

EXPLORE   Ask students to think about the order in which events happened in the
TV show they chose, and introduce the three parts of a story.

1. Beginning: How does the story start? Where are the characters
when the story begins and what are they doing?

2. Middle: What actions happen in the story (the plot)?

3. End: How does the story come to a close?

Choose a familiar story, and ask students to name its three parts.

DEVELOP   Introduce the term *audience* and its meaning (at least one person, perhaps
many more, who watch and form opinions about a performance). A play
must have a good beginning to involve the audience; a believable sequence
of actions to keep the audience interested; and an ending that fits with the
characters and the actions, so that the audience members will feel satisfied
with the story.

Ask the students if they have ever been audience members. Where? When? Were there parts of the performance they liked or didn't like? Were the parts at the beginning, the middle, or the end?

Choose a TV program or theatrical performance that most students have seen. Ask the class, "As an audience member, did you like the story (performance)? Can you tell us why you liked the show? After the students have commented briefly, continue, "Just as we did with the TV show earlier, let's change something about the show that you didn't like. First of all, tell us whether it was at the beginning, middle, or end of the story." After identifying the incident, ask how it could be changed. Select one suggestion and ask, in acting it out, what would happen first, second, and so on. Have the necessary number of students immediately get to their feet and act out the revised situation. Ask the students whether they felt the change improved the story. Did it make them, as the audience, more satisfied with the story? Repeat the exercise as time allows.

EVALUATE

Student evaluation: Ask students to evaluate the last movie or TV program they saw by asking, "Did you enjoy it? What would have made it better? Could it have had a different ending?"

Teacher observation: Were the students able to suggest valid criticisms of TV shows? Did they seem to understand the role of an audience in critical evaluation?

CONNECTIONS

Language Arts: To help students set standards for aesthetic valuing, list on a large chart criteria that students want to use. Give examples to get them started: stand up straight; speak loudly enough so everyone can hear; pronounce words clearly; speak slowly enough for everyone to understand; and so on. Using selected poems familiar to the whole class, have small groups each present one of the poems orally. Guide the remaining students (the audience) to compare the performance with the list of criteria. Help students to recognize characteristics of the performance that strongly reflect the desired criteria. Then encourage them to identify what could be changed to further comply with the criteria.

Exploring Common Themes in Stories

COMPONENT   Historical and Cultural

SUBJECT   Common Themes

OBJECTIVE   Students compare stories from different countries and cultures that deal with similar themes.

MATERIALS   *Yeh Shen: A Cinderella Story from China,* by Ai-Lang Louie; *Cinderella,* by Marcia Brown and Charles Perrault

WARM UP   Discuss the term *theme* (the central thought or idea of a story) with the students as it relates to stories they know.

Give examples of common themes. One example could be love. Most people, when speaking about love, will think of feelings and emotions that one person has for another. Have students try to identify other themes—for example, courage, friendship, growing up. Discuss them and list them on the board.

EXPLORE   Discuss with the students how authors use common themes when they create a story. Say, "Think about the theme we just talked about. Can you think of a story about love? Can you create a story that has love as its theme? Who would be the characters in your story? How would they love each other? What could be happening in the story?" Ask for one or two volunteers to tell an idea they have for a story with love as its theme.

DEVELOP   Read *Yeh Shen: A Cinderella Story From China* and the traditional *Cinderella,* two stories from different countries that focus on the same theme. *Yeh Shen* was written from Chinese manuscripts 1000 years before its European counterpart. After reading both stories, ask such questions as, "Are the characters the same in both stories? How are the stepmothers alike? How are they different? How did they treat Cinderella? How does each story end?"

Select segments of each story and have the students act out those parts so that they can better visualize how each story deals with the same theme. Discuss, evaluate, and compare other parts of each story.

EVALUATE   *Student evaluation:* Have students fold a piece of construction paper down the middle and draw two scenes, one from each *Cinderella* story, that illustrate a similar theme. Help students identify themes, if necessary.

Teacher observation: Were students able to identify the themes in the two stories? Were they able to generalize that many stories and cultures use the same themes? Could students compare some of the similarities and differences in two stories?

CONNECTIONS   *Social Studies:* One common theme in literature that helps children build a sense of self and self-worth is friendship and its responsibilities. Students can deepen their appreciation of their own ability to explore, solve problems, communicate, and assume responsibilities for being a friend to others through stories read to them such as *Will I Have a Friend?* by Miriam Cohen, *Friends* by Helme Heine, *It's Mine* by Leo Lionni, *Frog and Toad Are Friends* by Arnold Lobel, *George and Martha, One Fine Day* by James Marshall, *Amos and Boris* by William Steig, and *Thy Friend, Obadiah* by Brinton Turkle. After reading literature about friendship, the class can discuss and list words or phrases that describe the characteristics of a friend.

RESOURCES   Brown, Marcia, and Charles Perrault. *Cinderella.* Scribner (Macmillan), 1981.

Cohen, Miriam. *Will I Have a Friend?* Macmillan, 1967.

Heine, Helme. *Friends.* McElderry (Macmillan), 1982.

Ireland, Norma Olin, compiled by. *Index to Fairy Tales, 1949 to 1972, Including Folklore Legends and Myths in Collection.* Scarecrow, 1973.

Lionni, Leo. *It's Mine.* Knopf, 1986.

Lobel, Arnold. *Frog and Toad Are Friends.* HarperCollins Children's Books, Inc., 1970.

Louie, Ai-Lang. *Yeh-Shen: A Cinderella Story from China.* Philomel Books (Putnam Publishing Company), 1990.

Marshall, James. *George and Martha One Fine Day.* Houghton Mifflin Company, 1982.

Steig, William. *Amos and Boris.* Farrar, Straus & Giroux, Inc., 1971.

Turkle, Brinton. *Thy Friend, Obadiah.* Puffin Books (Viking Penguin), 1969.

Exploring Native American Literature

COMPONENT	Historical and Cultural
SUBJECT	Native American Literature
OBJECTIVE	Students dramatize a Native American story using a reappearing character in Plains Indian literature.
MATERIALS	*Iktomi and the Boulder,* by Paul Goble; visual arts materials such as paper, crayons, watercolor paints, and colored pencils

WARM UP

Introduce the Sioux Plains Indian character, Iktomi (ick-TOH-mee), to the students. The character of Iktomi is found in many stories. (Most cultures have a similar folk character.) Iktomi is very clever, with unusual magical powers, but he is also a mischief maker. He is forever trying to trick others, but many times he fools himself. Ask questions to help students understand Iktomi's various qualities: "What does it mean to be clever? If you had magical powers, what would they be? What could you do with the powers?"

EXPLORE

Read the story of *Iktomi and the Boulder.* Ask the students to recall specific parts of the story. Where in the story does Iktomi lie, or use his magic powers? Ask the students which parts of the story would be suitable for dramatization.

DEVELOP

Read again the parts of the story chosen to be dramatized. Using the techniques for dramatization in previous lessons, have students dramatize the scenes. After the scenes have been performed, evaluate the performances, and refer to the story to check perceptions of this well-known Native American character.

If time permits, or in another class period, allow students to brainstorm their own class story about Iktomi. For example, students may concentrate on Iktomi's magic powers. Say, "Make up your own story about a way that Iktomi uses his powers." Elicit from the students story ideas: Iktomi might be able to fly, or change into an animal or magic creature.

Let students create a class book of Iktomi and his adventures. Using visual arts materials, they can draw pictures, dictate or write captions, and make a cover for their book.

EVALUATE   *Student evaluation:* Allow the students as a group to evaluate their ability to act out the different parts of the story. Ask, "Was it hard or easy to convey some of the characters in the story? Why? What did you do in your dramatization to show that Iktomi was magical or mischievous?"

Teacher observation: Could the students understand what a reappearing character is? What kinds of scenes did the students create? Did the dramatizations reflect the theme and content of the story?

CONNECTIONS   *Social Studies:* In social studies young students are developing a sense of historical and cultural empathy. Through stories representing the many cultures of the world, students begin to imagine what it might have been like to live in other times and places. Through drama/theatre students can "put on someone else's shoes or moccasins." Books that provide stories for such dramatization are: *The Weaving of a Dream: A Chinese Folktale* by Marilee Heyer, *The Adventures of Charlie and His Wheat-Straw Hat* by Berniece Hiser, *Cornrows* by Camille Yarbrough, and *Buffalo Woman* by Paul Goble. Read aloud some of these stories in class and help students dramatize scenes from them.

RESOURCES   Goble, Paul. *Buffalo Woman.* Bradbury (Macmillan), 1984.

_____. *Iktomi and the Boulder: A Plains Indian Story.* Orchard Books (Franklin Watts, Inc.), 1988.

Heyer, Marilee. *The Weaving of a Dream: A Chinese Folktale.* Viking, 1986.

Hiser, Berniece. *The Adventures of Charlie and His Wheat-Straw Hat.* Dodd, 1986.

Yarbrough, Camille. *Cornrows.* Coward (Putnam Publishing Group), 1979.

Improvising Movement to Poetry

COMPONENT	Creative Expression
SUBJECT	Rhythm/Movement
OBJECTIVE	Students use poetry to improvise move-ment activities that reflect ideas and feeling.
MATERIALS	"Who has seen the wind?," by Christina Rossetti, or other poem with strong visual imagery

WARM UP　Poetry represents a rich collection of material which can be integrated with drama/theatre activities. Read a poem such as "Who has seen the wind?" to the students.

> Who has seen the wind?
> Neither I nor you:
> But when the leaves hang trembling
> The wind is passing thro'.
>
> Who has seen the wind?
> Neither you nor I:
> But when the trees bow down their heads
> The wind is passing by.

Talk about the poem with the students. Ask, "Can you describe how the wind feels when it is blowing on you? What is wind? What does the poet mean by 'the leaves hang trembling'? By 'the trees bow down their heads'?"

EXPLORE　Read the poem again. Ask students, "If we were to dramatize this poem, which parts could you act out?"

In an open space have the students move to different parts of the poem. For example, read, "when the leaves hang trembling," and ask the students to put their bodies into the shapes of trees with leaves dangling from their branches. When the wind comes along (another student or students could be the wind, if desired), the trees bow and shake and the leaves tremble. Ask the students to imagine the feeling of the wind on a tree and the different effects it would produce. Ask students to demonstrate these effects. Comment on the different interpretations.

DEVELOP

Review how actors have to imagine being different people (see Lesson 16, "Creating a Scene from Imagined Objects" and Lesson 10, "Exploring Different Environments Through Movement"). Sometimes they imagine being an object, such as a tree. Sometimes they show how the same object would move in several different environments. Actors pretend that they are all kinds of things in all kinds of environments to practice communicating.

Move the class to a large open space. Give them descriptions of a muddy field, a city street in the rain, a snowy mountaintop, a hot desert, or other interesting environments. Ask students to show how a particular object, such as a flag, a flower, or a piece of litter, would move in each of those conditions.

At the conclusion of the class, read the poem "Who has seen the Wind?" again and let individual students, groups of students, or the entire class recreate specific parts of the poem.

EVALUATE

Student evaluation: Ask the students which part of the poem was the easiest to dramatize. Why? Can they tell how a tree feels when it is being tossed about by the wind?

Teacher observation: Did the students' understanding of the poem increase with each portrayal of it? As you watched the movement activities of the students, did it seem that the words of the poem limited or enhanced their creative expression?

CONNECTIONS

Language Arts: Locate poems composed of words that elicit strong visual and kinesthetic imagery. Read these poems to the children. Let students help select several poems for memorization and translation into movement. After some focused work, small groups of students could further select one poem they would like to express through body movements while the rest of the class recites the poetry chorally. A final activity could involve a performance combining the oral presentation of the poems together with improvised movement.

Selected poems might include: "The Bat" by Theodore Roethke; "Mrs. Peck-Pigeon" by Eleanor Farjeon; "A Bird" by Emily Dickinson; "If I Were A..." by Karla Kuskin; "Mice" by Rose Fyleman; "Fireflies" by Mary Ann Hoberman; "Conversation" by Buson; and "Snow" by Issa from *Sing a Song of Popcorn: Every Child's Book of Poems*. Additional poems might be: "The Zipper," "Up and Down," "Five Enormous Dinosaurs," "Moving," and "Wiggles and Squiggles" from *I Wish I Had a Computer That Makes Waffles* by Fitzhugh Dodson.

RESOURCES

de Paola, Tomie. *Mother Goose Story Streamers*. Putnam Publishing Group, 1984.

de Regniers, Beatrice Schenk, ed. *Sing a Song of Popcorn: Every Child's Book of Poems*. Scholastic Inc., 1988.

Dodson, Fitzhugh. *I Wish I Had a Computer That Makes Waffles: Teaching Your Child with Modern Nursery Rhymes*. Oak Tree Publications, 1978.

Frank, Josette, ed. *Poems to Read to the Very Young*. Illustrated by Dagmar Wilson. Random House, 1988.

Jones, Hettie. *The Trees Stand Shining: Poetry of the North American Indian*. Illustrated by Robert Andrew Parker. Dial Books for Young Readers, 1971.

Rossetti, Christina Georgina. *Sing-Song: A Nursery Rhyme Book*. Macmillan, 1924 (contains "Who Has Seen the Wind?").

Revisiting the Five Senses

COMPONENT   Aesthetic Perception

SUBJECT   Sensory Awareness

OBJECTIVE   Students explore and communicate ways in which the senses are used in creating stories.

MATERIALS   None required

WARM UP   Review the five senses (smell, taste, sight, touch, and hearing). Examine and compare the five senses and how they affect our lives. Have the students pick one sense and imagine what it would be like not to have that sense, being careful of the feelings of students who may not have the full use of their senses. For example, what would it be like not to have the sense of taste? (All food would be tasteless; tasting would not be a pleasurable experience.) Ask some of the students to share their ideas.

EXPLORE   Review a simple story that students know, such as "Little Red Riding Hood," and talk about how the characters use their senses in the story. For example, if a character is in the forest smelling the flowers, which sense is being used? What does the character see around him or her? What does the character hear in the environment? Is there anything that the character could taste? and so on. Discover parts of the story in which a character's actions are based upon the use of one sense or another.

DEVELOP   In an open space have the students recreate various parts of the story in which they must use their senses and react to them imaginatively. If the students are in the woods smelling the flowers, ask them to concentrate on the sense of sight to determine other things in the environment. Ask some of the students to tell briefly what they see, then move on to another sense. Say, "Now let's concentrate on the sense of touch in the same forest. What objects could be in our forest that have different textures (rough, smooth, fuzzy, and so on)?" Continue this process with the other senses.

EVALUATE   *Student evaluation:* Discuss with the students the differences among the senses. Ask them what their favorite senses are, and why. Ask the students if they have discovered that more than one sense can operate at a time. Ask for examples.

Teacher observation: Were students able to understand the difference between experiencing the real and experiencing the imagined senses? Refer back to Lessons 1 through 5, in which the students experienced the senses with real objects, odors, and so on. Were students able to create the imaginary environment and to use their imaginary senses within that environment?

CONNECTIONS   *Language Arts:* After the students have fully explored sensory experiences in the story, review with them their descriptions of sensory experiences. Create a webbing map to capture graphically the vocabulary responses from the children related to each sense. Write on the board around clusters labeled Smell, Taste, Sight, Touch, and Hearing the descriptive words students used. Divide the class into five groups and assign a sense to each. Using the descriptive words for its sense, each group can cooperatively write or dictate a portion of the story. Let all the groups together create a beginning and ending to the story for framing the five sensory segments. The entire group story could be read to an audience of one or more as a culminating activity.

Exploring the Five W's

COMPONENT	Creative Expression
SUBJECT	The Five W's: *Who, What, Where, When,* and *Why*
OBJECTIVE	Students identify and act out the five W's in a story.
MATERIALS	*Pinocchio,* retold by Margaret Hillert; *The Nicest Gift,* by Leo Politi; *The Snowy Day,* by Ezra Jack Keats

WARM UP

Introduce *Where, When,* and *Why* as used in drama/theatre.

Where refers to the setting in which the story takes place.

When refers to the time of day, the time of year, and the time in history.

Why refers to the reason for something happening in a story.

Read aloud a story such as *Pinocchio, The Nicest Gift,* or *The Snowy Day.* Ask students to think about the *Where's, When's* and *Why's* in the story. Ask such questions as, "Where does the story happen? Do you think it is a different country from ours? What time of day does the first scene take place? Did the story happen in the present day or a long time ago? Why do you think (Pinocchio) behaved as he did?"

EXPLORE

Review *Who* and *What* as used in drama/theatre (Lessons 15 and 19), and continue to analyze the five W's with the story that you read.

Who Say to the students: "Let's name all the characters that were in the story." Write students' answers on the board.

What Ask students: "Can you remember what the characters in our story did? What was the first thing that happened? The next?" and so on.

Where Challenge students: "Think about all the places, such as the country, the city, or town, where our story happened. Can you name any specific places, such as a kitchen, a road, a workshop?"

When Have the students tell when the story took place—the time in history, the time of year, and the time of day.

Why Explain that there is always something that makes a character do what he does. Help the students find the reasons for certain actions they have identified in the story read.

DEVELOP	Choose several students to act out various "five W" questions. Ask the student to act as though she or he were in a particular setting from the story, perhaps a hot, dusty road. "When you are walking on the road is the air cool or hot? Is the road hot? Are there crowds of people? How can we tell that you are on the road?" Use the same process to bring to life the *Who, What, When,* and *Why* responses from the students.

EVALUATE	*Student evaluation:* Ask students, "Which of the five W's was easiest to recall? Why? Why were the others more difficult?"

Teacher observation: Were students able to understand the differences among the five W's? Could students pick out the five W's in the story you read to them? How effectively did students portray the five W's?

CONNECTIONS	*Language Arts:* Students' comprehension of stories that they read or hear depends upon their understanding the five W's. After reading a story to the students, have them identify each of the five W's in it—*Who, What, Where, When,* and *Why.* After these have been discussed and/or listed, have the students act out the story. A narrator or group of narrators can improvise a prologue to set the stage for the actors. The prologue might introduce the characters (*Who*), establish an anticipatory set for the action (*What*), tell of the setting (*Where*), the time of year, time of day, or time in history (*When*), and finally lead the audience to anticipate *Why* the action will take place. Stories to be used in this way could be *Goldilocks and the Three Bears* and *I'm Coming to Get You!* by Tony Ross.

RESOURCES	Cauley, Lorinda Bryan (retold and illustrated by). *Goldilocks and the Three Bears.* Putnam Publishing Group, 1981.

Center Stage: Creative Dramatics Supplement. (contains Five W's poster) Available from Dale Seymour Publications.

Hillert, Margaret (retold by). *Pinocchio.* Curriculum Press, 1981.

Keats, Ezra Jack. *The Snowy Day.* Viking Children's Books, 1962.

McCaslin, Nellie. *Creative Drama in the Classroom.* Longman, 1990.

Politi, Leo. *The Nicest Gift.* Scribner (Macmillan), 1973.

Ross, Tony. *I'm Coming to Get You!* Dial Books for Young Readers, 1984.

Solving Problems Creatively

COMPONENT   Creative Expression

SUBJECT   Problem Solving

OBJECTIVE   Students enact stories requiring problem solving.

MATERIALS   None required

WARM UP

Discuss a number of popular TV programs featuring family situations. During the show decisions are usually made that involve one or more of the family members. Have students name a few of these shows and list them on the board. On each of these the audience is given the opportunity to see how that family would solve a particular problem.

Select one show from the list and give students the kind of problem that might arise in it (or ask students what kind of problem might arise), such as: "One child in the family wants to go to the movies and everyone else wants to go bowling." Ask, "What might happen now? How might the family decide which activity to do?" Let the students suggest answers. Write their solutions on the board or on chart paper.

EXPLORE

Discuss the solutions presented by the students. Possible solutions could include: Parents say no to the child, and everyone goes bowling; the other members of the family talk the one child out of going to the movie, and they all go bowling; they leave the one child home with a baby sitter and go bowling; one parent takes the child to the movies and the other parent takes everyone else bowling; and so on.

DEVELOP

After discussing the simple problem and the different solutions, decide on the best solution. Put a star next to this solution. Have a student act out a portion of the conversation with you that could take place between the child and the parent. You take the role of the parent. For example:

PARENT: Well (child's name), what do you think? Everyone wants to go bowling except you. What are we going to do about that?

CHILD: (child may respond) I don't care what everyone else wants to do. I'm the youngest, so I should get my way.

Respond to what the child says, letting her or him develop the argument as much as possible.

After a few minutes of dialogue with one student, let another play the role of the child. Don't worry if the dialogue is similar. The purposes of the activity are:

1. To present a variety of ways to solve the same problem.
2. To have the child listen to what is being said and respond appropriately using oral language.
3. To give the child an opportunity to speak as a particular character.
4. To give children an opportunity to imagine how they might respond to the problem in real-life situations.

Continue with various students, but abdicate the parental role as soon as possible, allowing a student to be the parent. Other students may take the parts of other members of the family, offering their own solutions. Give as many students as possible an opportunity to interact. This exercise could also be used over a period of time in the classroom. Talking and listening are continuous processes in drama/theatre.

EVALUATE

Student evaluation: Have students list the problems that seem to arise on their favorite family shows on TV. Do they find that everyone involved in the problem is satisfied by the solution? Do the solutions make family members happy or unhappy?

Teacher observation: Did students find a number of different ways to solve the same problem? Were the solutions appropriate to the problems and characters presented? Could the students use oral language effectively in acting out the problems and solutions?

CONNECTIONS

Language Arts: The process of creative problem solving through active dialogue provides a rich opportunity for the development of language skills. Read a piece of literature; stop before the end of the story and ask students in small groups to plan and then act out possible endings. Stories that might provide a situation for created endings are: *Stevie,* by John Steptoe; *Nick Joins In,* by Joe Lasker; *Alexander Who Used to Be Rich Last Sunday,* by Judith Viorst; *A Color of His Own,* by Leo Lionni; *Knots on a Counting Rope,* by Bill Martin, Jr. and John Archambault; *Anansi the Spider: A Tale from the Ashanti,* by Gerald McDermott; *A Penny a Look: An Old Story,* by Harve Zemach; and *Leo the Late Bloomer,* by Robert Kraus.

Read the ending from the original story, and have one of the groups act it out. Then let students vote on the ending they liked the best.

SPECIAL NEEDS   Teachers of socially/emotionally impaired students should be prepared for possible introduction into the discussion of severe family problems in the lives of these pupils.

RESOURCES   Kraus, Robert. *Leo the Late Bloomer.* HarperCollins Children's Books, 1971.

Lasker, Joe. Kathleen Tucker, ed. *Nick Joins In.* Albert Whitman & Company, 1980.

Lionni, Leo. *A Color of His Own.* Pantheon, 1976.

Martin, Bill Jr., and John Archambault. *Knots on a Counting Rope.* Henry Holt & Co., 1987.

McDermott, Gerald (retold and illustrated by). *Anansi the Spider: A Tale from the Ashanti.* Henry Holt & Co., 1972.

Steptoe, John. *Stevie.* HarperCollins Children's Books, 1964.

Viorst, Judith. *Alexander Who Used to Be Rich Last Sunday.* Aladdin (Macmillan), 1987.

Zemach, Harve. *A Penny a Look: An Old Story.* Farrar, Straus & Giroux, Inc., 1971.

Celebrations Around the World

COMPONENT   Historical and Cultural

SUBJECT   Celebrations and Holidays

OBJECTIVE   Students participate in visual or performing arts activities from various cultural celebrations and holidays.

MATERIALS   Books with pictures of various cultural celebrations to illustrate those that might be unfamiliar to class members (see Resources)

Note: Arrange for a parent volunteer to visit the classroom and share various cultural holiday celebration activities with students.

WARM UP   Ask the students to name all of the holidays or occasions that they celebrate and to tell briefly about the activities associated with the celebration. Try to elicit from students the role the arts play in the celebration (for example, masks on Halloween; singing during Rosh Hashana services). Show pictures of some of these, if available.

EXPLORE   Define a cultural holiday as one that has grown out of the traditions and customs of a people. Tell the students there are many cultural holidays and celebrations, such as:

Chinese New Year: a celebration of the end of winter, when the dragon play is performed, using costumes and music;

Halloween: an American version of All Souls' Day, when ghosts and witches roam the earth and children wear masks;

Cinco de Mayo: a commemoration of the victory of the Mexican soldiers over the French at the Battle of Puebla on May 5, 1862;

Kwanzaa (African-American): a celebration of harvest, lasting from December 26 to January 1. Each of the seven days is dedicated to learning a different value: unity in the family, self-determination, responsibility, cooperative economics, purpose, creativity, and faith.

Ask your students whether they are familiar with any or all of the holidays and celebrations you have talked about. Can the students add to the list?

As you consider each celebration, show pictures and ask students if they can tell which arts are an integral and important part of it. Ask the students regarding the Chinese New Year, for example, "Do you see people dancing in the pictures? Do you think music might be playing? Are props and costumes used?" Ask which ones they see in the picture.

DEVELOP Continue the activity by leading the students to realize that art is very important in all of the celebrations. Let those who celebrate a particular holiday at home explain to the others what arts are used. Ask students for ideas for celebrating any holiday without the arts. For example, could Halloween be celebrated without costumes, masks, storytelling, and scary sounds? Is there a way to celebrate the Chinese New Year without a parade and dragon dancing? Ask if anyone knows what special art forms Kwanzaa and Cinco de Mayo use in their celebrations. Let students in whose culture the holiday occurs be the sources of information if possible.

If possible, plan several activities associated with a celebration of a cultural holiday. Invite family members from that culture to involve the students in either the performing or visual arts associated with the celebration. For example, a parent could teach the students a dance or song that is associated with Cinco de Mayo. Invite family members from different cultures into the classroom often to share their experiences and traditions.

EVALUATE *Student evaluation:* Have the students share with one another the different kinds of holiday experiences in which they participate. Encourage them to compare similarities and differences in the different art forms used.

Teacher observation: As you listen to students' discussion, note whether they seem to connect art experiences with particular celebrations. Are they appreciative and respectful of others' cultural heritages?

CONNECTIONS *Social Studies:* Develop a large calendar for a wall of the classroom so that the festivals and events studied can be noted on the appropriate days and months. Symbols and realia can be attached to the calendar for easy reference during the remainder of the year. Students could make some of these as appropriate during the year.

Students can be introduced to the idea that there is similarity of purpose in certain festivals that exist or have existed historically in several cultures: for instance, a need to recognize a beginning point for a new year, or a festival to express gratitude at harvest time.

Studying literature related to each festival and event will greatly enhance students' understanding of activities.

SPECIAL NEEDS   This lesson provides a wonderful opportunity to have family members of special children involved with the school's activities. All students will gain a sense of pride by having their parent(s), relatives, or other important adults in their lives participating in the activity.

RESOURCES   Barth, Edna. *Turkeys, Pilgrims and Indian Corn: The Story of the Thanksgiving Symbols.* Clarion (Ticknor & Fields), 1981.

Behrens, June. *Fiesta! Ethnic Traditional Holidays.* Children's Press, 1978.

Brown, Tricia. *Chinese New Year.* Henry Holt & Co., 1987.

Greene, Carol. *Holidays Around the World.* Children's Press, 1982.

Madhubuti, Haki R. *Kwanzaa: A Progressive and Uplifting African-American Holiday.* Third World Press (revised), 1987.

Newton, M. Deborah. *Kwanzaa.* Children's Press, 1990.

Politi, Leo. *The Nicest Gift.* Scribner, 1973.

Introduction To Grade Two

The sequence of lessons in Grade 2, as in every grade, is cumulative. Students begin with sensory experiences, move to emotional awareness, and on to the development of kinesthetic and oral communication skills. Students use these experiences to express original ideas in situations requiring problem solving. The resource materials provide opportunities for further development of creative ideas and for developing an awareness of the cultural heritage of America.

Lessons at the Grade 2 level offer experiences in:
- an awareness of the senses and their relationship to the creative process;
- the perception that rhythm and movement are the external expression of an inner idea or feeling;
- the use of the voice as an instrument of communication, both in speech and nonverbal sound;
- spontaneous and creative responses to problem-solving situations;
- an awareness of students' own cultural heritage.

Grade 2 students will bring to the lessons a higher level of sophistication than those at Grade 1. It may be necessary to spend more time introducing concepts to those students who have not had the creative dramatics experiences offered at Grade 1. However, the Grade 2 students will most probably learn quickly because of their already developed learning skills, and because of the influence and encouragement of other students in the classroom.

Contents of Grade Two

GRADE 2

Sense Abilities: Touch and Smell

COMPONENT   Aesthetic Perception

SUBJECT   Touch and Smell

OBJECTIVE   Students increase their perception and sensory awareness by imagining smells and textures in the environment.

MATERIALS   Small classroom objects with different textures (pencils, erasers, paper clips, chalk, and so on)

WARM UP

Briefly discuss with students the five senses. (Touch, sight, smell, taste, and hearing were introduced in the first five lessons of CENTER STAGE, Grade One.) Tell them that you will be focusing on two of these senses, touch and smell. Ask the students to give examples of objects they touch and smell every day.

Touch: Give students a small object, or ask them to pick up their pencils. Then have them close their eyes and explore the object with their fingers. Ask one or two students to describe what they felt.

Smell: Ask students to imagine the smell of food items that they will have for lunch. Encourage them to be specific with the re-creation of the imaginary stimuli. Ask one or two students to describe in detail how one item from his or her lunch smells.

EXPLORE

Say, "Let's explore the power of our imaginations. Just as you imagined the food that you're going to have for lunch, let's see whether you can imagine some other things." Name several distinctive smells, and challenge students to associate each smell with an event, situation, or story. Ask, for example: "What scene do you think of when you imagine the smell of burning leaves?" One or more students may associate the smell of burning leaves with the coming of the fall season. Another student may think of a forest fire. Ask what pictures come to mind when they imagine the smell. Continue this exercise suggesting other familiar sensory cues, such as buttered popcorn, perfume, fertilizer, and the ocean.

Repeat the above activity using the sense of touch. Ask, "Does the feel of certain objects bring a certain scene to mind?" Name such examples as hot sand, a shaggy dog, a feather, dry crunchy leaves, and so on.

GRADE 2

DEVELOP   As a class, create an event that focuses on a number of sensory associations cited by the students. For example, a student's association with hot sand might be: A child is playing on the beach, near the water where the sand is cool. Then the child decides to go up the beach to a blanket, and the sand begins to get very hot! The child runs through the sand reacting to the heat, until he or she reaches the blanket and stands on it for relief.

Provide an open space and ask three or four students to demonstrate such a scene. Tell the students to give each other ample room and to try not to touch each other.

Continue building the scene, giving other students the opportunity to perform. Experiment with action that is motivated by the sensory experience. Encourage increasingly more detailed information, including what the students smell in the environment (at the beach: the ocean, seaweed, someone's hot dog, suntan lotion, and so on). After each demonstration, encourage students to tell what they liked about the scene. Then ask, "How can we change it? What can we add to it?" As time allows, continue to experiment with the scene until enough details have been added to make the scene realistic.

EVALUATE   *Student evaluation:* Ask students to identify their favorite smells and discuss the similarities and differences. Ask the students to identify and compare the objects they enjoy touching in the classroom.

Teacher observation: How effective were the students in using their sensory associations in creating a scene? Did their awareness of the senses of touch and smell seem to increase?

CONNECTIONS   *Science:* Show students a drawing of the nervous system, focusing on nerve endings in the nose and hands, and discuss with students how the nerve endings send messages back to our brains, where we store sensations that we remember. Have students make an outline of one of their hands on a piece of paper and then draw the nerves in it.

RESOURCES   Broekel, Ray. *Your Five Senses.* Children's Press, 1984.

Kaufman, Joe. *Joe Kaufman's Big Book About the Human Body.* Golden Books, 1987.

Sense Abilities: Taste and Sight

COMPONENT	Aesthetic Perception
SUBJECT	Taste and Sight
OBJECTIVE	Students become aware of the relation of the senses of sight and taste by picturing objects "in the mind's eye" and by recalling specific foods seen and tasted.
MATERIALS	None required

WARM UP   Review the five senses (touch, taste, smell, hearing, and sight). Focus on tasting and seeing. Ask the students how tasting and seeing are different (taste—the sensations perceived by the tongue; sight—the sensations perceived with the eyes). Tell the students, "Close your eyes and picture a ripe yellow banana (or other fruit). Think of how it tastes." Then tell students to open their eyes. Hold up a real banana or other fruit. Ask students again to think a moment about how the fruit tastes. Did they think the taste seemed more real when they imagined the banana, or when they actually saw the banana?

EXPLORE   Tell the students that throughout the school year they will be asked to see objects, scenes, and images with their "mind's eye." This process involves getting a picture one sees in the mind of a person, object, or scene that is imagined. Seeing "in the mind's eye" is a great help in becoming aware of the other senses.

Ask one student to see in the "mind's eye" a particular plate. Then ask that student to describe it. Ask another student to "see" and then describe a specific food on the plate. Ask a third student to imagine and describe how the food tastes. Repeat this exercise three or four times (or more, if desired).

DEVELOP   Have the students picture in their minds, then draw pictures of a particular food that is grown in the ground, or a food that grows on trees. Let the students share their pictures, describing the food and its taste. If possible, put the pictures up for display. Ask the students whether seeing the food "in the mind's eye" helped them to draw the picture and to describe its taste.

GRADE 2

EVALUATE   *Student evaluation:* How easy or difficult was it to picture the foods in the imagination? Do seeing and tasting sometimes go together?

Teacher observation: Have the students developed an understanding of imagining an object and seeing it "in the mind's eye?" Can they grasp some of the interrelationships of the senses?

CONNECTIONS   *Language Arts:* Ask students to suggest descriptive words for each sense, and list them on the board. Note that some of the words can be used for several senses. Invite students to write a short poem or story using some of the descriptive words, and illustrate it if they wish.

SPECIAL NEEDS   Allow visually impaired students to handle the banana. Ask them to describe the tastes of foods, and ask whether they can identify the foods by using other senses (smell and touch).

RESOURCES   Brooks, Charles Van Wyck. *Sensory Awareness.* Viking Press, 1974.

Espy, William R. *A Children's Almanac of Words at Play.* Potter, 1982.

Kaufman, Joe. *Joe Kaufman's Big Book About the Human Body.* Golden Books, 1987.

Sense Abilities: Sound and Hearing

COMPONENT	Aesthetic Perception
SUBJECT	Hearing
OBJECTIVE	Students develop categorizing skills by identifying specific sounds in the environment.
MATERIALS	Art and writing materials, such as paper, colored pencils, and pens

WARM UP

Review the five senses (touch, taste, smell, hearing, and sight). Focus on the sense of hearing. Tell the students that sounds can be divided into two categories: mechanical sounds and natural sounds. Ask whether any of the students can describe the two types of sounds and explain the difference. If they have trouble doing this, define the two and ask students to give examples of each type.

Mechanical sounds: all those sounds caused by manufactured objects. Examples: airplanes, jackhammers, air conditioners, TV sets, radios, leaf blowers, car alarms.

Natural sounds: All those sounds that occur in nature. Examples: wind, rain, thunder, dogs barking, woodpeckers hammering, ocean waves.

EXPLORE

Suggest a number of settings and write a word or phrase on the board to describe them. Ask the students to imagine possible sounds that one would hear in each setting. For example, tell the students, "I am writing *restaurant* on the board. I want you to list all the sounds that you might hear in a restaurant. Think carefully of as many different sounds as you can so that we can list them on the board." Students' responses may include sounds made by people, such as laughing, talking, and babies crying. Other sounds might include silverware clacking and food sizzling in a frying pan.

DEVELOP

Continue the activity, listing sounds that might be heard in other places with which students are familiar, such as city streets, a school bus, a barn, a department store, and a library.

Challenge the students to be more specific with their descriptions of sounds in the different locations. Ask them to close their eyes and imagine the particular place where they hear certain sounds. Say, "Take a moment to see the environment in your mind's eye, and to listen to all the sounds that are there. Listen not only for the obvious sounds, but also for the sounds that are a constant background noise that you might not hear right away. For instance, in that restaurant, at first you may not hear the hum of the air conditioner or the sound of the freezer, but when you concentrate on sorting out the noises, those sounds are heard loudly and clearly."

As an extension, give each student the opportunity to create an imaginary location with imaginary sounds. Have students write and/or draw about a place where specific sounds are heard, and describe the sounds. Encourage imaginative and original exploration about locations. Ask several students to describe the place they imagined and the sounds that might be heard there, and to share their writings and drawings with the class.

EVALUATE

Student evaluation: Have the students describe a location they all pass each day, such as the entrance to the schoolyard. Ask them to describe the sounds they hear there and to differentiate between the natural and the mechanical sounds.

Teacher observation: Do the students seem to understand the difference between mechanical and natural sounds? Did they develop an awarenesss of the less obvious sounds in various locations? Can they use their imaginations to create locations and sounds?

CONNECTIONS

Science: Introduce the idea of sound waves to students by drawing a representation of sound waves on the board. Use the example of a violin string vibrating to convey the idea of pitch. (The greater the frequency of vibration, the higher the pitch.) Loudness is measured in units called decibels. Students can construct their own stringed instruments from milk cartons and rubber bands, and experiment with tightening the rubber bands to make the pitch higher.

Exploring Specific Environments

COMPONENT   Aesthetic Perception

SUBJECT   Selected Environments: Land, Air, and Sea

OBJECTIVE   Students increase their perception and sensory awareness by imagining objects or animals that exist in specific environments.

MATERIALS   Writing materials (pencils and paper)

WARM UP

Ask the students to name animals, plants, and other objects that might exist in different environments such as land, air, and the ocean. Write the names of these environments on the board, then list the objects found in each environment.

Have students pretend that they are looking out of a car window. What might they see? (trees, cars, buildings, animals, people) If they were flying in an airplane, what might they see out the window? (birds, clouds, stars, other airplanes) If they looked out the porthole of a submarine, what would they expect to see? (fish, other ships, water, whales). Ask students to think of as many objects as possible.

EXPLORE

As students are looking at the land, air, and sea lists, ask them to think of the ways each item named might move. Have a few students try moving as the items they selected. Say, "Without using any words, demonstrate an object or animal listed on the board." Class members should try to guess the object and tell whether it exists on land, in the air, or in the sea.

Discuss the different ways that students found to demonstrate their chosen objects. Did they use sound? Did they use specific movements that described the object? Were some objects described without movement?

DEVELOP

Tell students, "We have been working with animals and objects that really do exist in different environments. Now we are going to create an imagined object or animal that could exist on land, in the air, or in the sea.

"Each of you will create your own imaginary object or animal. You may either draw a picture or write down a description, or both. Give your creation a name and an action or movement. Think of questions such as:

Can it be found on land? In the air? In the sea? Why would you find it in that environment? Does it fly, swim, crawl? What does it do in its environment? What color is it? How large or small is it? Does it move quickly or slowly? Does it move in some unusual way? The creation of the object and the answers to the questions are completely up to you."

An example could be: "My animal is called a Flip Flop because it can exist wherever it wants—in the air, on the ground, or in the sea. When it is on land, it flip flops its wings to turn them into fins and jumps into the water."

Give students some time to think and then have them draw a picture or write about their imaginary objects or creatures. Have students share their creations, demonstrating them if they wish.

EVALUATE

Student evaluation: Ask students to share their ideas with one another. Ask them to compare all the differences in the imagined objects and to categorize them according to environment: land, air, or sea.

Teacher observation: Were the students able to make a substantial list of items existing on land, in the air, and in the sea? Were students able to give logical reasons as to why their creations would be in a particular environment (e.g., method of locomotion or breathing)?

CONNECTIONS

Social Studies: Discuss with students the effect the environment has on all the creatures that live in it. Contrast the lives of people and animals in as many environments as students can think of: desert, jungle, plains, mountains, islands, and so on. Divide the class into small groups of four or five and ask them to pantomime people and animals in a certain environment. The rest of the class is to guess who and where they are.

SPECIAL NEEDS

Help mentally impaired students as a group to create an imaginary object or animal. Ask very specific and descriptive questions to help them form an idea of the imaginary object and the environment where it exists. Draw the imaginary animal or object as it is being described to give form to the abstract idea. Let visually impaired students create an imaginary object or animal from clay or modeling dough.

RESOURCES

All the World's Animals. Torstar Books, 1985.

Simon, Seymour. *Oceans.* Morrow Junior Books, 1990.

See also *National Geographic, Nature Conservancy,* and *National Wildlife* magazines.

Exploring Rhythm and Movement

COMPONENT   Aesthetic Perception

SUBJECT   Rhythm/Movement

OBJECTIVE   Students develop flexible and diversified physical movement in response to rhythmic patterns.

MATERIALS   *Waves of the Danube,* by J. Ivanovici (or other waltz music); *The Stars and Stripes Forever,* by John Philip Sousa (or other march); *The Circus Is Coming* or *Catch the Brass Ring* (calliope music); tape or disc player or rhythm instruments

WARM UP

Define *rhythm* as a regular pattern, occurring over and over, in sound and movement. As an example, show students how to clap their hands in a simple ONE, two, three waltz rhythm, making a louder clap on the "ONE." Vary the activity by clapping another rhythm (ONE, two, three, four). Point out that rhythm comes from the repetition of a pattern.

Choose a student's name (Susan Jameson, for example). Clap the rhythm of the name, the loudest clap on the stressed syllable (SU-san JA-me-son). Try Miguel Lopez (Mi-GUEL LO-pez). Repeat the claps three or four times to establish the rhythm. Use several students' names.

EXPLORE

In an open space, have the students move around to strongly marked rhythmic music—a march or a waltz, for example. (Use rhythm instruments or hand clapping if music is not available.) Caution the students to respect each other's space and to avoid touching one other. As the music plays, direct the students to walk, hop, jump, and tiptoe to the rhythm.

DEVELOP

Without the music, have the students move like bouncing rubber balls. Comment on the use of the space—how high they moved, how low. Comment on the rhythm of a bouncing ball.

Move the students into a large circle. Point out to students that horses or other animals on a merry-go-round also go up and down in rhythm, but the animals are always at a fixed distance from one another. Tell the students to imagine a merry-go-round turning and that they are animals on it going up and down. Have the students practice moving up and down only.

Select one student to set the pace of the merry-go-round (be the leader). Tell students that when the music starts, they are to follow the leader, moving like merry-go-round animals around in a circle, their bodies going up and down to the rhythm of the music. Play the music for several minutes, giving students time to adjust their paces to stay in a circle, and to experiment with moving up and down at the same time.

Stop the music and comment on how well the students responded to the rhythm of the music, and how well they moved up and down. Ask the students how they could improve their movements.

Repeat the exercise, but suggest to the students that this time the animals are jointed so that their legs can make high steps while their bodies are moving up and down. Play the music again with the students making the amplified movements. Repeat the comments about students' response to the rhythm of the music.

EVALUATE

Student Evaluation: Ask the students if knowing about rhythm helped in the bouncing ball exercise. Did hearing the merry-go-round music help when they were trying to be merry-go-round animals? Was it easy or difficult to maintain the spaces between the animals?

Teacher observation: Were the students able to adapt the concept of rhythm to movement? Could students move up and down at the same time as they were moving around in a circle? Did they move imaginatively and in a rhythmic pattern?

CONNECTIONS

Language Arts: Ask students to look for words of three or more syllables, using dictionaries, magazines, library books, or just words they know. Write these words on the board, dividing them into syllables and accenting the stressed syllables. Have the class say each word together and then clap the rhythm. See if they can speak the words in a monotone, without any accent. Then erase all the accents and see whether students remember which syllables are stressed.

RESOURCES

Catch the Brass Ring. Klavier 566, Vols. 1 and 2 (tape).

The Circus Is Coming. Klavier Records, KCD 11020 (compact disc).

Ivanovici, J. *Waves of the Danube.*

Sousa, John Philip. *The Stars and Stripes Forever.*

Expressing Emotions

COMPONENT	Creative Expression
SUBJECT	Improvisation
OBJECTIVE	Students communicate feeling through drama by improvising facial expressions and postures that convey different emotions.
MATERIALS	Masking tape; four cardboard signs, each with one of four emotions written on it ("happy," "sad," "frightened," "angry"); upbeat jazz or popular musical recording such as *Sounds,* by Quincy Jones, or *The Electrifying Eddie Harris,* by Eddie Harris; cassette tape recorder

WARM UP

Ask the students to name some different kinds of feelings. Suggest that students think about a time when they were very happy. As they take some time to think, ask if they can remember what made them feel that way.

Select one student to tell about the time he or she was happy and why. For example, a child's parents may have given him or her a surprise birthday party, and the child was excited and happy because of it. Ask, "Can you tell us how 'happy' feels? Do you feel happy now when you remember the party?" Select another student to share with the class a time when he or she was happy, and why.

EXPLORE

Continue the discussion by selecting another emotion, e.g., anger, and ask the students the question: "Has anyone in the room ever been angry? When and why?" Ask them some of the reasons that might cause them to be angry, and list them on the board.

DEVELOP

Divide a large open space into four equal squares. Masking tape can be used to indicate the four squares. In the middle of each square, place a sign that has the name of an emotion such as "happy," "sad," "frightened," or "angry" written on it. Read them aloud with students, and define any unfamiliar words. Play an upbeat musical recording such as the ones listed in Materials, or other popular music of your choice, and encourage the students to move freely throughout the space, passing through the different squares. They should begin moving when the music starts. Challenge students not to anticipate when the music will stop or which square they will be on when the music stops. Remind the students that they are to respect one another's spaces.

At a certain moment either stop the music or say, "Freeze." The students must freeze wherever they are and make living statues with their bodies that represent the emotion written on the card in the square in which they are standing. For example, if a student finds herself standing in the square labeled "happy" when she hears "Freeze," she creates a living statue with her body that conveys happiness. Students continue to stay frozen until told to relax, or until the music begins again. Repeat this activity a number of times so that students have opportunities to convey all four emotions.

While they are "frozen," ask various students what could have happened to make someone feel the emotions they are representing.

EVALUATE

Student evaluation: Ask the students how they conveyed the different emotions. Ask also, "What reactions did you have to other students' movements? Tell how some of the statues showed the students' feelings."

Teacher observation: In your opinion, did the movement activities in Lessons 4 and 5 help students with this activity? Were the movements of students distinctive in conveying the various emotions?

CONNECTIONS

Music: Select some appropriate classical music, and some contrasting modern recordings. Ask the students to listen for emotion expressed in the music. Some may wish to create a drawing or story to go with the music. Let students who wish share their creations and tell how the music made them feel, and how the drawing or story represents that feeling.

SPECIAL NEEDS

For visually impaired students, create a safe environment that will allow them to move freely in that space. Provide tactile aids to assist in identifying the different emotions in the four squares.

RESOURCES

Center Stage: Creative Dramatics Supplement. (contains "How Are You Feeling Today?" poster) Available from Dale Seymour Publications.

Harris, Eddie. *The Electrifying Eddie Harris.* Atlantic, 1968.

Jones, Quincy. *Sounds.* A & M Records, 1978.

LESSON SEVEN

Movement with Imaginary Objects

COMPONENT	Aesthetic Perception
SUBJECT	Sensory Awareness, Pantomime
OBJECTIVE	Students work in pairs, using perceptual skills to imagine objects and stimuli in acting out a scene.
MATERIALS	None required

WARM UP

In an open space, have the students stand in a circle. Tell them that you have an imaginary beach ball that they must catch and toss back to you. Stress the importance of imagining the size and weight of the ball as they catch it and toss it back. Throw it to one student, and when it is returned, throw it to another. Continue this procedure until everyone has had an opportunity to catch and to throw the imaginary ball back to you.

Ask the students to imagine that each has her or his own ball. Say, "Hold your ball up so I can see it. I should be able to tell its size and weight by the way you are holding and handling it! When I count to three, I want all of you to bounce your balls. Make sure you don't disturb anyone else. Stay within your own spaces. Ready... one, two, three." As students bounce their imaginary balls for a few minutes, comment on what seems to be the size and weight of each one.

EXPLORE

Have the students choose partners, or choose partners for them. The students in each pair should stand a few feet away from one another and throw the imaginary ball back and forth.

Once the students have experienced throwing the ball to one another, have half the class continue the activity, while the other half watches to see whether partners are aware of the size and weight of the balls they are throwing.

Ask questions such as, "Could you tell the size of each imaginary ball? How did a person show that a ball was heavy or light?" Following a few minutes of observation and discussion, have the observers perform the activity while the other half of the class watches.

DEVELOP   Continue this activity by challenging pairs of students to handle other objects or demonstrate tasks. Other objects and tasks could include lifting a large rock or barbells together, playing soccer with one another, pulling or pushing a large object, and so on. Allow the partners a few moments to plan what their action will be and how they will do it. Give enough time so that the partners can rehearse their actions once or twice.

Let one set of partners share their simple nonverbal scene with the rest of the class. Give viewing students an opportunity to identify the action and to comment on the various ways students conveyed their ideas. Choose another pair and continue sharing.

EVALUATE   *Student evaluation:* Ask the students how they showed the size, shape, and weight of objects. What worked? Why did it work?

Teacher observation: Were students able to sustain a concentrated effort in conveying awareness of the size, shape, and weight of an imaginary object? How well were the different pairs of students able to work together? Could each pair work independently of the whole class in discussing, rehearsing, and sharing ideas? Why or why not?

CONNECTIONS   *Mathematics:* Have a ruler, tape measure, and scales available. Select some objects—for instance, large and small rocks, chalkboard eraser, oatmeal box, ruler, crayon, golf ball, baseball—and have students weigh and measure them. The tape measure can be used to measure circumference. Let students suggest other objects to weigh and measure, and make a chart of the measurements.

SPECIAL NEEDS   With physically challenged children, the emphasis may be on establishing the size, shape, and weight of the object, rather than trying to throw or kick it. Adapt the exercise to suit the movement capabilities of the children.

The Five W's: What and When

COMPONENT   Aesthetic Perception

SUBJECT   The Five W's: *What* and *When*

OBJECTIVE   Students identify the *What* and *When* as two of the basic elements and principles of drama/theatre and its vocabulary.

MATERIALS   *Hattie Be Quiet, Hattie Be Good,* by Dick Gackenbach, or other contemporary story with simple action

WARM UP

Explain to the students that there are five W's in a story—*Who, What, When, Where,* and *Why.* Today they are going to explore the *What* and the *When.*

Ask the students to think about beginnings of stories they know. Ask, "What are often the very first words of a story?" When the reply, "Once upon a time" is offered, ask students if they can tell you when "once upon a time" is. Most of the answers will reflect the concept of the past. (For most young children, "a long time ago" is any time before they were born.)

Tell the students that every story and scene takes place at a particular time. The time of a story helps to tell what the characters did, what they wore, and what customs might have been in use. Many stories that the class knows take place "now"—the time in which the students are living. Ask the students how "now" can be shown in their stories and scenes. (The characters will look and act very much as people today do.)

EXPLORE

Read aloud "Something Nice from Hattie," from *Hattie Be Quiet, Hattie Be Good.* Ask the students when the story takes place. (the present) Ask what in the story tells them the *When.*

Say, "We know the *When* of the story, but now we need to know the *What.* The *What* of a story is all the happenings in the story, one after the other. These happenings are also called the *plot.* We know that the events in our story could happen only in the present time, but what did happen? What is the plot or *What* of our story? Tell in as few words as possible." (The students should be able to outline the events briefly.)

GRADE 2

DEVELOP   Move the students to an open space with enough room to move freely without interfering with each other. Let students each choose one event or happening from the story and act out that event. Remind the students that in earlier lessons they practiced showing how all the senses are used in performing an action and that they should demonstrate the five senses when they act out their event. Give signals to start and stop the action.

Tell the students that you are going to read the story aloud to them again. Each student must listen very carefully to follow the plot—the *What*—and as his or her part of the story is read, perform the action just practiced. (If there is a specific action that no student has chosen, have all the students perform that action.) Reread the story, giving students time to act out the events in sequence as you read.

EVALUATE   *Student evaluation:* Ask students, "Can you tell what in the story would be different if the *When* were a long time ago? Was it easy to act out your part of the story as it was read the second time? Did acting it out help you understand the plot?

Teacher observation: Were the students able to understand the influence of *When* on *What*? Did the students move freely and demonstrate knowledge from past lessons? Were the students able to work individually to demonstrate their chosen sections of the story?

CONNECTIONS   *Art appreciation:* Provide some art prints or interesting photographs from magazines of people involved in some activity, and have students imagine a *What* and *When* from the characters' clothes and what they seem to be doing in the pictures. Select the pictures from different periods of time so that students can look for clues in the type of dress. It is also helpful to choose pictures with some kind of action around which students can establish a plot.

RESOURCES   Gackenbach, Dick. *Hattie Be Quiet, Hattie Be Good.* HarperCollins Children's Books, 1977.

Locker, Thomas. *The Young Artist.* Dial Books for Young Readers, 1990.

Sullivan, Charles. *Imaginary Gardens: American Poetry and Art for Young People.* Harry Abrams, 1989.

Nonverbal Communication: Pantomime

COMPONENT	Aesthetic Perception
SUBJECT	Pantomime
OBJECTIVE	Students create a story by pantomiming specific actions.
MATERIALS	None required

WARM UP

Ask students what they see when they look into the mirror. Generally, the answers will be that they see themselves and their movements and facial expressions. Tell them that they are going to work with a partner to practice being that person's reflection in a mirror.

Have the students pair off and face one another. Tell them to extend their hands towards one another, but not to touch. One of the pair then moves his or her hands very slowly. The partner tries to follow the movements of the first person as if she or he is that person's reflection in a mirror.

Stress that students should not try to outsmart or trick their partners but instead make it possible for their partners to follow their movements by performing the movements very slowly. After a few minutes of one person leading and the other following, have partners switch roles.

EXPLORE

Extend this activity to include moving other parts of the body besides the hands: the head, arms, legs, and the torso. Change actions frequently.

Continue with the mirroring activity to include simple actions the students do every day, such as combing their hair, brushing their teeth, and putting on their shoes. Have students think of some simple actions themselves, and do them slowly and carefully for their partners to follow.

DEVELOP

Define *pantomime* simply as "actions without words." Ask students to create a story from their actions to pantomime. Ask what could happen before and after one of the activities they mirrored to expand it to a scene or story. If the activity is brushing teeth, the story could begin with a little girl waking up, getting out of bed, and moving very slowly towards the bathroom. She opens the door to the bathroom and walks inside to the sink. She then begins putting toothpaste on the toothbrush, and so on.

Have the class continue to build a story, paying attention to the *What* and *When*. Ask, "What happens after the little girl brushes her teeth in the bathroom? What other pantomimed actions could be shown in developing this story?" Add other actions and an ending that students suggest.

Have students find an open space in the room where they can move freely without bumping into each other. Tell the story the students created and have all the students pantomime it as you tell it. Name specific actions as you tell the story. For example: "Once upon a time there was a little girl asleep in her room. Morning came. She woke up, yawned, got out of bed, and put on her bathrobe and slippers. She was cold. The little girl walked slowly toward the bathroom, opened the door, and went in. She turned on the water in the sink, grabbed her toothbrush, and put toothpaste on it," and so on.

Continue directing the students as they individually mime specific actions of a made-up story such as the one above. Remind the students of elements learned in previous lessons, such as conveying the size, weight, shape, and texture of objects.

EVALUATE   *Student evaluation:* As a class, discuss the mirroring activity. What parts of the exercise were the most difficult, and why? What would help in doing it again? Ask the students what they enjoyed about pantomime.

Teacher observation: Were the students able to follow one another during the mirror exercise? Did the leaders in the mirror exercise concentrate on moving slowly instead of trying to outsmart their partners? Were students able to incorporate the simple movements into a sequence of action?

CONNECTIONS   *Music and movement:* Provide an open space where students can all stand facing you. Play some expressive music, and ask students to copy your movements as you move to the music. Then ask for volunteers to lead the others with movements that express the mood of the music. Divide the class into groups of four or five and let different students in turn lead their group in expressing different moods and emotions. Try this with a variety of musical recordings.

SPECIAL NEEDS   Have visually impaired students give each other verbal commands and allow their hands to touch slightly to indicate direction and speed.

RESOURCES   *Flamenco, Cameo Classics.* Moss Music Group, 1988.

Kipnis, Claude. *The Mime Book.* Meriwether Publishing Ltd., 1988.

The Five W's: Exploring the Who in Stories

COMPONENT	Aesthetic Perception
SUBJECT	The Five W's: *Who*
OBJECTIVE	Students identify the *Who* in a story as one of the basic elements and principles of drama/theatre and its vocabulary.
MATERIALS	None required

WARM UP

Explain to the students that every story, scene, and play is about someone. The "someone," the *Who* in the story, scene, or play, is called a *character,* and the story tells what happens to that person, or perhaps several persons. Write "Who = character" on the board. Sometimes characters are like ourselves or people we know, but often they are not. An actor, the person who pretends to be a character, must think about how that person behaves, looks, and feels.

Ask the students to think about a favorite character in a story, and to see that character in their mind's eye. What does he look like? What is he wearing? How old is he? How does he walk? Stand? What kind of expression does he have on his face? Is he something other than a human being?

Make a list on the board of the students' favorite characters. (Accept duplicates.)

EXPLORE

Select one of the characters from the list, and ask the student(s) who named him or her to tell about the character, answering the questions listed in Warm Up.

Move the students to an open area where they can move freely without contact with each other. Ask the students, on signal, to walk about as the character described for a minute or two. Remind the students that they should "stay in character"—that is, be the other person all the time they are doing the exercise. This will be easier if the student constantly keeps a mental picture of the character.

Stop the students, and ask a few questions about the characterizations. For example: How do people of that age walk? Is the expression on your face reflected in the way you walk? Does what the character wears help you move in a certain way? Repeat the exercise, noting changes, if any, in the movements.

DEVELOP Select another, different character from the list, and repeat the exercise. This time have the students, as that character, greet each other with, "Good morning. How are you?" Comment on how the voice must reflect the character in age, gender, and emotion. If time allows, have students choose a third character for the exercise, and have each of them respond to the greeting of the second character with, "I am very well (ill, angry, happy, busy, and so on)."

EVALUATE *Student evaluation:* Was it easy or difficult to move as the character? Why? How did you make your voices sound like the characters' voices? Was it easy or difficult?

Teacher observation: Were the students able to grasp the concept of "being" someone else? Did picturing the characters in the mind's eye seem to help? Were the students able to change their voices to match the characters? Did each move about freely without infringing on others' spaces?

CONNECTIONS *Social Studies:* Prepare a list of characters from history with whom the students are slightly familiar. Review details surrounding each character and let small groups of students choose a scene to act out. For example, they may choose Abe Lincoln trying to study by firelight, Florence Nightingale taking care of wounded soldiers, Puritan children going to church, or a Sioux teaching young boys how to become braves. Help students do any research needed to get information about their chosen character. Provide time for students to share their scenes with the rest of the class.

SPECIAL NEEDS Often actors must portray characters who are physically challenged. Ask those who are visually impaired, if they feel comfortable doing so, to work with sighted students, sharing some of their movement limitations. The hearing impaired could work with hearing students, and so on, so that the nonchallenged students can become more sensitive to those students with special needs.

Character Development

COMPONENT	Creative Expression
SUBJECT	Improvisation
OBJECTIVE	Students transform ideas, feelings, and values into artistic forms by improvising a scene with specific characters.
MATERIALS	None required

WARM UP

Ask the students whether they enjoy going shopping. What are some of their favorite stores to visit? List the students' favorite stores to visit on the board. Responses may include an ice cream store, a toy store, a pet store, and a clothing store. Have each student imagine and tell briefly what it would be like to own his or her favorite store.

EXPLORE

Divide the students into pairs. Have each pair find an open space in the room and stand facing one another.

Say, "We are going to be different characters in a story. One person is going to be a customer coming into a store to buy something. The other person will be the owner of the store and salesperson."

Let each set of partners decide who is the customer and who is the owner. The owner decides what kind of store it is and what is sold in the store. Pairs need to decide possible dialogue and action that could happen between the two characters in the story. For example, if one "owner" decides on a shoe store, he or she will also be the salesperson who greets people as they come in, and the other the customer who enters the store looking for a particular type of shoe.

Say, "When I give the signal, the customer will enter the store to buy something. If you're a customer, make sure you get what you want. If you're the store owner, be sure to listen to the customer." Remind students of their practice being the *Who* in the story in Lesson 10. Tell the pairs that for now, they will all practice their scenes at the same time, and show them to the class later. Give the signal. Give the pairs a few minutes to rehearse their scenes before giving the signal to stop.

DEVELOP

Following the discussion, planning, and rehearsal, allow each pair to present their improvised story to the class. Remind students to convey the weight, size, and shape of any object used in their scenes by the way they handle it. Ask the viewing students to tell what they liked about the way each pair portrayed their characters.

Select one student to be a salesperson, and let the rest of the class be the customers. Have the salesperson select one imaginary object to sell to the class. The salesperson should tell the class everything he or she knows about the object. Information about the product may include the size, shape, weight, color, price, what the object is used for, and the reason we should buy it. Remind students, if they are handling the product, to be aware of the size, shape, and weight of the object.

As time allows, give a number of students a chance to present to the class a characterization and dialogue concerning an imaginary product.

EVALUATE

Student evaluation: Ask, "How hard was it to play two different roles? Which character did you enjoy playing most? Why?"

Teacher observation: Did all of the pairs actively participate in the activity? Were the members of the pairs able to cooperate? Did students use movement, imaginary objects, and oral language to create their characters?

CONNECTIONS

Mathematics: Let students continue to work in pairs to make up some word problems that would be appropriate in their store. These may involve money, or numbers of items for sale, or time, or space—encourage students to be creative. Ask them to write down the problems. If desired, some of these problems could be put on a blackline master for others to work out.

SPECIAL NEEDS

With mentally and emotionally impaired students, the leader may want to choose specific stores for each pair to allow a more focused participation with the creative activity. Care should be taken to pair each student with another one who will be supportive.

RESOURCES

Cook, Marcy. *Cooperative Learning Seminars and Materials.* California Elementary Education Association, 3420 Kashiwa St., Suite 3000, P.O. Box 3168, Torrance, CA 90510.

The Five W's: Exploring the Why in Stories

COMPONENT	Aesthetic Perception
SUBJECT	The Five W's: *Why*
OBJECTIVE	Students identify the *Why* in a story as one of the basic elements and principles of drama/theatre and its vocabulary, and develop an understanding of the effect of the *Why* on the *What.*
MATERIALS	*Wave,* by Margaret Hodges; *The Little Red Hen* and *The Three Billy Goats Gruff,* by Paul Galdone.

GRADE 2

WARM UP

Review the five W's in drama/theatre. *Who* refers to roles and characterizations. *Where* refers to setting or environment. *What* refers to the events in a story. *When* refers to time of day or year. *Why* refers to motivation.

Explain to students that the *Why* of a story is the reason for what happens in it. Reasons may be physical events such as a tidal wave or earthquake. They can also be the feelings of a character—a need, an emotion, or an idea—that cause a certain behavior. The character's behavior starts the action, or the *What* of a story. For instance, what made Goldilocks go into the three bears' house? Was it hunger? Curiosity? Whatever made her go into the house was the *Why*; her actions were the *What.*

Read a story such as *Wave* and ask students to explain why a character acted as he did in the story. For example, in *Wave,* why did the farmer set his field on fire? What was inside him that made him do it? What were the results? Did the results create other *Whys* in the story?

EXPLORE

Read or talk about another familiar story such as *The Little Red Hen* or *The Three Billy Goats Gruff* and have students find the reasons for specific characters' actions in the story.

DEVELOP

While the students are seated at their desks or in a circle, say, "I'm going to give you some information about a story we are going to make up. Your job will be to create the story from what I tell you. Here is the information: There is a little girl looking through a window of a toy store with a big smile on her face. Why do you think the little girl is smiling?"

Encourage the students to find a variety of answers to your question. One student may say, "The little girl sees a beautiful doll, one that she's always wanted." Another student may say, "The little girl is smiling because as she is looking through the window, all of the toys come to life."

Use one of the students' reasons why the little girl might be smiling to create a story with the class. Ask, "What could happen to begin our story? What happens next? What happens to end the story?"

Suggest another reason why the little girl is smiling. How would this new story begin? Would what happens next be the same as what happened in the first story? Why not? What happens to end the story? Why is the ending different from the first story?

EVALUATE   *Student evaluation:* Ask students to give reasons why the two stories were different, even though they both began with the little girl smiling as she looked through a toy store window. How did the reasons for the little girl smiling affect what happened?

Teacher observation: How well were students able to recognize the *Why* in a story? Did they understand that changing the reasons for a character's behavior will change the content of a story as well?

CONNECTIONS   *Science:* Encourage students to ask *Why* questions about everyday occurrences, such as: Why does the wind blow? Why is the sky blue? Why does the tide go back and forth? Why do some trees grow taller than others? Put their questions on sentence strips and pin them up them around the room. Discuss possible answers in class, and encourage students to research the answers. Discuss how we know when an answer is correct. When a question has been answered, clip the answer to the back of the question with the name of the student who provided it.

RESOURCES   Addison-Wesley Big Book Programs, Level B. *The Little Red Hen.* Addison-Wesley Publishing Company, Inc., 1989.

Galdone, Paul. *The Little Red Hen.* Clarion (Ticknor & Fields), 1985.

_____. *The Three Billy Goats Gruff.* Clarion (Ticknor & Fields), 1981.

Hann, Judith. *How Science Works.* Dorling Kindersley Limited, Readers Digest, 1991.

Hodges, Margaret. *Wave.* Houghton Mifflin Company, 1964.

Why Things Are: Understanding the World Around You. Simon & Schuster, 1991.

The Five W's: Identifying the Where

COMPONENT	Aesthetic Perception
SUBJECT	The Five W's: *Where*
OBJECTIVE	Students identify the *Where* in a story as one of the basic elements and principles of drama/theatre and its vocabulary.
MATERIALS	*Harry, the Dirty Dog,* by Gene Zion; a set of about thirty 3-by-5-inch cards with different story settings written on them.

WARM UP

Tell the students that the *Where* of a story is the setting, or the place in which the action happens. Ask the students where they were on Saturday or Sunday, or the last day they had off from school. List the different places on the board. Examples may include the park, a hospital, the beach, or their home.

EXPLORE

Read a simple story such as *Harry, the Dirty Dog,* and ask the students to identify the different places in the story where the action occurs (the house, a railroad yard, a construction site, a coal chute, and a restaurant). List the students' responses on the board and if necessary, read the story again.

DEVELOP

Use *Where* cards (3-by-5-inch cards with various places written on them such as "the beach," "a horse barn," "a toy store," or "Mars"). Have one student pick a card and look at it, or privately read the card to the student so that the rest of the class will not know what it is.

Tell the student, "Think how you will show us, or act out, being at the place on the card. If you were really at that place, what would you be doing there? Show us what you would be doing."

For example, the *Where* card may say, "a farm." A student may show a farm setting by using an imaginary pitchfork and hauling hay from the barn to the horses' stalls. After a few minutes of watching the student act out the *Where* situation, other students should try to identify the setting of the story.

Discuss specific actions the student used to convey the setting to the audience. Ask, "What did (name) do to show she was on a farm? How did she move to show where she was? Did she use any of her senses to show where she was?" Following the discussion, continue the activity with other students acting out the *Where* on their cards.

EVALUATE   *Student evaluation:* Ask the students for other settings that could be written on 3-by-5-inch cards for a follow-up activity. Choose one suggestion and ask the class to think of at least four or five different actions that could be done in that location to identify it.

Teacher observation: How well did the students understand *Where* as it relates to identifying locations in stories? How imaginative were the students in suggesting different activities that could be done in the same setting?

CONNECTIONS   *Social Studies:* Show the class some pictures of people dressed in ways that suit their environment. Help students try to match these people's clothes to a place they might live, using a globe or relief map, or one that is color coded to show physical features such as deserts, ice, mountains, and plains. *National Geographic* is a good source of pictures and maps. Let students work in small groups to create their own relief map of a particular environment, using clay or play dough.

SPECIAL NEEDS   For special students whose experience may be limited to their immediate environments, make sure the *Where* cards include only places to which they have been.

RESOURCES   Aruego, Jose, and Ariane Dewey. *We Hide, You Seek.* Greenwillow, 1979.

Graham, Alma. *Discovering Maps.* Hammond Inc., 1990.

Zion, Gene. *Harry, the Dirty Dog.* HarperCollins Children's Books, 1956.

Exploring Sequence in Stories

COMPONENT   Creative Expression

SUBJECT   Sequence

OBJECTIVE   Students develop a beginning, middle, and end to a story and dramatize it.

MATERIALS   *Where the Wild Things Are,* by Maurice Sendak

WARM UP   Introduce the word *sequence* to students (the order that events happen or tasks are performed—first, second, third, and so on). Read a story such as *Where the Wild Things Are* and discuss the sequence of actions in the story. Ask the students, "What happened first in the story?" Questions could include, "What was Max doing to get him sent to bed without eating? What happened next in the story? What began to grow in Max's room? What did Max do next? Whom did Max meet as he was sailing in the boat? Then what happened? How did the story end?"

EXPLORE   Discuss the fact that stories have beginnings, middles, and endings. Say, "When we are discussing the sequence in a story, we could also ask, 'What happened at the beginning, middle, and end of that story?'"

Read students another story of your choice and ask students to identify the beginning, middle, and end.

DEVELOP   After identifying the parts of the story that represent the beginning, middle, and end, focus on the ending of the story. Talk about all the different events that led directly to the ending. Review a few stories you have read in class. Focus on their endings and decide whether the ending is happy or sad, satisfying or unsatisfying, and so on. Point out that one word cannot always describe an ending; for example, an ending can be both happy and sad.

Review the meaning of *sequence*. Say to the class, "I am going to give you an ending to a story. Your task is to create a middle and a beginning. For example, if at the end of a story, a child takes some beautiful flowers from the garden into the house and gives them to his or her parents, what could have happened to make the child think of doing this?" Encourage many suggestions.

Select one of the suggestions, and ask the students to think of what the characters would say and do in the scene. Plan the sequence of action within the scene, and select the appropriate number of students to act it out. Ask the students whether everything necessary to the scene was said and done; if not, repeat the scene with appropriate adjustments.

As time allows, repeat this process with other scenes, carefully establishing the beginning, middle, and end scenes, until the story is complete.

EVALUATE

Student evaluation: Ask the students to name different stories that the class has read and identify the beginning, middle, and end of each one. Ask, "Is it easier to make up a story when you start with the beginning or the end? Why or why not?"

Teacher observation: Were the suggestions offered by the students appropriate to the different endings? Were students able to begin at the end of the story and work backward to the beginning? Do the students have a clear understanding of *sequence?*

CONNECTIONS

Language Arts: Tell each student to think of a sentence that might be the beginning of a story and write it down. Then have each student pass the paper to another student, who writes down something that could happen next—the middle of the story. Again ask students to pass their papers on, and have the third student write an ending to the story. Ask for volunteers to share a whole story, and have other students comment on whether the events in the story seemed to follow each other well.

SPECIAL NEEDS

Grasping a sequence of events is often a problem for developmentally disabled students. Keep the story simple.

Many special students are visual learners. Write the ending of the story on the board. Give suggestions for a beginning or middle of the story, record the responses on the board, and give students an opportunity to talk about and/or act out the different parts.

RESOURCES

Sendak, Maurice. *Where the Wild Things Are.* HarperCollins Children's Books, 1988.

Creating a Story

COMPONENT	Creative Expression
SUBJECT	Story Development
OBJECTIVE	Students develop personal insight and satisfaction by creating a simple sequence in a story.
MATERIALS	Cassette tape and tape recorder

WARM UP

Ask students to find words that describe their feelings and thoughts about particular objects or foods. Say, "For instance, if you had to tell me only one word that describes how you feel or what you think about ice cream or chicken soup, what would that word be?" Elicit a variety of responses from the students. For ice cream, they may include such words as *good, cold, vanilla;* for chicken soup, *winter, warm,* and *sick.* Write a number of the responses on the board under the stimulus words, and comment on the words and feelings.

EXPLORE

Ask the students to make shapes with their bodies, either in an open space or standing by their seats, to demonstrate one of the words written on the board. For example, a child may make a very closed-in shape with crossed arms to show *cold.* Or to show *summer,* a student might make a statue of someone swimming or diving into a swimming pool. Discuss the relationship that the shapes have with the one-word responses.

DEVELOP

Together as a class, select several of the words and shapes the students made and use them to create a story. Have students talk about the different parts of the story, using the five W's (*Who, What, Where, When,* and *Why;* Lessons 8, 10, 12, and 13) and decide on a beginning, middle, and end (Lesson 14). Then ask selected students or groups of students to develop various parts of the story into scenes. For example, the class might choose *summer, cold,* and *happy.* The story could begin with happy children playing about a swimming pool, having a wonderful time, when all of a sudden a large cloud approaches. It gets very cold, people hurry out of the pool, and so on.

Give the students a specific amount of time to plan and rehearse their scenes before sharing them with the class. Present the scenes sequentially,

GRADE 2

if possible, so that the story is completed, and write down or tape record the sequence of events to review later.

Evaluate the effectiveness of the improvisations and change, adapt, and try them again if necessary. Give each student a chance to act out a part of the story.

EVALUATE   *Student evaluation:* Ask, "How did the one-word responses stimulate your imaginations to create a story? How did knowing the five W's and sequencing help in making the story?"

Teacher observation: Were the students able to use the one-word responses to motivate and shape the body? What associations did the students use in making their shapes? Were students able to add on to one-word responses to create a short story?

CONNECTIONS   *Language Arts:* Use the stimulus words on the board and ask students to name more descriptive words such as *ghastly, fresh, prickly,* and *homey.* List at least 20 words. Show students how to fold a piece of paper in half 4 times to make 16 squares. On each square they are to write one of the words from the board. Any "favorite" word they may put in twice. They are to leave one square blank or draw a picture in it for a free square. Call out the words, and have students put a check in the square if they have it. When they have 4 in a row in any direction, they are to call out "WORDO!" The game can be repeated with an X or underlining or circling.

RESOURCES   Espy, William R. *A Children's Almanac of Words at Play.* Potter (Crown), 1988.

Performing Without Words

COMPONENT	Creative Expression
SUBJECT	Pantomime
OBJECTIVE	Students use pantomime to explore real and imagined situations that require problem solving.
MATERIALS	None required

WARM UP

Ask students to look around the room to see if they can tell by their classmates' expressions how they are feeling. Explain that we express ourselves without using words. Tell the class that with our bodies we can express an action, showing what we are doing; we can express a character, showing who we are; we can express emotions, showing how we feel. Say, "For instance, if a boy playing baseball misses a fly ball, we might see him sit down on the ground and pull his hat over his face. How do you think this player is feeling?" Elicit the thought that the player's actions alone indicate that he felt unhappy because he missed the ball. Ask the students to recall a situation in which they knew how someone was feeling through the person's body movements.

EXPLORE

Have students use the situations they recalled in Warm Up to demonstrate what a person's body movements might be. For instance, if someone were trying on a pair of very tight shoes, that person might move gingerly about the room, grimacing with each step. Have the class identify the feeling being conveyed through body movements.

DEVELOP

Remind the students that the *Where* (or environment) of a story (Lesson 13) influences how a character moves. Ask for examples of a *Where* that could do so. Answers might include outer space, hot asphalt, sand, water, and weeds. In an open space have the students move through a specific environment as you name it. Repeat this activity using several different environments.

Divide the class into groups. Assign each group an environment, and ask the group to decide on an event that causes a problem as they move through their environment. For example, a group is walking through a muddy field looking for a treasure when someone gets stuck in the mud.

A solution to this problem might be: the characters in the story make a human chain by holding onto each other's arms and pull the stuck person to safety. Ask students for other solutions to the problem.

After each group determines the problem in its environment, have the members of the group offer a number of possible solutions. Then the members must agree on a solution to use in their story.

Have each group plan its story from the beginning. Members will need to plan the action, choose characters in the story, rehearse it, and then share it with the class. Remind the students that the acting should show what is happening, who the characters are, and how they feel.

Challenge the groups to tell their stories through actions only.

EVALUATE   *Student evaluation:* Have groups compare their experiences in planning their presentations with other groups' experiences. What did each group like about its own presentation? What would they change about it if they were to do it again? Why?

Teacher observation: What cooperation skills did students use in deciding on their group's problem and solution? Were solutions creative? Were observers able to identify the environment, the problem, and the solution? Did all the groups use similar themes in their stories, or were the stories diverse?

CONNECTIONS   *Social Studies:* Focus on a culture from your social studies curriculum and have children work in groups of four or five to solve some problem that people from the culture being studied might encounter. Write a list of sample problems on the board, letting students suggest as many as possible. Each group should choose a different problem, and pantomime the solution for the class.

SPECIAL NEEDS   Problem solving may be difficult for many special students, depending on their mental capabilities and/or sensory impairments. Accept simple solutions to problems given.

RESOURCES   *Center Stage: Creative Dramatics Supplement.* (contains "How Are You Feeling Today?" poster) Available from Dale Seymour Publications.

Developing Stories Through Movement Activities

COMPONENT	Aesthetic Perception
SUBJECT	Dramatic Movement
OBJECTIVE	Students become aware of drama/theatre as a means of communication, and use movement to express feelings and explore characterization.
MATERIALS	None required

WARM UP

While students are all seated in the classroom, leave briefly and re-enter. Walk slowly into the room with your head back, looking at the ceiling. After a few moments, look at your students and ask them what they thought or felt was happening. Expect varied responses, such as: "I thought you saw something strange on the ceiling," or "I thought your neck hurt," or "You were trying to get our attention." Comment on the different responses.

EXPLORE

Explain to the students that people respond to other people by the way they move and carry themselves. Say, "I wanted to see what you thought was happening." Ask students what they would have thought if you had run or crawled into the classroom. Compare students' responses to these scenarios and the one in Warm Up.

DEVELOP

Ask for a volunteer to leave the room and re-enter in a different way from yours. For example, a student could enter the room crouched over and moving slowly or could enter moving backward, taking small steps. Ask students who are watching why they think this person entered the room in that way. After eliciting a number of responses, have the volunteer tell the class what he or she had in mind by moving in that particular way.

Now have another volunteer exit and enter the room in a different way. Again ask the students to think of possible reasons. Point out that people (in this case, the audience) respond to the manner in which others move.

Extend the activity into a discussion of possible stories that could go along with the way a particular student entered the room. Make a chart of the five W's (*Who, What, Where, When,* and *Why*) on the board. Fill in all the pieces of one of the stories. Ask "Who is the character? Give him or her a name. Give other details about that person entering the room. What is the action? (A child enters the room backward, taking very small steps.) What could be happening at the beginning of our story? Where is the character at the beginning of the story? Where is the story taking place? Why would that character be moving backward?" Have the student leave the room and enter again the same way.

When the chart is complete, have the class write or draw the story. Give the students an opportunity to share written or drawn stories with one another.

EVALUATE   *Student evaluation:* Ask the class to comment on how the movements of individual students helped to convey a story. Ask positive questions such as "What did you like about the way (name) used his body to convey a certain character?"

Teacher observation: Were students eager to participate in this activity? How effectively did students convey various characters by the way they entered the room? Did students develop the understanding that how people carry themselves gives an impression to others?

CONNECTIONS   *Music:* Play two or three different kinds of expressive music, and encourage students to move the way the music makes them feel. Discuss the images the music brought to mind. Ask if anyone had a whole scene or story come to mind, and ask that person to narrate the scene, concentrating on the *Who, What,* and *Where* as the music is played quietly. The rest of the class then moves to the music and the narration. Point out that often composers do have scenes and stories in mind when they write their music.

SPECIAL NEEDS   A few descriptive words will be required for the visually impaired student (e.g., "Bill is walking in backwards.").

Students whose movement is restricted may need some help to enter the classroom in their chosen way. Another option is to have a student carry out a particular movement at his or her seat.

Poetry and Nature

COMPONENT   Aesthetic Valuing

SUBJECT   Poetry

OBJECTIVE   Students investigate the relationship of nature and the fine arts by using movement to interpret poetry.

MATERIALS   *Haiku Anthology* by Cor Van den Heuvel; "Swift Things Are Beautiful," from *Away Goes Sally*, by Elizabeth Coatsworth; *Chariots of Fire* (recording), by Vangelis; cassette tape recorder

WARM UP   Give examples of the beauty and order in nature and talk about them with the students. Ask, "Have you ever watched a sunset? What colors did you see? Have you watched the trees swaying gently in the wind? How did that make you feel? Have you ever watched a flock of birds flying in formation? What did that make you think about?" Elicit from the class other examples of natural phenomena and find out why the students thought them beautiful. Examples may include flowers of different colors blooming in a yard or field, large clouds floating by in the sky, or snow falling very quietly to the ground. Encourage a variety of answers.

EXPLORE   Tell the students that many artists use images from nature as subjects for their art. Some examples include: the mime (pantomime artist) physically reacting to imaginary wind; the visual artist drawing a sunset; the dancer moving like a bird or other animal; and the actor using movement and language to convey the onset of winter or nightfall to an audience. The artist is motivated by what he or she sees, hears, smells, tastes, and touches in nature. Ask students to describe some examples of art that they have seen that have tried to recreate the beauty found in nature.

DEVELOP   Remind the students that rhythm is often a part of nature. (Refer to Lesson 5.) Birds' wings moving as they fly and the rhythm of sunrise/sunset are examples of rhythm in nature. Poetry is a special way of saying things in which the writer often uses rhythm. Poets use words to explore various relationships between art and nature.

Read aloud poetry such as haiku that speaks specifically to the beauty in nature and/or read other poems such as *Swift Things Are Beautiful* by Elizabeth Coatsworth.

Swift things are beautiful,
Swallow and deer,
And lightning that falls
Bright veined and clear.

Rivers and meteors,
Wind in the wheat,
The strong-withered horse,
The runner's sure feet.

And slow things are beautiful,
The closing of day,
The pause of the wave
That curves downward to spray.

The ember that crumbles,
The opening flower,
And the ox that moves on
In the quiet of power.

Ask the students to see "in the mind's eye" the images in the poem and to think about how they could convey the images through movement. Ask, "How could we show the line 'Swift things are beautiful' through movement?"

Encourage the students to try different ways of moving to the first line of the poem. Point out that there are no right or wrong ways to interpret the images. Students should be encouraged to present a wide range of movements that may speak creatively to the images in the poem.

Continue this process with other parts of the poem. Once the students have had a chance to interpret each line, give individuals and/or small groups the opportunity to move to the poem as you or the class read it aloud.

If time allows, replay the scene with other students. If desired, use expressive music, such as *Chariots of Fire,* to enhance the movement experience.

EVALUATE

Student evaluation: Ask the students to name art forms other than poetry that use images from nature to create art (dance, the visual arts, music). Ask the students whether they saw the images from the poem in their mind's eyes as they did the movement. How did seeing an image in the mind's eye help in creating the movements?

Teacher observation: Did the students freely explore movement activities? What connections did they make between images in art and nature? Which worked better—individual students exploring ways to create images, or small groups creating a movement piece?

CONNECTIONS

Science: Bring into the classroom some natural objects that have specific patterns or symmetry: a sand dollar, a chambered nautilus, several different kinds of leaves. With the students, discover the patterns in each of the objects. Ask students to bring in their own found objects that have rhythm and pattern. Have each student make a drawing of one of the objects, and create a bulletin board of patterns in nature.

RESOURCES

Coatsworth, Elizabeth. *Away Goes Sally.* Macmillan Publishing Company, 1934 (contains the poem, "Swift Things Are Beautiful").

Van den Heuvel, Cor. *Haiku Anthology: Haiku and Senryu in English.* Simon & Schuster, 1986.

Vangelis. *Chariots of Fire.* Polygram Records.

The Role of Evaluation in Drama/Theatre

COMPONENT	Aesthetic Valuing
SUBJECT	Evaluation
OBJECTIVE	Students discuss and evaluate a story that has been performed to help them learn to use objective criteria when analyzing drama/theatre.
MATERIALS	None required

WARM UP

Introduce the word *evaluation* and its meaning to the students. Define it as "judging one's own work as well as reflecting on and making judgments about the efforts of others."

Explain to students how evaluation is important in many things that we do. In drama/theatre we evaluate our own and others' work so that we have a better understanding of what we are doing, and so that we can find ways to make dramatic activities clearer and better. Remind students that they can evaluate an activity by asking themselves, "What did we like about what we did? Could we change it or add to it to make it better in any way?" Students can also use the five W's (*Who, What, Where, When,* and *Why*) to evaluate whether they've included all the necessary elements of a story.

Name a class activity that you have evaluated—for example, projects made for a science fair. Ask students to comment on whether the evaluation affected subsequent similar activities. Did your suggestions help students revise their project, or make the next one better?

EXPLORE

Explain that evaluation is a very important process in the arts as well as in science, social studies, and math. During a rehearsal for a play or scene, for example, the actors often discuss the way they performed in the play or scene. They will consider what they did well, what needs improving, and how to improve their performance. As a result of the discussion and evaluation, a certain part of the dramatic activity may be changed, adapted, or reordered.

Say, "Without evaluation, you will never know whether what you are doing is being done well, could be done better, or be done differently."

Ask the students for examples of times they evaluated their own and others' work. How did the students being evaluated feel about the evaluation and its effect upon their performances? Compare examples given by the students. Students may refer to a writing project, a drama activity, or a visual arts experience that they discussed and evaluated, either as a class or in small groups, and then decided to change in some way.

Impress upon the students how important it is that evaluation be constructive and not destructive. The point of evaluating is not to put someone down, or to make any individual or group feel bad about what they have created, but to strengthen students' ability to look constructively at their own and others' work. The object of evaluation is to reinforce the positive aspects of their own creations, and to help them improve on what they have done so that they will feel even more successful.

DEVELOP

Using a previously completed exercise in which the students created stories (perhaps Lesson 15), replay one of the stories or scenes. Remind students to use the five W's as they replay the scene. Lead the students in evaluating their performance. Ask questions such as, "What is your favorite part of the story or scene? What do you like best about what you did, and why? What could you change to make the story better? What could you do to make your own performance better?" Have the students who played the scene evaluate the story and performance first. Then have some of the students who watched answer the questions.

Following the evaluation of the scene or story, the students should plan, rehearse, and repeat the scene, incorporating suggestions from the evaluation. Students may adapt, insert new parts, or delete existing parts.

If time permits, choose another group story and continue giving students opportunities to use evaluation techniques to improve their dramatic work.

Constantly stress the positive, constructive attitudes necessary for effective evaluation. (These techniques are adaptable to all subject areas.)

EVALUATE

Student evaluation: Ask, "Did you use the five W's (*Who, What, Where, When,* and *Why*) to focus on all parts of a scene or story being evaluated? Were you positive in your evaluation?"

Teacher observation: When evaluating the works of others, were students positive and constructive in their evaluation? Were students able to talk about and evaluate their own work as well? Were students able to incorporate suggestions into subsequent performances?

CONNECTIONS *Mathematics:* Extend the concept of critical evaluation to the process of doing and checking word problems. Help students think of some questions for improvement when they get an incorrect answer: Did they understand the key words? Did they plan the steps to the problem? If those steps didn't work, did they try something different? Did they do the calculation carefully? Did they check the calculation? Ask students for their own methods of self-evaluation.

SPECIAL NEEDS With certain students, such as those who are emotionally impaired, evaluation can be especially devastating if not used properly. Making any kind of judgments, positive or negative, should be done very carefully to assure proper sensitivity to those children's specific needs.

LESSON TWENTY

Exploring Creativity

COMPONENT   Creative Expression

SUBJECT   Creativity

OBJECTIVE   Students create stories using music to gain personal insight and increased appreciation of their own and others' accomplishments.

MATERIALS   Recordings such as *Pat Metheny Group (Offramp)*; *2001 (A Space Odyssey)*; *Jazz Crusaders 1 (Put It Where You Want It)*; and *Close Encounters Of The Third Kind*

WARM UP   Remind the students of the importance of rhythm and movement in drama/theatre. If necessary, refer to Lesson 5, in which these basic concepts are explored; also see Lesson 18, in which rhythm in poetry is covered.

In an open space have students move to an up-beat jazz recording such as *Jazz Crusaders 1*, or other popular music. Allow the students to experiment moving to the music for a few minutes. Then stop the music and say, "I will play the music again. This time when the music stops, I will say 'freeze.' When you hear the music this next time, think about how it makes you feel. See if you can express your feeling in the way you move."

After the students have been moving for a few minutes, challenge them to vary their movements. Suggest different options such as moving just their legs, moving within their own space, using their arms to propel them around the room, moving in place, or experimenting with different levels—high space, middle space, and low space. Remind students to be careful not to bump into or hit anyone as they move.

After a few moments, put on a different record, such as *2001 (A Space Odyssey)* and invite the students to move to the different style of music.

EXPLORE   Say, "I noticed that when the style or mood of the music changed, your movements changed as well. Could we create a story from the different ways we moved to each kind of music? Would the two stories be the same? Why or why not? Will the music help us to determine the characters and the action of our story?"

GRADE 2

Discuss some possible scenes and/or stories that seem to fit the specific music selections played. For instance, the music played and the resulting movements may prompt the students to create a story about a circus. Brainstorm a few scenes and actions that could be part of such a story.

DEVELOP

In small groups or as a class, continue to experiment with creating story content from movements that match a variety of musical styles. After a selection is played and students have moved to it, ask them to suggest a story that would fit with the specific movements and music. Choose one of the stories suggested and have selected students improvise parts of the story, using the music to interpret story content. Plan, rehearse, and share the stories with the entire class. Evaluate, adapt, and replay the scenes.

EVALUATE

Student evaluation: Ask the students, "Would your stories have stayed the same if the music used to create the stories changed? Would the different music change the ways you moved in the story as well? Is there anything in the story itself you would change? Why or why not?"

Teacher observation: Were the students aware of the effect that the different styles of music were having on their movements? Did all of the students participate in developing the story themes?

CONNECTIONS

Art Appreciation: Bring in some prints of artwork and put them up around the room. Include a variety of artists, such as Rembrandt, Cassatt, Bearden, Picasso, Rivera, and O'Keeffe. Number the pictures, and as you play several different kinds of music, ask students to write down the number of the picture they think best suits the music. Then play the music again, and compare students' choices. (There is no right or wrong.) Ask different students how they thought the music and the art brought out the same feelings and images. Let students draw their own pictures to the same music.

SPECIAL NEEDS

Hearing impaired students should become attuned to music by sensing the variations in its vibrations felt through the floor and chair. Give these students labels for the various types of music to enable them to participate in the activity.

RESOURCES

Close Encounters of the Third Kind. Arista Records.

Jazz Crusaders 1 (Put It Where You Want It). Chisa Records.

Pat Metheny Group (Offramp). ECM Records.

2001 (A Space Odyssey). MGM Records.

Common Themes in Literature

COMPONENT	Historical and Cultural
SUBJECT	Folklore
OBJECTIVE	Students recognize that people of diverse cultures have dealt with common themes throughout the ages.
MATERIALS	"Loo-Wit, the Fire Keeper," from *Keepers of the Earth,* by M. Caduto and J. Bruchac; "The God Brings Fire to Man," from *In the Beginning,* by V. Hamilton.

WARM UP

Ask, "Do you ever wonder about how certain things came to be, such as where rain comes from or why the stars don't fall from the sky? What are some things you have questions about?" List a few of the students' questions on the board. Ask whether other students have wanted to know the same things. Lead students to recognize that although each of them is unique, many of them share the same thoughts and questions.

Explain to the students that many stories attempt to answer such questions as how people first got fire, or how the camel got its hump, or how the sun got in the sky. Such stories are called "how and why" stories.

EXPLORE

Explain to students that children from different countries ask the very same questions. No matter where they live, all children want to know the hows and whys of the world. Focus on the subject *fire*. Ask the students how they think human beings discovered fire to keep warm, to cook food, and to make tools and other useful items. Invite students to imagine different scenes or events that led to the discovery of fire. Encourage creative responses and record the students' suggestions on the board.

DEVELOP

Read "Loo-Wit, the Fire Keeper" and "The God Brings Fire to Man," two stories from different cultures dealing with same theme, the discovery of fire. (If appropriate, define *theme* as the basic idea, thought, or subject of a story or play.) When two brothers quarrel over who should marry Loo-Wit, the gift of fire is taken away from them and they are turned into mountains. Loo-Wit is also changed into a mountain. She separates the two brothers and becomes the keeper of the fire.

In the Greek myth, "The God Brings Fire to Man," Prometheus has a plan to make humans better and wiser than the animals. He steals fire from the heavens and gives it to mortals.

Compare the similarities and differences between these two stories and between students' imagined scenes of how people discovered fire. Point out that each culture's story answered the "how and why" for those people. Other stories with the same theme include: *The Stolen Fire,* from Hawaii, in which Maui defies the gods, and the Native American tale, *The Fire Bringer,* in which a coyote obtains fire for the people. These two stories are out of print, but can be found in most libraries.

If you have a classroom aide, divide the class into two groups and let each plan a dramatization of one of the stories. Each of the groups should rehearse briefly and present the drama to the class. If two presentations are impractical, work with the whole class on one dramatization. Evaluate the presentation(s).

EVALUATE   *Student evaluation:* Discuss and list all the similarities and differences of each story's approach to the subject of how human beings obtained fire. Have the students share with one another some other questions that might be answered through "how and why" stories.

Teacher observation: Did the students offer a variety of questions about how and why phenomena occur in the world? Did the students see the relationship of the two stories? Did they understand the idea of themes? Did they understand the concept of "how and why" stories, and that most cultures have stories to explain physical and cultural phenomena?

CONNECTIONS   *Social Studies, Language Arts:* Ask students to name some other natural events besides fire that they think every culture would try to explain. What would be important in everyone's lives on this earth? (changing seasons, day and night, rainfall and water sources, and so on) Turn these into "How and Why" titles and list them on the board. Then choose one of the titles and create a group story to explain the natural event. Tell students to think about how people who didn't know the answer might make something up. Encourage students to be as imaginative as possible. Write the story on the board, and let students copy and illustrate it. They may also wish to create their own "How and Why" stories.

RESOURCES   Caduto, Michael J., and Joseph Bruchac. *Keepers of the Earth.* Fulcrum Publishing, 1988.

Hamilton, Virginia. *In the Beginning.* Harcourt Brace Jovanovich, 1988.

Folklore in Literature

COMPONENT	Historical and Cultural
SUBJECT	Folklore
OBJECTIVE	Students become familiar with fables, folk tales, myths, legends, and fairy tales.
MATERIALS	*The Girl Who Loved the Wind* (fairy tale), by Jane Yolen; *Mythology* (myths), by Edith Hamilton; *The Three Billy Goats Gruff* (folk tale), by Paul Galdone; and *Johnny Appleseed* (legend), by Steven Kellogg; chart paper

WARM UP   Introduce the different kinds of stories that represent folklore in children's literature. Include in the discussion folk tales, myths, fairy tales, fables, and legends.

Folk tales: Any stories about a culture passed on from generation to generation. Myths, fairy tales, fables, and legends can also be folk tales.

Fables: Stories that teach a lesson and that often have animals with human traits.

Myths: Stories that explain the unknown.

Fairy tales: Stories about supernatural beings.

Legends: Greatly exaggerated stories about people who really lived.

List the five categories of stories on the board or on chart paper for students to refer to. Ask the students to name stories they know in the various categories. Help them to categorize the stories if necessary.

EXPLORE   Discuss a story you have read to your class recently, or choose one of those listed under materials and read it aloud. Determine with the students whether that story is a considered a folk tale and/or a fable, a myth, a fairy tale, or a legend. Ask the students to tell why the story fits into a particular category.

DEVELOP   Divide the students into several groups, and using the stories that were either read or discussed with the class, assign each group a different genre. Say, "As a group, decide on a specific part of the story that would be good for dramatizing. Choose parts, plan, and rehearse, so that we can share your story with the entire class."

Encourage all the students to take part in the dramatization of the stories. If a story does not have enough parts for everyone to participate, create other action in the story so that more students can be included. For example, in *The Tortoise and the Hare,* students can be the race officials or the spectators of the race.

Allow adequate time for the planning and rehearsal process. When the groups are ready, share the dramatizations.

Following the presentations, have students discuss the genre, the different characters in the story, and what the students may have added to the original story. Evaluate the dramatizations.

If time permits, replay the stories after the evaluation so that the students may add or delete material according to the suggestions made.

EVALUATE   *Student evaluation:* Ask students to identify and compare the different genres of stories presented to the class.

Teacher observation: Were students able to comprehend the differences among the types of stories? Did students incorporate any changes in their stories that were prompted by the general discussion? Are the students' evaluative skills progressing (see Lesson 19)?

CONNECTIONS   *Science, Language Arts:* Discuss the balance of nature, the food chain, and the interdependency of living things. Ask students what they do at home to contribute to saving the environment. They will probably have a wealth of ideas on recycling, eating properly, carpooling, and so on. Help students formulate a lesson to be learned from what they do, and then create a modern fable to go along with the moral of the story. This activity can be done either individually or as a group, depending on students' abilities.

SPECIAL NEEDS   To the mentally impaired student, the various genres are abstract and therefore difficult, especially when presented at the same time. Simplify the activity by focusing on only one story game.

RESOURCES   Asbjornsen, Peter Christen, and Jorgen Moe. *Norwegian Folk Tales.* Pantheon Books, 1982.

Galdone, Paul. *The Three Billy Goats Gruff*. Clarion (Ticknor & Fields), 1981.

Hamilton, Edith. *Mythology*. Little, 1942.

Kellogg, Steven. *Johnny Appleseed*. William Morrow Junior Books, 1988.

Rackham, Arthur (illustrated by). *Aesop's Fables*. Outlet Book Company, 1985.

Yolen, Jane. *The Girl Who Loved the Wind*. Trophy Picture Books, 1987.

GRADE 2

Native American Stories

COMPONENT	Historical and Cultural
SUBJECT	Native American Folklore
OBJECTIVE	Students read and dramatize a Native American myth to help them understand how a myth attempts to explain a natural phenomenon.
MATERIALS	*Keepers of the Earth* ("How Grandmother Spider Stole the Sun"), by Michael Caduto and Joseph Bruchac

WARM UP

Define *natural phenomena* as those events in nature that seem difficult to explain: the sun rising and setting, birds flying south for winter and north for summer, the change of seasons, the changing color of the sky. Talk about the sun and how it is important to us for food, energy, heat, and light. Ask the students for examples of how sunlight (or lack of it) affects us and the food we grow. (We need sunlight—Vitamin D—to stay healthy; sunlight affects our moods; sunlight is needed by plants for growth; and so on.)

EXPLORE

Read the Native American story "How Grandmother Spider Stole the Sun," which explains how the sun came to be in the sky. Ask the students to identify the genre, as learned in Lesson 22.

Choose specific parts of the story to discuss, such as Fox and Possum grabbing a piece of the sun. Ask, "What happened? What did Grandmother Spider do differently in the story?" After the story discussion, lead students to recognize that natural phenomena are themes not only for many Native American stories, but for stories from cultures around the world, because the phenomena themselves are so important in people's lives. (Refer to Lessons 21 and 22.)

DEVELOP

After the discussion of natural phenomena and their place in Native American folklore, read the story to the class again. Assign scenes from the story to small groups, allowing the students to improvise the scenes. Have the students develop the scenes, cast parts, rehearse, and then share their scenes with the entire class. Have groups present their scenes in the order they occurred in the story.

EVALUATE   *Student evaluation:* As a class, evaluate the performances. Ask the students if they know of any other stories based on natural phenomena. Discuss the meaning the sun had for Native Americans.

Teacher observation: Were students aware of what natural phenomena are? Were their reactions different after discussing the story and then rereading it? Were students able to work in small groups to improvise parts of the story? Were they able to evaluate their work (Lesson 19)?

CONNECTIONS   *Social Studies:* Native Americans lived in harmony with nature and identified closely with the world around them. Their stories often had animals as the main characters, such as the possum and the fox in "How Grandmother Spider Stole the Sun." Native Americans often took names of animals that they felt suited their personalities. Post pictures of animals around the room so that students can select one with which to identify. They can add other words to the animal name, such as "Running Deer," or "Brave Wolf." Let students make a name tag for their desks with their animal name on it, and tell why they chose it.

RESOURCES   Caduto, Michael, and Joseph Bruchac. *Keepers of the Earth: Native American Stories.* Fulcrum Publishing, 1988.

(The illustration on page 120 was done by Jane Bush for the book *If Rocks Could Talk.*)

GRADE 2

The Oral Tradition of Storytelling

COMPONENT	Historical and Cultural
SUBJECT	Storytelling in the United States
OBJECTIVE	Students study American folklore in order to understand oral and written traditions.
MATERIALS	*Jack Tales,* by Richard Chase; *North American Legends*, by Virginia Haviland

WARM UP

Tell students a story you know from memory. The story could be one that your parents told you when you were a child, or one that you read recently. Then read a story from a resource such as *Jack Tales* or *North American Legends.*

Ask students if they noticed any differences in the way you told the first story and the way you read the second one. Answers may include a difference in the length, how you used your voice, eye contact you made with the listeners, and gestures.

If students do not mention that a story told orally can change in each telling, say, "Another difference could be that in the story I told you from memory, the words may not be the same each time I tell the story. Depending on who the listeners are, I may leave out certain parts or add new parts to make the story more interesting. A story that is read from a book stays the same no matter who is reading it or who the audience is."

EXPLORE

Review the definition of folklore: stories and information about a culture that have been passed on from one generation to another. As time passes, especially if a story is not written down, many of the details of the original story may change.

Refer to the story that you told the students from memory. Say, "I want you to tell me all the details of the story that you can remember. Here are a few questions to get started: Who were the different characters in the story? Where did the action take place? When? Why?" Remind students of details they may have forgotten. Then talk about how stories are changed when told orally. Point out that students used words different from yours when they retold your story.

DEVELOP   Review a few stories all the students have read as part of a reading assignment, or in previous drama/theatre lessons.

Many stories, especially those classified as folklore, may have started in the oral tradition. Later someone wrote them down so that they would not be lost as years passed.

Although the United States is a young country compared to others in the world, it has a rich supply of folklore. The stories in the United States also represent a world perspective because when people from other countries came or were brought to this country, they brought their stories with them.

The recommended resources include many stories of America that were told orally, just as was folklore of other countries. Read and discuss with your students a number of the stories with subject matter appropriate for your students that focus on the American experience and culture(s).

If time allows, have one student tell a brief story. On the following day, have the same student repeat the story. Have the class point out any differences in the two tellings.

EVALUATE   *Student evaluation:* Ask the students how stories told today are similar to or different from the stories used in the last two drama/theatre lessons. Ask, "What might happen to a story if you were the only person who knew it?"

Teacher observation: How well did the students understand the concepts of oral and written traditions? Did trying to recall the content of the story that you told give the students an understanding of what happens to stories when they are passed on orally?

CONNECTIONS   *Music, Social Studies:* Many cultural traditions are passed on through music. Select some American folk songs from the resources listed and teach the songs to the students, sharing information about United States history and culture at the time the song was written.

RESOURCES   Chase, Richard. *Jack Tales.* Houghton Mifflin Company, 1943.

Glazer, Tom. *Tom Glazer's Treasury of Songs for Children.* Doubleday, 1988.

Haviland, Virginia. *North American Legends.* Philomel Books (Putnam Publishing Group), 1979.

Seeger, Ruth. *American Folk Songs for Children.* Doubleday, 1980.

Legendary Characters

COMPONENT   Historical and Cultural

SUBJECT   Legends

OBJECTIVE   Students create stories of legendary characters in order to understand how a legend is created.

MATERIALS   *Johnny Appleseed,* by Steven Kellogg; *John Henry: An American Legend*; by Ezra Jack Keats; *William Tell,* by Felicity Trotman; writing materials

WARM UP   Explain that a *legend* is a greatly exaggerated story about someone who actually lived that has been handed down through generations. It has been added on to and retold so many times over the years that it's hard to know what really happened in the event and to the character. People may believe the story to be true, but at least some information in it is not actually provable. A legend usually tells about the culture as well as a particular person. Often the real actions of the person or particular events are exaggerated, or are changed so much that they become unbelievable. Give the students a few examples of legendary characters, such as Johnny Appleseed, John Henry, and William Tell.

EXPLORE   Read brief accounts of a number of legendary characters such as Johnny Appleseed, John Henry, and William Tell. Ask the students, "Do you think the stories about these characters could be true? Why or why not?"

Ask for a volunteer to act out a deed one of the characters performed, such as John Henry swinging his hammer so fast that he cut a hole through the mountain faster than a machine could.

DEVELOP   Tell the students, "We are going to create our own legend. Remember that a story becomes a legend by having so much information added to it over the years that people forget the original and start thinking that the story heard now is the real story. To understand how this happens, we are going to play the 'Add-On Game'."

To play the game, the first person selects one object or animal, perhaps a cow. Have each person add on to this word. For example, the second person may say, "A blue cow," the third person, "A big blue cow," and so forth. Tell the students that a legend can change and grow in very much the same way as the description of the cow changed and grew. People add information each time they tell the story.

Now explain to students that they will be building a story in the same way that a legend is created. Give the class a simple statement such as, "_____ scored five touchdowns last Sunday!" or "_____ sang on her own TV show last night." Write the sentence on the board.

Choose names for the blanks and ask for suggestions of actions and descriptions that could be added to the story. For example, "Last Sunday _____ caught passes for five touchdowns with one arm tied behind his back," or "_____'s voice last night sounded like an entire chorus singing together." Write these new sentences on chart paper or on the board.

Tell students to continue adding on to the original sentence by selecting, evaluating, and including more information. Stop at an appropriate place and read the "legend" to the students. Continue to refine the original ideas with the students.

If time allows, have the students create and write about their own individual legendary characters. If desired, give the entire class one simple sentence about a character, such as one used in the examples above. Or encourage the students to find their own statements to develop. Say, "Write about your own legendary character by adding on to the sentence. Feel free to add information that no one would ever believe."

Assist individual students in developing ideas and content for their stories, if necessary. Following the writing, have students share their legendary characters with the class.

EVALUATE   *Student evaluation:* Ask the students to explain how legends grow. Do they know of someone now who is becoming a legendary figure? Do they think legends have anything to do with history? If so, what?

Teacher observation: Is the concept of *legend* clear to students? Do they believe that the legends about William Tell, Johnny Appleseed, and John Henry are true? Were the students able to create legends?

CONNECTIONS   *Music:* Legendary characters are often immortalized in song. Some familiar examples are Davy Crockett, Clementine, John Henry, and Paul Bunyan.

Stories are embellished as verses are added. Teach students songs about some of these characters and let them pantomime the action in the stories (songs). They might also try making up a fantastic verse themselves.

SPECIAL NEEDS   Let your special needs student, even if in a wheelchair, be the one to act out John Henry swinging his hammer with all his might, to provide a reminder to that student and others that effort brings results, even if the odds are against you.

RESOURCES   Glazer, Tom. *Tom Glazer's Treasury of Songs for Children*. Doubleday, 1988.

Haviland, Virginia. *North American Legends*. Philomel Books (Putnam Publishing Group), 1979.

Keats, Ezra Jack. *John Henry: An American Legend*. Knopf, 1987.

Kellogg, Steven. *Johnny Appleseed*. William Morrow Junior Books, 1988.

Seeger, Ruth. *American Folk Songs for Children*. Doubleday, 1980.

Trotman, Felicity, illustrated by. *William Tell*. Raintree Publications, 1989.

Dramatizing "The Deer and the Tortoise"

COMPONENT	Historical and Cultural
SUBJECT	Folklore
OBJECTIVE	Students investigate and dramatize a story from another country and compare it with other stories to gain understanding of drama/theatre and folklore.
MATERIALS	None required

WARM UP   Encourage the students to share their feelings about running in a race. Do they participate in races at school? At home? Ask the students to name familiar stories about running races, such as "The Tortoise and the Hare."

EXPLORE   Tell students that they will have a chance to listen to another story about a race, called "The Deer and the Tortoise." This story is a Brazilian folktale. Help students locate Brazil on a map or globe, and share some information about the country with the class:

Brazil is the largest country in South America.

Most of the Brazilian people today speak Portuguese. Those who are not Indians came from other countries, starting about 1500.

Indians have lived in the Amazon jungle for thousands of years. They speak a language called Tupi. *Suasu* (soo-ah-SOO) and *yauti* (yah-oo-TEE) are the Tupi words for "deer" and "tortoise," respectively.

In the story, "The Deer and the Tortoise," a tortoise challenges a deer to run a race. Ask, "How are deer different from tortoises? How are deer and tortoises alike? Who do you think would win in a race between the two? Why?"

Read aloud to the class "The Deer and the Tortoise" from the Appendix of CENTER STAGE. After the reading, ask students, "What do you think this story was trying to teach?"

DEVELOP   Read aloud another story such as *The Amazon* or *The Turtle and the Monkey*. Discuss with students the role of the underdog in the story, and how that character finds ways to outsmart the other character(s).

GRADE 2

Now tell the class to listen carefully as you reread "The Deer and the Tortoise," so that they can select parts of the story to dramatize.

Develop the dramatization by asking what happens first in the story, what characters are needed, and what words the characters say.

Then divide the class into groups, giving each the opportunity to create a part of the story. Plan, rehearse, and share the scenes with the whole class. Have students evaluate their performances.

EVALUATE *Student evaluation:* Ask the students, "Did hearing the story read again help you develop your improvised stories? What would you change if the scenes were to be played again?"

Teacher observation: Did students understand the concept of the underdog in the story? Were students able to transform the narrative presentation into a dramatization? How effectively were students able to work together? Are they developing evaluative skills?

CONNECTIONS *Science:* Provide books and pictures about tortoises and where they live. If possible, bring a tortoise to class to observe how it moves and how its legs are structured. Have students time the tortoise's pace over the same distance on different surfaces (sand, polished floor, grass, cement) to see on which surface it is most effective.

SPECIAL NEEDS Your special needs student, without a doubt, will relate to the underdog in the stories discussed. Share with the class some instances when you have felt like an underdog, and encourage students to do so, too. Point out what a good feeling it is to overcome difficulties, and how it helps when other people have faith in you.

RESOURCES *Center Stage: Creative Dramatics Supplement.* (contains audiotape of "The Deer and the Tortoise") Available from Dale Seymour Publications.

Cheney, Alan Glenn. *The Amazon.* Franklin Watts, Inc., 1984.

Galdone, Paul. *The Turtle and the Monkey.* Clarion, 1983.

Osborn, Steve. *Story Chest: Treasured Tales from Many Lands.* Addison-Wesley Publishing Company, 1992.

Using Costumes and Props

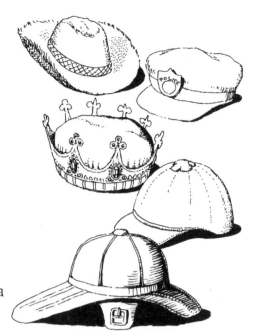

COMPONENT	Aesthetic Valuing
SUBJECT	Technical Theatre
OBJECTIVE	Students create characters and stories using costumes and props.
MATERIALS	A large box of costume pieces and props, including such items as a train whistle, a drum, a firefighter's cap, a police officer's cap, a witch's cape, a construction hat, a walking cane, and a magic wand

WARM UP

Define *costume* as the actor's stage clothing. A costume can reveal much about the character: for example, that person's taste, how rich or poor he or she is, and the character's station in life (a king or a beggar). Ask students what other information a costume might give them.

Define *personal* or *hand props* as those objects used by the actor while on stage, and *stage props* as all those items on the stage that help create the setting. Also tell students that *prop* is a short form of the word *property*.

Bring out a police officer's hat or a construction hat and ask the students, "Is this a costume or a prop? Who would wear this type of hat?" Continue with other costume pieces that identify characters, such as a witch's cape, a farmer's hat, a king's crown, and cowboy boots.

EXPLORE

Show the students examples of such props as a magic wand, a walking cane, and a teacher's pointer. Identify and discuss the types of characters who would use such props. Ask, "Who would use this prop? How would that person use it? How would it help to understand the character? What might be other characters' reactions to it?"

Describe the jobs of costume and prop persons in the theatre. Explain that the costumer is assigned to look for, collect, make, and/or buy all the costumes needed by the actors in a dramatic performance. The costumer must also see that the costumes fit and look right on the stage. The property manager must look for, collect, and/or buy all the props needed for the actors. He or she must see that the props are in good condition and ready for use.

Refer to a story or scene the students have performed, or a story the class has read. Have students think about all the different props and costumes that would be used by the characters in the story. Ask, "What costumes would the characters wear? Do any of the characters need more than one outfit? What props would the characters use? Which props help establish the setting? Will they all be on stage at once?" As students discuss the costumes and props, list them on the board.

DEVELOP   Have available a large box of props and costumes. Ask each student to choose one costume piece and one prop that he or she would like to use to create a character in a scene or story. Ask the students to act out a short scene or tell a brief story describing the character who would wear the costume and use the selected prop. Remind them to use the five W's in determining content.

For example, a student may choose a firefighter's hat and a nozzle. That student should tell what a character who uses this hat and nozzle would do for a living, and act out a short scene that would be typical of the character's life. Then that student returns the prop and costume to the box, and another student uses a different prop and costume piece to create another story.

If time allows, let small groups of students create their own scenes. Ask each group to choose a number of costume pieces and props to indicate characters in a made-up story or scene. Have the groups plan the characters suggested by the costume pieces, and determine how the props would be used. After students plan, cast, and rehearse, have them share the scenes or stories with the entire class. Evaluate each presentation briefly.

EVALUATE   *Student evaluation:* As a class, discuss how costume and prop pieces were used to create a story or scene. Ask the students, "How would your story change if you switched one prop or costume piece for another?"

Teacher observation: Could students associate the costume and prop pieces with specific characters? Were the characters imaginative? Did the students move freely in their characterizations?

CONNECTIONS   *Social Studies:* Ask students what "props" they need to be students (books, pencils, paper, rulers, crayons, and so on). Tell them that any job has tools or instruments, just as they do. Ask students to suggest all the careers they can, and list them on the board. Let each student select a career, then make a list of all the items he or she would need for that job. These can be either written or drawn.

Designing a Set

COMPONENT	Aesthetic Valuing
SUBJECT	Technical Theatre
OBJECTIVE	Students visualize and draw pictures of different story settings to help them understand one of the specific arts integral to drama/theatre.
MATERIALS	Visual arts materials

WARM UP

Remind students that every story and scene has a *Where*. Ask students to explain the *Where* (a setting in which the action takes place). Tell the class that they are going to identify and plan some settings. Ask them to think of and name a number of possible environments where stories and scenes take place, such as a forest, a desert, a palace, a certain room, or outer space. If desired, list the settings on the board.

EXPLORE

Ask, "What might we see in the different environments you mentioned?" For example, in outer space there might be a sun, stars, other planets besides the earth, and a rocket or a comet.

Select a setting suggested by the students, and ask them to picture it in their mind's eye. Say, for example, "Think about a playground as a setting. What would be on your playground? A swing? A sandbox?"

Ask students to draw a quick picture of the items they want to have on their playground. Tell them not to be too concerned about drawing each object perfectly. Give the students some time to draw all the items that would be on their playgrounds. When the students have completed their drawings, have some volunteers show their work and describe what they have drawn. Compare the objects students chose for their playgrounds.

DEVELOP

Explain what a set designer's job is in the theatre. This person is responsible for creating a space on the stage for the dramatic action to happen—the *Where* of the scene or play. Before the set designer actually paints the backdrop (a curtain at the back of the stage sometimes painted to look like scenery) or builds the sets, he or she often draws a sketch of the environment to show how the finished space will appear.

Encourage students to name additional items that could be included in their set designs. Have the students add to their drawings from the suggestions made, or make new, more detailed drawings. Have students share their work.

EVALUATE   *Student evaluation:* Divide the class into small groups and ask them to compare their drawings. Tell students to look for both similar and different items in the selected environment. Ask, "How would you take what is in your picture and transfer it to an actual performing space? What needs to be done to make that happen?"

Teacher observation: Were students more concerned about making their pictures perfect or their ability to create an environment suitable for a story? Were the kinds of objects appropriate to the environments? Do the students seem to have a better understanding of a set designer's job in the theatre following this experience?

CONNECTIONS   *Mathematics:* Have students use their set sketches to measure the amount of space a piece of furniture they are using (a sofa, for instance) will take up on the stage. Then have them plan how much more space is needed if a character will have to walk around the sofa in the play. Measurements need not be in numbers; they could be done with string or tape on the floor. If students are able, have them plan for several items on the stage and the movement around them to get a sense of what set designers do.

SPECIAL NEEDS   Pair a visually impaired student with a sighted classmate. Using tactile materials and a small carton, have the two design a three-dimensional set. Spatial relationships on the set should be emphasized.

RESOURCES   Parker, Oren. *Stage Lighting: Practice and Design.* Holt, Rinehart and Winston, Inc., 1987.

Comparing Dramatic Media

COMPONENT   Aesthetic Valuing

SUBJECT   Dramatic Media

OBJECTIVE   Students investigate the characteristics of theatre, TV, film, and radio, and create and record a radio drama.

MATERIALS   Cassette Recorder
Note: Contact the local National Public Broadcasting station in your area for possible radio programs appropriate for your students.

WARM UP

Ask students to name four ways—other than through the printed word—that people communicate with one another. Elicit from the students the following four media: theatre, TV, film, and radio. Then ask students to identify unique features of each.

Theatre: Usually a live performance, with actors "in the flesh." The audience responds to the performers.

TV: The electronic medium with the shows either live or prerecorded. There is no performer-audience interaction. Many people have one or more TV's in their homes; TV is probably the most common medium.

Film: The photographed performance usually shown in a movie theater (or from cassette tapes on the home VCR). The film in the movie theater is sometimes shown on a very large screen.

Radio: An auditory experience only. We hear music or voices or sounds without seeing the person(s) performing.

Ask the students to compare a play and a movie. What do they know about each? How are they different? Ask students to compare a TV program and a radio program. How are these two different?

EXPLORE

Continue the discussion of the similarities and differences among the four media. Make a chart listing the features of each one. Which one is most familiar to students? Why? (Students probably see more TV than anything else.) Which is the second most watched or listened to? Which is the third? Which medium do the students like most? Why?

DEVELOP   Contact your local public broadcasting station for storytelling programs that are age-appropriate for your students, and select some of those programs for your students to listen to. Ask students to listen for the different voices used to portray characters and particular sound effects.

Using a tape recorder and a well-known story, such as "The Bremen Town Musicians" from the Appendix of CENTER STAGE, create your own radio drama. Assign students to be different characters in the story. Tape record their voices as they read from the script. Select various students to be the sound makers. Experiment with creating sounds that would fit specific parts of the story. Tape the sounds and listen to them.

Retape the story, adding the different sound effects students created. Replay the performance for the entire class. Then evaluate, adapt, and retape until students have produced a satisfactory "radio program."

EVALUATE   *Student evaluation:* Ask students what they think is the most important quality of each of the four media. Ask whether the students listen to the radio at home. Why or why not? Will they be more likely to listen now that they have become aware of radio theatre?

Teacher observation: Were students able to identify some differences among the four media? From their comments, could you determine the students' interest level in each? How well were they able to read material for taping and to create the sound effects for the story?

CONNECTIONS   *Language Arts:* Set up a screen of some kind behind which students can be hidden from view. In groups of four or five, let students plan and rehearse a scene, then present it behind the screen, changing their voices and creating sound effects while the class listens carefully to guess who is speaking or what kind of sound is being made.

RESOURCES   *Center Stage: Creative Dramatics Supplement.* (contains audiotape of "The Bremen Town Musicians") Available from Dale Seymour Publications.

Hansen, Merrily P. *Now Presenting: Classic Tales for Readers' Theatre.* Addison-Wesley Publishing Company, 1992.

Head, Sydney, and Christopher Sterling. *Broadcasting in America, Brief.* Houghton Mifflin Company, 1991.

Celebration! A Visiting Artist

COMPONENT Historical and Cultural

SUBJECT Theatre History

OBJECTIVE Students listen to and work with a visiting artist in order to understand the specifics of that person's job in drama/ theatre.

MATERIALS None required

Note: Arrange for an actor or creative drama specialist to visit the classroom to share the details of theatre professionals' jobs. (Contact a community or professional theatre group, radio station, TV station, or college theatre department for help in finding a visiting artist.)

WARM UP Review the art disciplines of music, dance, the visual arts (artwork that can be seen without the artist being present), and drama. Ask, "What does a musician do? A visual artist? A dancer? The actor in drama/theatre?" Encourage students to give examples they are familiar with from each art discipline.

EXPLORE Discuss the students' understanding of each art discipline and the professional people within that discipline. Ask questions such as: "What have we learned this year about acting and actors? What are some of the other jobs in the theatre we have learned about?"

DEVELOP Invite an actor or creative drama specialist (or other theatre professional) into the classroom to involve the students in the art discipline of drama/ theatre. Before the artist arrives, have students prepare a list of questions for the visitor. These questions may be shared with the visitor ahead of time, so that he or she will be prepared to address students' interests.

The visiting artist(s) may be:

- A performing company that would perform for the entire school and also do follow-up, hands-on experiences for your class and other selected classes in the school.

- A creative drama specialist who would involve your students in elements of drama/theatre that are supportive of the exercises and activities you have been doing with the students during the year.
- An actor from a community or professional theatre company to demonstrate, discuss, and share her or his profession with the students.
- Other support personnel in the theatre—the director, costumer, property manager, lighting designer, or set designer—to speak to the students concerning their specific jobs in the theatre.

After the visitor has left, review the questions students had, and how they were answered. Ask students to make a drawing or a clay model of something they learned about from the visitor.

EVALUATE

Student evaluation: Have the students compare the activities and exercises presented by the visiting artist to those experiences in drama/theatre done in class. Ask the students to look back at the entire year and recall which activities were the most enjoyable. Why did they think so? What did they learn from them?

Teacher observation: Through your observation, what skills have the students refined during the year? Do you feel that drama/theatre activities have improved the students' oral language development? Do the students understand better the various elements of drama/theatre, such as the beginnings and endings of stories, and the five W's? Do they know more about the technical aspects of the theatre? Have they gained in specific knowledge about storytelling and cultural references?

CONNECTIONS

Social Studies: Explore other careers besides those in drama/theatre by asking for parent or adult volunteers to come to the classroom to share what they do with the class. It is often helpful if they bring a few "tools of the trade" with them.

RESOURCES

Williamson, Walter. *Early Stages: The Professional Theater and the Young Actor.* Walker and Company, 1986.

Introduction To Grade Three

At Grade 3 students continue with the concepts introduced at Grades 1 and 2, but at a higher degree of sophistication. More sophisticated critical thinking skills are also introduced at this level.

Lessons are necessarily sequential and cumulative, and move quickly from the basic sensory, emotional, and movement areas into concepts of story development and dramatization. Some extra time may be required to introduce concepts of sensory and emotional awareness and rhythm and movement to students who did not have creative dramatics at the lower grades.

Lessons at the Grade 3 level offer experiences in:
- an awareness of the senses and their relationship to the creative process;
- the perception that rhythm and movement are the external expression of an inner idea or feeling;
- the use of the voice as an instrument of communication, both in speech and nonverbal sound;
- spontaneous and creative responses to problem-solving situations;
- the adaptation of simple materials for improvisations, and a recognition of some of the basic elements of drama;
- the development of critical evaluative skills;
- the development of an appreciation of the place of drama in the arts;
- an awareness of students' own cultural heritage and the heritage of others.

Contents of Grade Three

GRADE 3

LESSON ONE

Settings and Senses: Sight, Touch, and Hearing

COMPONENT	Aesthetic Perception
SUBJECT	Sensory Recall: Sight, Touch, and Hearing
OBJECTIVE	Students imagine and describe the visual, tactile, and auditory qualities of different settings.
MATERIALS	None required

WARM UP

Explain *sensory recall* as used in drama/theatre activities (the ability to remember experiences associated with physical sensations and emotional states). Tell the students that performers depend on their memories and imaginations to help them. For example, if actors have to portray being lost in the Arctic, they try to remember a time when they felt very cold and lost. Then they imagine themselves on a plain of ice, and show what they remember.

Ask students to shut their eyes and imagine that they are on a desert island alone. Say, "Using your imaginations, look around the island and describe what you see, touch, and hear. Be as detailed as you can." Choose individual students to share with the class some of the feelings and objects that they are imagining on their desert island. A student might say, "It's very hot here. The sand is sticking to my feet. I see a large brown camel running across the sand. I can hear its hoofbeats as it comes toward me, and then it brushes by me so closely that I can feel its hot fur."

EXPLORE

Once you have discussed the desert island with the group, have the students shut their eyes again and imagine a location of their choice (desert, ocean, forest, outer space, underground, and so on).

After students have had a few minutes to imagine what is in that setting, ask them to write two or three sentences to describe it. Give them an example: "I'm in a large train station. The ceilings are very high, and there is an oddly shaped window in the ceiling made of many different colors of glass. As the trains click and clang into the station the building shakes and the glass rattles and I can feel the vibrations in my legs."

Ask some of the students to share what they have written. Comment on the sensory aspects of their sentences.

DEVELOP Choose one of the environments described by the students. In an open space have the class as individuals, or in groups of two or three, create some action that would communicate that environment. For example, the location might be the seashore. The students might carry a small boat or raft from the beach to the water. They could get into the boat, grab the oars, and row away from the shore. Help the students define and organize the actions they will perform. Remind participants to show with their actions, for example, how heavy the boat is, how cold or warm the water is, and the weight of the oars in their hands as they row against the water.

When the scene is completed, ask the observers to identify the actions that communicated the setting. If time allows, repeat the activity with other settings.

EVALUATE *Student evaluation:* Ask the students whether keeping their eyes closed helped in imagining an environment. Ask individual students to share the different places they have been in their imaginations, and how they visualize different objects in each setting. Encourage them to describe the sensory experiences in their settings.

Teacher observation: Were the students more effective in writing about their environments or physically acting out where they were? Did the students cooperate with one another in planning and performing a scene or sequence of actions? Did all the students participate in the activity?

CONNECTIONS *Geography:* Using a large physical map as an aid, discuss color coding to designate geographical areas. Point out particular deserts, mountains, jungles, and very cold climates. Invite students to be explorers and to pick out a particular place to investigate. List a few locations on the board: the Sahara Desert, the Antarctic, the Rocky Mountains, and the Amazon. Help students locate their places on the map. Let them plan an adventure trip, drawing pictures of their environment, and listing clothing and supplies to take. Provide reference books if students need more information.

SPECIAL NEEDS Mentally impaired students may have some difficulty imagining and acting out a setting, due to problems integrating all the senses. Choose a setting and one sense for them, first to talk about, and then to perform. If possible, pair these students with supportive classmates.

Settings and Senses: Taste and Smell

COMPONENT	Aesthetic Perception
SUBJECT	Sensory Recall: Taste and Smell
OBJECTIVE	Students imagine and describe various tastes and smells and dramatize those experiences.
MATERIALS	None required

WARM UP

Ask students to define *smell* (the sensations perceived by the nose that distinguish odor). Have students think of real situations in which they use the sense of smell. Some examples might be: smelling food, enjoying the fragrance of different kinds of flowers and plants, smelling perfumes, and smelling the smoke from a fire.

In a similar manner, lead students to define taste as sensations perceived by the tongue that distinguish flavor, and ask them to give examples of times when they use their sense of taste. Because tasting is a more voluntary activity than smelling, students' examples will almost all be of food and drink, but they could also include medicines.

Explain that the senses of smell and taste are connected. Ask students to think what happens to their sense of taste when they have a cold and a stuffy nose. (When the sense of smell is lost, the sense of taste is lost as well.)

EXPLORE

Review Lesson 1, in which the students imagined a location or environment and acted out what objects would be in that setting. They also incorporated sensory recall in demonstrating what kinds of activities would take place in that specific environment.

Using the same settings discussed in Lesson 1—whatever locations the students suggested—have students identify all the different tastes and smells that could be found in a particular environment. Ask, for example, "What are some smells and tastes that might be associated with the train station?" List students' suggestions and ask the class if recalling a specific smell or taste helped them visualize the setting.

GRADE 3

DEVELOP Have each student decide on an imaginary object that has a specific smell or taste to it. Then ask each student to act out a scene using that object to convey the smell and/or taste. Provide an open space for the action.

One student may choose a lemon, for example. Perhaps this person enters the space and pretends to open a refrigerator and bring out a small object. The student then might go through the motions of cutting the lemon and licking his or her fingers. The puckered expression on the student's face indicates that the lemon is sour.

Let other members of the class try to identify the object. Discuss how the student conveyed the smell or taste of the object. Continue with other students sharing their scenes.

EVALUATE *Student evaluation:* Discuss with the students whether recalling different tastes and smells was helpful in identifying a particular setting. Ask them how easy or hard it was to act out how something tasted or smelled. Ask the students who were observers how they could identify what others were acting out.

Teacher observation: How much did the students remember and use from the previous lesson to help them with this activity? Could students associate smells with places and environments? Did all students participate by identifying a smell or taste and acting that out in front of the class?

CONNECTIONS *Science:* Point out to students how smelling is related to breathing, especially inhaling. Describe briefly the breathing process. Then have students practice filling their lungs with air (inhaling) and pushing the air out (exhaling). Do some voice control exercises with the class, saying or singing different sounds—mmm, aahh, oooooh—breathing out as long as they can, inhaling and holding breaths for a count of ten, then breathing out slowly, and so on. Show students where their diaphragms are, and have them put their hands there as they inhale and exhale. Have students give examples of objects they might smell for which they would use deep breathing (smelling a rose) or shallow breathing (smelling a rotten egg).

RESOURCES Kaufman, Joe. *Joe Kaufman's Big Book About the Human Body.* Golden Books (Western Publishing Company), 1987.

Expressing Emotions

COMPONENT	Aesthetic Perception
SUBJECT	Emotions
OBJECTIVE	Students identify the emotional content of a story—what the characters are feeling—and experiment with changing it.
MATERIALS	*The Giving Tree,* by Shel Silverstein

WARM UP

Choose a story that the students have read in class recently and determine its emotional content. Ask, "What events in the story made you feel happy? What made you sad? Angry? Did you have other feelings? In addition to the events, did anything else in the story make you feel a certain way? Was it the description of how the character felt? Was it because something similar happened to you?" Ask students to show with their faces different emotions.

EXPLORE

Read a story that has a specific emotional content, such as *The Giving Tree,* by Shel Silverstein. In this story, the character experiences both happiness and sadness. Choose one section that focuses on a particular emotion. For example, read, "The young boy is very happy when he can swing from the branches of the tree." Ask, "Why is he happy when he can swing from a tree? What else in the scene might make him happy?" (his sense of freedom, the enjoyment of the movement, being out-of-doors, and so on)

Read the entire story. Discuss and compare the different emotions experienced by the character in the story.

DEVELOP

Ask, "Would you consider *The Giving Tree* (or whatever story that was read aloud) a happy or sad story? What other emotions were the characters in the story feeling? How could you tell?"

Invite a few students to tell which parts of the story made them think the character was happy or sad. Can students discover the reasons for a character's feeling the way she or he does?

Now ask the students to change the emotional content of the story. What could be changed, added, or deleted to make the reader feel happier, sadder, or angrier? If the students changed part of the story, discuss what the change was and how it affected the story.

EVALUATE *Student evaluation:* Ask students how difficult or easy it was to identify the parts of a story that made the reader feel an emotion. Which story do the students like better, the original or their adaptation?

Teacher evaluation: Were the students able to revise the story to show a specific emotion more clearly? Do the students understand how changing an emotion changes the content of a story?

CONNECTIONS *Social Studies:* Ask students to identify the feelings that they think everyone has in common. Lead students to agree that whatever their backgrounds, all human beings have similar feelings. Describe a real or made-up situation in which someone was discriminated against because of a physical characteristic. (If the situation is real, do not mention the person's real name.) Ask students to describe how such a person might feel, and to suggest ways to avoid discrimination.

RESOURCES *Center Stage: Creative Dramatics Supplement.* (contains "How Are You Feeling Today?" poster) Available from Dale Seymour Publications.

Silverstein, Shel. *The Giving Tree.* Harper & Row Publishers, Inc., 1964.

Spolin, Viola. *Improvisation for Theatre: A Handbook of Teaching and Directing Techniques.* Northwestern University Press, 1963.

Patterns in Rhythm and Movement

COMPONENT   Aesthetic Perception

SUBJECT   Rhythm/Movement

OBJECTIVE   Students develop flexible and diversified movements in response to rhythmic patterns.

MATERIALS   Small drum or other rhythm instrument

WARM UP   Define *rhythm* as a regular, recurring pattern in sound and/or movement. As an example, use a small drum to beat out a simple rhythm (ONE, two, three, four), repeating it many times. In an open space, have the students walk to the repeated pattern you are beating. Then change the rhythm to a slightly more complex one (ONE, two, three, with the second and third beats twice as fast as the first one). Ask the students to join you by clapping or moving to the rhythm as soon as they perceive it.

EXPLORE   Have the students sit in a circle. Tell them you are going to beat a very simple, slow rhythm on the drum (ONE, two). Each student in turn is to join in by clapping a rhythm that fits into yours. Each student's rhythm will be different from yours and from the others. For example, another rhythm might be ONE-two-three, four, fitting the first three beats into the same time as your first ONE. The secret of doing this exercise is for each student to concentrate on the rhythm that just precedes his or hers, and to fit the new rhythm into that one. You may wish to do this activity two or three times.

Ask the students to think of another way to make a noise without using their voices. Tell them they must stay seated. Responses may include hitting the floor with the hands or feet, slapping thighs, and snapping fingers. Again, start a simple rhythm and have the students join in one at a time, fitting their own rhythms into the one you started.

DEVELOP   Ask the students to think of some activities or tasks in life that are made easier by using rhythm. The answers might include dancing, playing basketball, jumping rope, working on a production line, counting out items, or hiking up a steep hill.

Ask the students to stand in an open space, with enough room for moving without infringing on one another's space. Tell the class that they are going to perform actions in a rhythmic fashion. Ask students to pretend that on each one's left there is a box filled with small bags of peanuts. Students are to reach into the box with their left hands, pick up three bags at once, and hand them out one at a time with their right hands to imaginary students filing past them. To help the students establish a rhythm, say, "Reach, hand, hand, hand; reach, hand, hand, hand."

Repeat the exercise with a variation. Ask the students to pick up small boxes from an imaginary conveyer belt and put them into a larger box. You might say, "Reach, pack; reach, pack; reach, pack," to help establish the rhythm. Encourage large movements.

EVALUATE

Student evaluation: Ask the students whether moving or clapping in unison helped them when they later tried to make up a new rhythm to fit into an existing one. Did moving to a rhythm help them understand how rhythm plays a part in everyday situations?

Teacher observation: Did the students gain a clear understanding of rhythm from the activities? Did they use imaginative ways of making sounds? Did they move freely within their spaces? Were they able to establish rhythms when performing a specific action?

CONNECTIONS

Language Arts: Rhythm is a key element in poetry and choral speaking. Choose a short verse and write it on a chart or the board so that everyone can see it. Have the class recite it as a group. Then ask for one volunteer to read it aloud. Remind the volunteer to say the words slowly and clearly, with an identifiable rhythm, and to use gestures. Then have the student choose one or two classmates to recite the poem along with him or her. They should all say the verse together without looking at each other, trying to keep together. (Gestures will make this easier.) Let small groups choose other poems to read chorally. Point out that the rhythm of the verse helps the group stay together.

SPECIAL NEEDS

Students with limited motor skills could speak their invented rhythms.

RESOURCES

De La Mare, Walter. *Rhymes and Verses: Collected Poems for Young People.* Henry Holt & Co., 1988.

Lear, Edward. *The Nonsense Verse of Edward Lear.* Crown Publishers, 1984.

Inventing Body Machines

COMPONENT   Creative Expression

SUBJECT   Improvisation

OBJECTIVE   Students work together as a group to
create with their bodies an imaginary
machine.

MATERIALS   Pictures of some common machines

WARM UP   Ask the students to name a few machines that they see and use in their
daily lives. Examples may include garage door openers, electric mixers,
lawn mowers, bicycles, cars, and buses. List them on the board. Have
available some pictures of common machines for students to look at.

Ask the students what these machines have in common (some kind of
power to make them work, moving parts; they are tools designed to make
our lives easier). Make a list of the common characteristics of machines so
that students can refer to it later. What are the differences in these machines? (Some are electric, some mechanical, some use gas, and so on.)

EXPLORE   After discussing a few machines that we use, ask, "If you could have or
invent a machine that could do anything, what would you want it to do?"

Responses could be as varied as, "I want a machine to do my homework; I
want a machine to take me anywhere I want to go instantly; I want a
machine that would do all my chores at home for me."

List the students' responses and compare them.

DEVELOP   Divide the class into groups of four or five each. Tell students that they are
going to create and build an imaginary machine using all the members of
the group as the machine's moving parts. Stress that everyone in the group
should be part of this imaginary machine in some way. The machine
should be one that has never been seen before.

Tell students their first task is to decide what their machine does. Then
they should give it a name. They should determine how they can use their
bodies to represent the moving parts of the machine. Tell students that
the activities they performed in Lesson 4 can help them think of ways to
show how their machine moves. Remind students that the machine must
go through its motions in appropriate sequence.

Following the planning and rehearsal, each group should share its imaginary machine with the class. Have the class guess what the machine might be called and the work it does. Then give each group the opportunity to describe the function of the machine, what its cost is, and where the imaginary machine might be purchased. Allow members of the audience to ask questions about each improvisation and each machine.

EVALUATE

Student evaluation: Compare each group's machine with the others. Did any groups use the same movements? What were similarities of all the machines? How difficult was it to convey machine functions through body movements?

Teacher observation: Were the students able to use their bodies effectively to create imaginary parts of a machine? Did each member of the group represent a working part of the machine? In describing the particulars of each machine, did the students use interesting and creative oral language?

CONNECTIONS

Science: Introduce the idea of a simple machine as something that makes work easier for people by changing the application of energy, such as a lever, a pulley, or an inclined plane. This is slightly different from the machines discussed in the lesson. Give students examples of simple machines that they would find familiar (e.g., a bottle opener for prying off a bottle cap, the mechanism for raising a flag on a flagpole, and a ramp put over stairs to wheel up something heavy) and see if they can think of some others. Let students build a model of a simple machine to be used for a particular purpose and label it. Provide a place in the classroom to display the models.

RESOURCES

Macaulay, David. *The Way Things Work.* Houghton Mifflin Co., 1988.

Developing Pantomime from a Word

COMPONENT	Creative Expression
SUBJECT	Communication Skills
OBJECT	Students explore verbal and nonverbal communication by transforming a single word into an idea for action and dramatic form.
MATERIALS	None required

WARM UP

Explain that *pantomime* is a form of communication without words. Pantomime shows the action, who is doing the action, and how that person feels about the action.

Choose a student and say, "Let me hear you say *hello*. Let me see you say *hello* nonverbally." Have the students communicate another simple word such as *stop* or *go* verbally and nonverbally.

EXPLORE

Select a group of words that could be expressed in a variety of ways and write them on the board. Examples could include *hello, stop, watch, no, yes, come, and goodbye*. Choose one of the words and invite several students to explore different ways that word could be communicated verbally. Then ask other students to demonstrate different ways it could be communicated nonverbally.

DEVELOP

Extend this activity to create a series of actions using the single word. For example, ask a student to develop the word *stop* beyond a simple gesture of putting up the hands. Tell students to create a *Who*, a *What*, a *Where*, and a *Why*. It could be that the character is a police officer directing traffic. After a few minutes of directing the flow of traffic by motioning to cars, the officer stops oncoming cars with a direct gesture so that an elderly person can cross the street.

After students have pantomimed the set of actions leading up to the gesture or movement that highlights the selected word, have them repeat the exercise, but this time they should verbally use the selected word in the story. For instance, using the previous scene, the police officer directs traffic for a minute or two, and then at an opportune time, puts up his or her hands and says the word *stop* to oncoming traffic.

Have students each plan a short improvisation to be shared with the entire class. Students may choose the same word, but insist that they not repeat any of the improvisations that went before them.

Share, then comment on the positive aspects of the improvisation, and ask each student what he or she could do to add to or delete from the scene to make it better. If time permits, replay the scenes with the suggested changes.

EVALUATE

Student evaluation: Ask students how difficult it was to put the one-word responses within a scene or story. Have them tell which way they preferred telling their "story," verbally or nonverbally, and explain why.

Teacher observation: How effectively were the students able to express words verbally and nonverbally? Did all the students participate in this activity? Were students more enthusiastic about the verbal or nonverbal method? Were there any surprises in student involvement? Did the improvisations improve after the discussion and replaying the scenes?

CONNECTIONS

Mathematics: Have students pantomime math problems: for example, they may add and subtract by moving students from one group to another, or by moving objects. Challenge students to act out fractions, such as half of me, one fifth of my fingers, one fourth of these coins, and so on. Put problems on the board for students to pantomime.

SPECIAL NEEDS

Give hearing impaired students the opportunity to share sign language with the class, as a form of nonverbal communication. Have them teach other students a few common words.

RESOURCES

Durland, Francis Caldwell. *Creative Dramatics for Children: A Practical Manual for Teachers and Leaders.* Kent State University Press, 1975.

Imagining with a "Magic Box"

COMPONENT   Creative Expression

SUBJECT   Imaginary Objects

OBJECTIVE   Visualizing their own remembered experiences, students create drama with imaginary objects.

MATERIALS   None required

WARM UP   Remind the students of Lesson 6, in which *pantomime* was defined as nonverbal communication that shows an action, the character who is doing the action, and how that person feels about the action. Tell the students that you are going to create a magic box. Outline with your hands an imaginary box with four sides, about two feet deep. Say, "What you see before me is a magic box. The reason this box is magic is that with your imaginations, you can find anything you want in this box."

Pause, then continue, "I can go inside this magic box and bring out anything! There is nothing I can't bring out of this box." Pause again. Then go on, "I am going to bring something out and use it. See if you can guess what it is. Pay attention to the shape, size, and weight of the object, and also to the way I use it."

Put your hand into the magic box and bring out an imaginary horn. Begin to play the horn. After a few moments have the students guess what your imaginary object is. Once the students have identified the object and its purpose, put it back into the box and bring out another, completely different imaginary object for students to identify—for example, a dog.

EXPLORE   Once you have brought out a number of imaginary objects from the box, invite individual students to come up in front of the class and take other objects out of the box. Each student should use an object in the way it was intended to be used. After a few minutes of viewing, the other students may guess what they think each object is. Students might imagine a kite, marbles, a bicycle, an umbrella, or a telephone.

DEVELOP   Once the students are familiar and comfortable with using the magic box, introduce a variety of tasks and challenges. For instance, say, "I want you to take an object out of the box that we usually use inside the house. You must take it out of the box and show how it is used. When you have finished using the object, you must return it to the box." Examples may include an iron, a mop, a toothbrush, a TV set, and a frying pan. Continue the activity giving a number of students the opportunity to take something out of the box.

Other tasks and challenges could include:

Taking something out of the box that is usually used outside of the house.

Taking something out of the box that is very big—that is very small—that is very straight—that is curved.

Taking an emotion out of the box—happiness, sadness, anger, surprise. Tell students to put that emotion on and make a living statue out of that emotion.

Give as many students as possible an opportunity to participate in this activity. Comment on how well each student conveys the imaginary object or emotion taken out of the box.

EVALUATE *Student evaluation:* Ask students how they decided what their object would be. Did they choose objects or feelings that would be easy or difficult to identify? Why? Ask students to think of other objects or feelings that could have been taken out of the box.

Teacher observation: Did students convey the size, shape, and weight of each object taken out of the box? Did they use creative ways to help others identify their objects? Did the students accept the idea of the magic box and taking different objects out of it?

CONNECTIONS *Social Studies:* Take out of the magic box historical figures from the class' current social studies unit. "Put on" a character and present some identifying dialogue, and let students guess who you are. Then let a student take another personality out of the box and present it to the class. Invite the rest of the class to ask questions as the student stays in character and gives answers.

SPECIAL NEEDS Severely visually impaired students will be unable to guess what objects or emotions others have taken out of the Magic Box, but will be able to take a turn at pantomime with their own.

Dramatizing Traditional "How and Why" Stories

COMPONENT	Historical and Cultural
SUBJECT	Dramatic Literature
OBJECTIVE	Students develop an awareness of common themes in diverse cultures by comparing "How and Why" stories.
MATERIALS	*Why the Sun and the Moon Live in the Sky,* by Elphinstone Dayrell; *How the Sun Made a Promise and Kept It,* by Margery Bernstein and Janet Kobrin

Note: Lessons 8 and 9 use the same materials. Lesson 9 is a continuation of Lesson 8. The content of both these lessons will be referred to again in Lesson 11.

WARM UP

Ask students what *how* means and what *why* means. (*How* describes a way or means of doing something; *why* explains the purpose for doing something.) Explain that people all over the world have made up stories to answer the *how* and *why* of physical or cultural phenomena. Say, "The two stories we are going to dramatize today and in our next lesson come from two very different places and cultures. *Why the Sun and Moon Live in the Sky* comes from Africa. *How the Sun Made a Promise and Kept It* comes from the Bungee Indians in Canada." Show the locations of Canada and Africa on a map or globe.

EXPLORE

Read the two stories listed in Materials to the students. Ask, "What 'how' or 'why' does each story explain? How are the stories alike? Who are most of the characters? (animals or beings from nature) Isn't it interesting that people from such different parts of the world, and from such different cultures, explain almost the same thing through a folk tale!"

Let students select one of the stories to dramatize.

DEVELOP

Ask the students to retell the part of the story that most clearly describes *how* or *why* the sun is in its place in the sky. Ask, "What is happening in that part of the story (the action)? Who are the people involved in the action (character development)? How do they feel about what they are doing (emotional awareness)?" Ask, "What would (one character) say to (another character) to start the action in this scene? What would the other character reply?" Elicit responses from several students.

Designate as many students as are necessary to play the chosen scene, using their own words and movements. Encourage the students to focus on bringing out the *how* or *why* of the story (plot) in their lines and their actions.

Let other students repeat the scene, adding necessary lines and movements to develop the scene further. The lines will vary, as will the movements, with each developmental repetition. Replay the scene until the students are satisfied and the scene is complete.

Tell the students that they will hear more about the other story in the next lesson. Ask students to think about how the stories are the same, and how they are different.

Some students may want to dramatize the entire story. As time permits, follow the procedures outlined in Develop for each additional segment of the story. Put the scenes together sequentially for the dramatization of the entire story.

EVALUATE   *Student evaluation:* Ask the students how their dramatization demonstrated *how* or *why*. Can they recall in which cultures the stories originated? Did dramatizing help them understand the *how* and *why* of this story?

Teacher observation: Did the ideas presented in the students' improvisations relate to the concepts of *how* and *why*? Do the students have a better understanding of "How and Why" stories following this activity? Did the students work together effectively? Did all students participate, and were all ideas listened to respectfully, even though not all ideas were acted upon?

CONNECTIONS   *Social Studies, Mathematics:* Have students make a time line of their own lives. This will only be about 8 years long, so they can divide into half years or even months if they wish. Have them mark it off in equal segments and label the years. Then ask them to identify the age at which they found out how or why something worked, add it to their birth age to identify the year, and mark it on the time line. Examples of key events might be, "When I found out that sunlight makes the daytime," "When I found out that rain comes from clouds," and "When I found out that milk comes from cows."

RESOURCES   Bernstein, Margery, and Janet Kobrin. *How the Sun Made a Promise and Kept It: A Canadian Myth.* Charles Scribner's Sons, 1974.

Dayrell, Elphinstone. *Why the Sun and Moon Live in the Sky: An African Folktale.* Houghton Mifflin, 1968.

Creating a "How and Why" Story

COMPONENT   Historical and Cultural

SUBJECT   Dramatic Literature

OBJECTIVE   Students develop an awareness of common themes in diverse cultures by creating a "How and Why" story with the same theme as the story from Lesson 8.

MATERIALS   *Why the Sun and Moon Live in the Sky,* by Elphinstone Dayrell; *How the Sun Made a Promise and Kept It,* by Margery Bernstein and Janet Kobrin

Note: Make a copy of the story that students develop in this lesson and use it for other classroom activities, such as a reading lesson, or for dramatization in Lesson 11.

WARM UP   Briefly review the meanings of *how* and *why,* and how the *how* and *why* were demonstrated in the dramatization of the story in Lesson 8. Read again the "How and Why" story not dramatized, and ask the students to identify the *how* and *why* of the story. Again locate both Canada and Africa on the map or globe. Reinforce the information that two cultures so far apart in the world had the same question to ask (how the sun got into the sky), and both developed stories to explain it.

EXPLORE   Ask the students if they have ever wondered how the sun seems to come up from the horizon in the morning and go down behind the horizon in the evening. Ask for volunteers to explain the process, then tell students that they can participate in a demonstration of the way it works.

Have students stand in a large circle, with one student in the center. Give the student in the center a large orange paper circle or ball to hold. The students on the outside of the circle are to turn around slowly in place. When they are facing the "sun" (the student in the center), it is daylight. When they are facing out, it is dark, or night. Explain to the students that as they turn toward the sun, the light seems to appear on one side of them, and as they turn away, it disappears on the other side. So it is with the earth and the sun. The earth turns toward and away from the sun. It seems to us that we are standing still because the earth is so large, and we are standing on it. But it is the sun that is stationary.

DEVELOP

Explain to students that many cultures did not know that the earth turned, making the sun seem to appear and disappear, so they created a reason to explain it.

If the class were a culture without the knowledge of how the earth turns, what kind of story might be created to explain the natural phenomenon? (It would be a "How and Why" story.)

Ask the students to make up a story to explain why it looks as though the sun comes up and goes down. Ask for volunteers to tell their ideas.

For example, a student might say, "The sun used to shine all the time, but one day it did something bad, so it had to run and hide." Another student might have the idea that Light and Dark had a fierce battle. Both were so strong that neither could win, so they decided to divide time between them. Or a student might say that the earth used to face the sun all the time, but the sun was so bright and splendid that the earth was frightened and blinded, and had to turn away to rest its eyes.

Select one of the ideas and develop it together as a class. Help the students establish a story line by asking, "Where does our story begin? Who is the main character? Where is he or she? What is that character doing? Is there another character who helps the main character? Does someone or something try to stop that character?"

What happens at the end of the story? How is the problem solved, or how does the main character get what she or he wants? What is the result of the action? (The resolution should be the answer to why the sun comes up in the morning and sets at night.)

EVALUATE

Student evaluation: Ask the class what was difficult in constructing a "How and Why" story. What was easy? Ask the students, "Did your knowledge about how the earth turns help you to create the story?"

Teacher observation: Were students able to solve the questions of how or why imaginatively? Did they understand the concept of "How and Why" stories from different cultures to explain natural phenomena? Were students aware of the commonality of ideas in different cultures?

CONNECTIONS   *Science, Language Arts:* Ask students for suggestions of other natural phenomena for which they do not know the causes, and have them predict what the real answers might be. Make a chart showing some of the "How and Why" questions students have suggested, with three columns. The first column should show the questions, the second should show the answers that students predicted, and the third column will be filled in when they discover the scientific answer. Give students reference materials. Let them work in small groups to discover the answers, and report back to the class.

RESOURCES   Bernstein, Margery, and Janet Kobrin. *How the Sun Made a Promise and Kept It: A Canadian Myth.* Charles Scribner's Sons, 1974.

Dayrell, Elphinstone. *Why the Sun and Moon Live in the Sky: An African Folktale.* Houghton Mifflin, 1968.

Dramatizing Original Who, What, and Where Stories

COMPONENT	Aesthetic Perception
SUBJECT	*Who, What, Where*
OBJECTIVE	Students use appropriate vocabulary to describe the basic elements of drama/theatre and to create stories using *Who, What,* and *Where.*
MATERIALS	Three sets of three-by-five-inch cards, one set with a different group of characters *(Who)* written on each card, one set with a different action *(What)* written on each card, and one set with a different setting *(Where)* written on each card (create about 20 cards per set); three boxes or bags, labeled WHO, WHAT, and WHERE

WARM UP

Review the five W's used in drama/theatre. If the students have not been introduced to those terms, define them as follows:

Who: the people or characters in the story

What: the action(s) that happen in the story

Where: the location of the action of the story

When: the time of day, year, and/or period that the story occurs

Why: the reasons a particular action happens; a character's motivation for acting in a certain way

EXPLORE

Tell the students that they are to focus on *who, what,* and *where.* Explain that they are to act out a situation they have made up in their imaginations. Each student is to choose a *who*—someone imagined, someone she or he knows, or a story character. Then the students should decide *where* the character is. Finally, students should decide *what* happens. (Have students make these decisions quickly.)

For example, a student may decide that she or he is a middle-aged woman who is being notified that she has won a million dollars in the state lottery. The student may begin the scene by entering a space, opening her door, listening to imagined messengers, registering shock with her expression, then realize that TV cameras are recording her reaction. Have each student act out the scene he or she decided upon.

DEVELOP

Divide the class into small groups and have one student from each group choose one card from each of three bags or boxes labeled "Who," "What," and "Where." After selecting the cards, the student should return to the small group and share the information on the cards.

Perhaps the group's three cards say: *(Who)* "You are spies"; *(Where)* "You are in a forest"; *(What)* "One person in your group has a broken leg." The challenge for each group is to create a story using this information. The group will know who they are in the story, where the story takes place, and what one or more actions in the story are.

Say, "Discuss the information that you have to create a story. What are a few different possibilities for using that information?" Tell students to decide on one idea and talk through what happens at the beginning, the middle, and the end of the story. Have them assign the different characters, rehearse the scene, and then share their story with the rest of the class. After each group has acted out its story, discuss the improvisation and whether the group utilized the information from all three cards in its story.

EVALUATE

Student evaluation: As a class, discuss how individual students conveyed the *Who, What,* and *Where* of a situation. Were they able to use the given information to create a scene? What made each method effective?

Teacher observation: Did students begin this activity with a general understanding of how the five W's are used in drama/theatre? Were students able to focus on using *Who, What,* and *Where* situations for creating a story? Why or why not? Did the stories that each group created have a beginning, middle, and end?

CONNECTIONS

Art, Social Studies: Show students some prints of paintings of historical events that have at least two people in them, and that show some action and a specific location. Identify for the class the *Who, What,* and *Where* of each painting. Ask for volunteers to create a tableau of one of the paintings. Remind students to freeze in the postures of their characters. Have the class see whether they can identify the painting and the *Who, What,* and *Where* of the historical event from the tableau that students make.

SPECIAL NEEDS   Independent group work will be difficult for the mentally impaired
student. Close supervision by an adult or helpful classmate will facilitate
success.

RESOURCES   Spolin, Viola. *Improvisation for the Theatre.* Northwestern University Press,
1963.

Understanding Theatre Terminology

COMPONENT   Aesthetic Perception

SUBJECT   Drama/Theatre Vocabulary

OBJECTIVE   Students use appropriate vocabulary to understand the difference between *drama* and *theatre*.

MATERIALS   A few costume pieces and props relating to the stories in Lessons 8 and 9; masking tape

WARM UP   Ask students what they think a *theater* is. Responses might include such comments as: "A theater is a place where we see movies and plays." or "A building to see shows in." If desired, list students' responses on the board.

Tell students that a theater is indeed a place where some kind of performance or show is held for an audience to see, but *theatre,* in a larger sense, means all the activities that need to happen to present a drama. Write both words on the board.

Tell students that *drama* consists of the plays and reenactment of stories, often presented in a theater, but not always. Drama in the school happens in the classroom. The stories of the plays tell the audience something about life and people. Refer to Lesson 8, in which the dramatization brought to life a story from a particular culture.

EXPLORE   Have the students set up the classroom as a theater. First, they will need to identify the stage area, and set it off in some way, perhaps with masking tape on the floor. Then students should arrange their chairs into position for an audience.

Referring to the dramatization in Lesson 8, ask what people besides the actors are needed to put on the play. Students' responses should include someone to plan the stage setup (the set designer); someone to decide what the actors will wear (the costumer); and someone to take care of all the objects the actors use on stage (the property manager). If no one mentions the director, tell the students that the person who helps actors say their parts and move about the stage so that they can be seen and/or heard by the audience is the director. Write these different jobs in the theatre on the board under *theatre.*

DEVELOP	Referring to the dramatization in Lesson 8, assign one or two students to arrange the furniture on the "stage" to represent the setting in the dramatization. If simple costumes are available, assign one or two students to decide what items the characters will wear. Have one or two students collect items from around the classroom to serve as "props" for the actors. Select the appropriate number of students to dramatize again one of the scenes from the story in Lesson 8. The remainder of the students are to sit in the chairs as the audience.

Let the director move the actors to the stage area and give them directions. Have the costumers help the actors put on the costume items to be used, and the property managers provide the props. Play the scene. Ask the audience if they could see what was done by the director, set designers, costumers, and property managers. Reinforce the idea that the acting out of the story is *drama,* which is only part of the group effort involved in the activity referred to as *theatre.*

EVALUATE	*Student evaluation:* Ask the students if they can define *drama* and *theatre.* Ask, "What are some of the tasks and who are some of the people needed to present a drama?"

Teacher observation: Did students understand the difference between *drama* and *theatre* following this lesson? Are they aware of some of the terminology used to refer to specific people who work in theatre?

CONNECTIONS	*Physical Education, Language Arts:* Compare the different jobs in drama/theatre to positions on a team. Ask students what players are needed to play softball or another team sport familiar to students. List the positions on the board (for softball: catcher, pitcher, first base, second base, shortstop, third base, left field, center field, and right field). Ask, "What happens if the shortstop misses the ball?" Divide the class into small groups and have each group choose a sport and make a list of the players and terms that are used for that sport. Ask them to decide whether one of the positions could be eliminated.

SPECIAL NEEDS	Simplification of terms, definitions, and applications may be necessary for the mentally impaired student.

Creating Specific Characters

COMPONENT	Creative Expression
SUBJECT	Characterization
OBJECTIVE	Students dramatize actions, ideas, and emotions by creating specific characters.
MATERIALS	*Jean Rides a Tiger to Washington,* by Jean Simmons Wear

WARM UP   Review that in drama/theatre the *who* is called the *character.* The characters are beings other than themselves whom actors must portray. Ask the students for ideas on different ways they could express a character. Make a list on the board. Answers might include: by the way they walk; by the way they talk; their posture, how quickly or slowly they gesture; their facial expressions; and how they dress.

EXPLORE   Tell the students that feelings are an important part of portraying a character. Emotions cannot often be separated from actions; feelings determine how we behave.

Move the students to an open space where they can move freely without bumping into each other. Tell the students to close their eyes and see in their minds' eyes (picture in their minds) somebody they know very well. Ask them to "see" that person walking and to imagine how that person is feeling as she or he walks. When the students have clear mental pictures, they may begin to walk as that person does. Have them add facial expressions or gestures, too. Stop the students, and make brief comments on some of their movements, such as, "_____'s character seemed to be a teenager happy to be with friends. Tell us about your character, _____." Give several students the opportunity to comment on their characterizations.

DEVELOP   Read the description of Charles Lindbergh in Chapter 17 of *Jean Rides a Tiger to Washington,* or read a description of another strong character from a familiar story. Then ask the students questions about the character. For example, in reference to President Coolidge, ask, "How tall or short is he? How fat or thin? What is his hair like? How is he dressed? What kind of expression does he generally wear on his face? Can people tell what he is feeling from his expression? Does he like to be inside or outside? How does this affect the way he moves? What kind of a voice does he have? Does he talk in long sentences or short ones?"

As soon as the students have defined the character, ask them to move about the open space in the manner of the character.

Group the students into pairs. Each pair is to choose a small incident from the reading (President Coolidge presenting the Congressional Medal of Honor or Jean meeting Mr. Lindbergh, for instance), and plan and rehearse it briefly. Remind each partner to "see" his or her character mentally, imagine how that person is feeling, and how she or he would respond to the other person. Have the students share their brief characterizations with the class. Comment on some positive aspect of each characterization.

EVALUATE

Student evaluation: Ask the students, "Did seeing the character in the mind's eye help in the characterization? Was it easy or hard to be someone else? Do you think you understood how that character might be feeling? Did portraying one character give you ideas for portraying several other characters?"

Teacher observation: Have the students grasped the concept of characterization? Were they able to assume some of the characteristics of the person discussed? Did they move about freely and unselfconsciously?

CONNECTIONS

Social Studies: Relate the *Who* in this lesson to famous people in history. Collect photos or paintings of famous people, such as Charles Lindbergh and Calvin Coolidge, Amelia Earhart, Chief Joseph, or people the class is studying for history. Briefly identify who each of these people were. Number the pictures and make a card with a number and a short identifying sentence to go with each one. Then turn the cards over and see how many students can identify each person. Let students take turns posing as one of the famous people in a picture for others to guess which one it is.

SPECIAL NEEDS

Ask students who are unable to demonstrate a character's walk to concentrate on expressions or other body movements, and interpret characters this way.

RESOURCES

Edeen, Susan, et al. *Portraits Series: Mathematicians, Scientists, Poets, Authors, Artists.* Dale Seymour Publishing Company, 1988–90.

Wear, Jean Simmons. *Jean Rides a Tiger to Washington.* Regina Books, 1990.

Creating a Play from a Story

COMPONENT	Aesthetic Perception
SUBJECT	Stories and Plays
OBJECTIVE	Students become aware of the structural differences between stories and plays, and create a play from a narrative.
MATERIALS	*The Princess and the Pea,* by Hans Christian Andersen

WARM UP Ask the students whether any of them have seen a play. How many have ever read a play? (Many students may never have read a play.) Ask, "What is the difference between a story and a play?" Answers might include: "You read a story, but you see (act) a play." "They look different on the page." "A play has live people in it." Make two lists on the board. Label one, "Story," and the other, "Play," and list students' responses under the appropriate head.

EXPLORE Lead students to compare the items in their lists. If they have not suggested the following differences, describe them and give examples:

In a play the action happens in only a few places—usually one or two—but there can be many settings in a story (several can be described in one sentence).

Another difference between a story and a play is that a story can give information about several time periods at once, but what an audience at a play sees can only be happening in one time period. A story may say, "Last week Jorge pulled weeds in his garden and this week he planted vegetables." A play can only show Jorge doing one thing at a time.

A story describes what happens, the setting, and how the characters look and feel. A play must transform all those descriptions into a live visual and auditory experience.

Tell the students that a story is written in narrative form, that is, it "tells," or "narrates" the events. Write "narrative" on the board under "Story." A play is written in dramatic form, which indicates words and actions to each of the actors. Write "dramatic form" under "Play."

DEVELOP	Read *The Princess and the Pea*, by Hans Christian Andersen. Tell the students it is in narrative form, and they will change it into dramatic form, or the form ready to be acted.

Ask students what players will need to know to act out the story, and develop the following list:

1. Where and when the story happens (the setting)

2. Who the characters are (the King, the Queen, the Prince, the Princess, servants, and so on)

3. What happens in the plot (the story of the play)

4. What the characters will say and how they say it

Help students write a script from the story. For example, students might say, and you write on the board for them, "The scene is...," (Write the description of the set.) "...the great hall of a castle. There is a large door to the outside, another door to the rest of the castle, and two thrones. The King and Queen are seated on the thrones. A servant is nearby."

Ask the students what the first action in the play is to be. Perhaps the King and Queen are discussing that the Prince has not yet found a wife. Write on the board the dramatic form of what the students wish the characters to say. For example:

QUEEN: The Prince must find a wife!

KING: He is the heir to the throne, and he must have children to rule the kingdom after him.

QUEEN: Send for the Prince!

Ask the students to specify the actions that go with each line. When the students decide, alter the lines accordingly, following the dramatic form. The result should look like this:

QUEEN (greatly upset): The Prince must find a wife!

KING (gets up from throne and paces up and down): He is the heir to the throne, and he must have children to rule the kingdom after him.

QUEEN (motioning to the servant): Send for the Prince!

(The servant exits. The king sits down on his throne.)

KING: He has traveled the world to find a wife, but with no luck.

(The Prince enters and bows.)

PRINCE: You sent for me, Father?

Continue the process as far as time allows, showing how the speeches are written out for actors, and how the action is described for the actors to perform.

If possible, you or the students might copy the play and put it away for further work and possible presentation at a later date.

EVALUATE   *Student evaluation:* Ask the students to describe how a story can be changed into a play. What are some of the differences between a story and a play?

Teacher observation: Were the students able to grasp the concept of the dramatic form? Are they aware of the differences between it and the narrative form? Were students able to change description into speech and action? Did all participate? Were students' vocabularies enlarged?

CONNECTIONS   *Language Arts:* To help students become more familiar with dramatic literature, find one story in both narrative form and dramatic form. Read the narrative form aloud, then let students read the dramatic form to themselves. To practice the dramatic form, ask students to write a script for a joke that they know.

RESOURCES   Andersen, Hans Christian. *The Princess and the Pea.* (Clarion) Houghton Mifflin Company, 1979.

Hansen, Merrily. *Now Presenting: Classic Tales for Readers' Theatre.* Addison-Wesley Publishing Company, 1992.

Creating New Endings for Literature Selections

COMPONENT	Creative Expression
SUBJECT	Story Development
OBJECTIVE	Students analyze the parts of a story and create different endings.
MATERIALS	None required

WARM UP
Review the elements of a story: The beginning, which introduces the characters, where they are, and the situation, problem, or conflict they are facing; the middle, which tells how the characters work to solve the problem; and the ending, in which the problem or conflict is resolved. The beginning, middle, and end of a story, the "what happens," is called the *plot*.

Discuss a few stories that you have read. Ask if there are any similarities in the beginnings. Then focus on the endings. What usually happens at the end of a story? For example, once all the conflicts are resolved between and among the characters, do they live happily ever after?

EXPLORE
Read aloud to the class "The Poor Turkey Girl" from the Appendix of CENTER STAGE. Ask students to identify the beginning, middle, and ending. Ask them to look for possible opportunities the story offers for dramatization. When the students have named specific events, focus on each of them and ask such questions as, "What happens to the girl's beautiful clothes and jewelry?" or "What happens to the turkeys when the girl does not return in time?" Ask students to think of ways they could change the beginning, middle, or end of the story.

DEVELOP
Ask the students to create a different ending for the story in some way. The story ends with the young girl waiting for the turkeys to return. Her clothes return to rags, and from that time forward, the turkeys run wild up and down Thunder Mountain.

Say, "You are the writer of the story and you want a different ending. What would that ending be?" Discuss with the students a number of the new endings suggested. If time allows, divide the class into small groups and have each group plan, rehearse, and act out one of the new endings.

EVALUATE
Student evaluation: As a class, compare all the different endings suggested by the students. Ask students what their reasons were for deciding on a particular ending. Did students prefer one of the new endings to the original one? If so, why?

Teacher observation: Were the students able to change the ending logically, in accordance with the events of the story? Were the new endings imaginative? Were the students aware of the story structure: beginnings, middles, and ends?

CONNECTIONS
Mathematics: Let students experiment with changing the beginnings, middles, or endings of word problems to see how the problem-solving processes and the answers are affected. For example, a problem could be: Rashad bought 4 dozen cookies, and Simone bought 3 1/2 dozen cookies. How many cookies did they buy in all? Students might change the problem to: Rashad bought 4 dozen cookies and his friends ate 3 1/2 dozen. How many cookies were left? Let students work in pairs, changing word problems they have had in their math lessons. Make a blackline master of some of the problems for the class to solve.

SPECIAL NEEDS
The hearing impaired could read the script of the story provided with CENTER STAGE.

RESOURCES
Center Stage: Creative Dramatics Supplement. (contains an audiotape of "The Poor Turkey Girl") Available from Dale Seymour Publications.

Communicating Meaning Through Spoken Words

COMPONENT   Aesthetic Perception

SUBJECT   Communication

OBJECTIVE   Students become aware of the communicative potential of drama/theatre by exploring the various ways to express a single word.

MATERIALS   None required

WARM UP

While the students are seated at their desks or in a circle on the floor, challenge them, one at a time, to see how many different ways they can say the word *help*. Tell them that *help* is the only word they may say. They may say it loudly, speak it softly, say it as if it were a question, whisper the word, and so on. After several students have offered interpretations, suggest that they make their voices go up or down as they say the word. When several students have tried this, ask, "When the word *help* is said the way _____ says it, what does it suggest? Why?" or "How does saying *help* _____'s way make you feel? Why?" Invite responses from as many students as possible.

EXPLORE

As a group, choose one of the ways of saying *help* and think of a story that could go along with that way of saying the word. For example, if a student says the word with the sound tapering off, sounding farther and farther away, he or she might create the following story: A group of mountain climbers is about to reach the summit of the mountain. One of the climbers loses hold of the rope and falls to a lower ledge of the mountain.

As the climber falls, a yell is heard: "HEEeeeelllllp."

Continue the activity with a number of students recalling specific ways in which they said the word *help*, and as a group, developing possible stories to match the interpretations.

DEVELOP

Point out to the students how voice inflection can change the entire meaning of any word.

Tell students that they can use other words to do the same kind of activity they did with the word *help*. Invite students to suggest some words that might be used, and create a class list on the board. Encourage imaginative thinking.

Then divide the class into small groups, and have each group use a different single word or short phrase as a stimulus to create a story. Each student in the group should speak the word with his or her own inflection, to give the group a variety of story ideas. After the groups have developed their stories, give them the choice of either telling it, or dramatizing a segment of the story for the class. Comment on the favorable points of each presentation.

EVALUATE

Student evaluation: Ask students, "Did hearing different ways of saying a word (voice inflection) make a difference in the way you felt when you heard it? How does changing the tone of voice, even though you say the same word, change its meaning? Can you think of more words or phrases that change meaning when the tone of voice is changed?"

Teacher observation: Did the students use their voices effectively in conveying specific meanings to words? Were the students free enough to use physical and vocal interpretations in creating their stories? Did students work together well in the small groups?

CONNECTIONS

Language Arts: Students have found that one word, expressed differently, can have different meanings. Many words have different usage, as well. A word like *sharp,* for instance, may be used as an adjective (a *sharp* knife), a noun (music: a *sharp* or a flat), or by adding endings, a verb (*sharpen*) or an adverb (to speak *sharply*). Have the class try to think of words with many meanings or usages. Students may want to keep and add to a homonym list for themselves.

SPECIAL NEEDS

Some hearing impaired students will be able to experiment with variations in voice inflection. Those who cannot can do a comparable activity using the same signs in different ways.

Creating Stories from "What If...?" Questions

COMPONENT	Creative Expression
SUBJECT	Fantasy
OBJECTIVE	Students use fantasy situations to create stories.
MATERIALS	Pencils and paper

Note: Save the written materials from this lesson and keep a record of the students in each group for Lessons 22 and 30.

WARM UP

Define *fantasy* as "imagination at work"; fantasy is an unreal and fanciful mental image based on no solid facts. It often deals with unreal or supernatural events or characters.

Ask students questions such as, "What if the moon were made of cheese?" or "What if the sky were the ground and the ground were the sky?" Have individual students respond to the questions.

Then explain the power of the phrase "What if...?" Tell students that we call the *If* in this phrase the "Magic If," because when such a question is asked, the answer can be anything our imaginations can dream up, and therefore, almost magic.

EXPLORE

Ask a "What if...?" question similar to one of those in Warm Up. Have the students write their answers in one or two sentences. Responses might include, "All the stars are bouncing all over the place." "People and animals can now fly." Have volunteers share what they wrote.

DEVELOP

List on the board other possible "What if...?" situations, either suggested by the students or from your own imagination. Some examples of "What if...?" situations might be, "What if school were 24 hours long?" or "What if everyone could travel in time?" or "What if giraffes were house pets?" Divide the class into groups of five or six students, and have each group choose a "What if...?" question that they like. Then ask each student in the group to answer the question by writing one or two short sentences.

Challenge the students to combine all of their group's "What if...?" sentences into one narrative or story that has a beginning, middle, and end.

Each group should decide what needs adjusting in their individual sentences so that when the sentences are combined, a clear narrative is formed describing a "What if...?" situation. Allow each group to read and discuss its story with the entire class.

EVALUATE   *Student evaluation:* Ask students how the idea of "The Magic If" helped encourage their imagination. Ask students to describe any problems they had combining their different ideas. Ask, "What is imagination, and how did it help you in this exercise?"

Teacher observation: How well were students able to grasp the concept of the "Magic If?" Could the students work effectively in small groups? Were students able to organize the narrative using parts from each member of the group? Did all the students participate in this activity?

CONNECTIONS   *Social Studies:* Connect the "What if...?" to the study of history. This will help students remember the actual events better. Ask questions like, "What if everyone had continued to think the world was flat?" and "What if the American colonists had lost the Revolutionary War?" Students could write or dramatize their stories. Use the "What if...?" device for current events as well as events in the past.

SPECIAL NEEDS   The final step of combining all of the "What if...?" sentences may prove difficult for learning impaired students, but they may be able to contribute their sentences to have others in the group combine them into a story.

RESOURCES   Ringgold, Faith. *Tar Beach.* Crown Publishers, Inc., 1991.

Using Props to Develop Stories

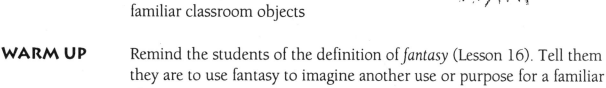

COMPONENT   Creative Expression

SUBJECT   Improvisation

OBJECTIVE   Students invent new uses for familiar objects and improvise a scene using an object as a prop.

MATERIALS   A light bulb, pencil, broom, and other familiar classroom objects

WARM UP   Remind the students of the definition of *fantasy* (Lesson 16). Tell them they are to use fantasy to imagine another use or purpose for a familiar object.

In front of the class, hold up a light bulb. Give the students a few seconds to look at it, then say, "We all know that this is a light bulb and we already know its use. Now I want you to forget how we usually use a light bulb. In a fantasy world, can you imagine what this could be (hold up the light bulb), and how it could work?"

After a few seconds, the students may have such responses as, "It's a new kind of candle; it's a frozen ice cream cone that softens up when you spin it around; it's a transformer that lets people travel through time."

EXPLORE   Continue the activity by holding up, one at a time, other simple objects available in the classroom such as a broom, a pencil, an eraser, and a book. Challenge the students to imagine a use for each object that was not intended by its inventor. Ask about each one, "In a fantasy world, what could this be? How might it work?" List on the board the various suggestions for each object. Let students handle the objects if they wish. Give several students the opportunity to imagine a new use for an object.

DEVELOP   Make available several objects in the classroom. Tell the students that in drama/theatre, objects used to help performers play their parts are called *props* and that they are going to have a chance to use one of these objects as a prop in a story.

Divide the class into pairs. Each pair should decide on one prop/object they will use to develop a scene with two characters. Tell the students that in the scene, each character must try to convince the other that his or her

GRADE 3

own use of the prop is the real and correct one. Remind students that they should try to forget the real use of the object, as they did in the Warm Up.

Each student must develop a convincing explanation and characterization to go with the use of the prop. The student should also give the object a new name. If, for example, the object is a broom, one character may be a witch who calls the broom a money tree. She plants the broom, straws up, by the light of a full moon so that it begins to grow and bears money fruit. The other character could be an astronaut who says that the broom is a rudder on a space shuttle. Each character should demonstrate his or her use of the prop and try to convince the other of the "correct" point of view. Emphasize that partners should not reveal the use of their props before the improvisations. Have each pair share their improvisation with the class.

EVALUATE

Student evaluation: Ask each pair of students why they chose the prop/ object they did. How did the object give them the idea for their improvisation? What other props/objects would be fun to use in developing another improvisation? What other stories could be developed around the same objects?

Teacher observation: Were the students able to come up with imaginative uses of the props? Did they understand how the use of props enhances a scene? Did the students work effectively in pairs? Did one member of the pair seem to dominate the other in some cases, or did both share the improvisation equally?

CONNECTIONS

Science: Carry over the idea of varied and imaginative uses of items into the study of nature. List several substances or objects, such as the ocean, trees, sand, and oil. Ask students to list as many uses as they can think of for each one. For the ocean they might say a home for fish and other animals; food, transportation, and recreation for people. In thinking of uses of trees, students might offer ideas like wood, paper, shade, homes for birds and other animals; and so on. Have students work as a group to illustrate one of these items and its uses as a display project.

Making Rod Puppets

COMPONENT	Historical and Cultural
SUBJECT	Puppetry
OBJECTIVE	Students increase their knowledge of drama/theatre arts and techniques by learning about puppetry used in other cultures, and by building simple puppets.
MATERIALS	Colored construction paper; tape, paste, or glue; stapler; 18-inch rods, such as bamboo garden stakes; *The World of Puppets* by Rene Simmen, or any book on puppetry with good photographs

Note: Ahead of time, invite the students to bring to class any puppets they may have at home.

WARM UP

Share the puppets brought in by the students. Most will probably be hand puppets (those operated by the hand inside the puppet). Define *puppet* as an artificial figure (not always, but often, a doll-like figure), often jointed, which is moved or manipulated by the hand, by wires, by strings, or by a rod or rods. Some puppets are manipulated by a combination of means.

Ask the students whether they have seen a live puppet show, or have watched TV shows in which puppets are used. What kinds of puppets did they see? (How were they manipulated?)

EXPLORE

Introduce students to the three types of puppets. As you describe each type, show pictures or hold up real examples.

1. *Marionettes.* Marionettes are figures attached to a frame by strings or wires. The operator manipulates the figures by pulling on the strings or wires. Marionettes were originally used in the Middle Ages. (The film, *The Sound of Music,* has some very fine marionettes in it.)

2. *Rod puppets.* Rod puppets are manipulated by rods and sticks. Sometimes the puppet is fastened to a single rod that moves the entire puppet; sometimes separate rods are fastened to different parts of the puppet's body so that the parts of the body can move separately. Japanese *bunraku*

(boon-RAH-koo) or doll theatre uses rod puppets that are four feet tall. Many cultures—China, Turkey, Indonesia, Cambodia, Thailand, and India—have developed rod puppets to a high art, and often use them in shadow performances.

3. *Hand puppets.* Hand puppets are manipulated by placing the hand inside the figure and moving all of the puppet or parts of it with the hand or fingers. These are the most common puppets. The English Punch and Judy, and the American Muppets are examples.

DEVELOP

Have each student make a three-dimensional abstract shape with a piece of colored construction paper. The paper can be folded, bent, torn, glued, stapled, or otherwise molded into the abstract shape. Students may wish to use several different colors of paper. Allow students approximately fifteen minutes to complete this exercise.

When students have made their shapes, fasten each one to a rod with tape. Have the student hold the rod and experiment with moving the shape puppet.

If a puppet theatre is not available in the school, turn a small table onto its side, and have the students operate their puppets from behind that. Or simply have the students hold the puppets away from their bodies as they manipulate them.

Have each student imagine a persona for the shape puppet and demonstrate it, answering the following questions: Who am I? Where did I come from? What do I do? What do I want most of all in the world?

If time allows, the students may wish to work in pairs to improvise a very brief scene or dialogue between two puppets. Tell the students that only the puppet who is speaking moves. The other puppet remains absolutely still until it speaks.

EVALUATE

Student evaluation: Ask students whether they can recall the differences among the three kinds of puppets, and how each is used. Can they remember some of the cultures that have a tradition of puppet theatre? How did students' shape puppets suggest a story to them? Ask students to tell what they liked about others' puppet presentations.

Teacher observation: Did students seem to increase their understanding of the cultural use of puppets? Were students able to manipulate materials creatively in making their own puppets? Were they motivated by the puppets to create original stories?

CONNECTIONS   *Art, Language Arts:* Have students create a set of simple puppets for a story they have read in class. Working in groups, they can decide on the necessary characters, and create simple figures out of tongue depressors, construction paper or fabric scraps, and glue. Help each group develop a script for their story and present a puppet show to the class.

SPECIAL NEEDS   Both visually and physically impaired students may need precut materials to help them create a puppet and to participate fully. In working with manipulative materials, severely visually impaired individuals find it helpful to position one hand in a certain spot on the table, e.g., by the paste or the paper, as a point of reference. This reduces the amount of time spent on continually searching for the materials with which they are working. Encourage the use of this technique.

RESOURCES   Currell, David. *The Complete Book of Puppet Theatre.* A. & C. Black, 1985.

Simmens, Rene. *The World of Puppets.* Elsevier Phaidon, 1975. This book is out of print, but it may be available in the library.

Von Boehn, Max (Josephine Nicoll, tr.). *Dolls and Puppets.* Cooper Square, 1966.

Music and Dramatic Action

COMPONENT	Aesthetic Valuing
SUBJECT	Movement Drama
OBJECTIVE	Students create and dramatize stories from their own interpretive response to various musical selections.
MATERIALS	Two contrasting musical recordings, such as *Close Encounters of the Third Kind,* by John Williams, and *Alice Coltrane with Strings,* by Alice Coltrane; cassette tape recorder or record or disk player

WARM UP

Say to the students, "Imagine that you are at a movie theater watching a film. All of a sudden the picture goes out and you are left with only the music." Tell the students that they will be creating pictures in their minds of what might be happening in a movie by listening to the music with their eyes closed.

Play an expressive recording such as *Close Encounters of the Third Kind.* (Different sections of the music are quite varied in expression, tempo, and volume.) Have the students close their eyes, listen to the music, and imagine what is happening on the screen. Let the students listen for three to four minutes. Stop the music and ask the students what images they saw in their minds' eyes. List their suggestions on the board and comment on a few of the images.

EXPLORE

Listen to another selection of music with a contrasting style, such as *Alice Coltrane with Strings* (very powerful, abstract music, with a variety of instruments), or another recording of your choice that is different from the first. Again, have the students shut their eyes to listen to the music, and to imagine what might be happening on the screen. List the students' responses and compare the images to those suggested earlier for *Close Encounters.*

DEVELOP

In groups or as a class, choose one of the musical selections just played to improvise a story without words (a nonverbal movement drama). Tell the students to make the action in the story fit the style and mood of the music.

If, for example, the music chosen is from *Close Encounters,* the improvisational scene may be astronauts walking on the moon, or a group of undersea divers discovering a sunken treasure ship.

Continue playing the music for motivation. In small groups or as a class, have students plan and rehearse the nonverbal story. Share the scene(s), and ask the students who were observers, "Do you think that the story fit the mood or atmosphere the music created? If the music changed, did the performers change their actions?"

You may wish to extend the activity, if time allows, or you may wish to continue the activity at another time. In either case, use the same story the students created with another musical recording of a different mood and style. Play the new music for students. Then let students perform the story again and decide whether the original story fits the new music. Ask the students, "Did different images come to mind when the new music was played? Could the original meaning of the story be kept? Did the old story fit the new music? Why or why not? Do you think changes should be made in the story to fit the new music? If so, what are they?"

EVALUATE

Student evaluation: Ask students, "What images did you see when the story was performed? Which music made it easier to create pictures in your mind's eye? Why? Can you think of other styles of music that could be used with this activity?"

Teacher observation: Were the students able to suspend reality to imagine that they were at the movies without a picture on the screen? How effective were the students in developing a story to fit each musical style? Did students seem to have an awareness of how music is used in movies to help create mood?

CONNECTIONS

Music Appreciation: Collect a variety of nature pictures or have students bring some to class, and display them on a bulletin board or wall. The pictures could be of clouds, volcanoes, glaciers, fields of flowers, lightning storms, starry skies, floods, and so on. Number each picture for identification. Play parts of the two musical selections from the lesson, and any others that would evoke imagery. Ask students to write down the number of the picture that they feel best illustrates each piece of music. They may write down several numbers if they wish. After each selection is played, have students give their reasons for choosing a particular picture.

SPECIAL NEEDS   With hearing impaired students, use pictures rather than music as stimuli to create a story. Once a story is created, change the picture and ask if the original story still fits. Compare the two pictures and ask students what part of the story would need to be changed.

RESOURCES   Coltrane, Alice. *Alice Coltrane with Strings*. Impulse ABC Records.

Williams, John. *Close Encounters of the Third Kind*. Arista Records.

Elements of Evaluation

COMPONENT   Aesthetic Valuing

SUBJECT   Evaluation

OBJECTIVE   Students analyze a performance in terms of drama/theatre to determine what props, sets, and costumes would best suit a performance.

MATERIALS   None required

Note: If the students have seen a school play or other performance together recently, use that as a basis for this lesson. If not, assign ahead of time a specific TV performance for all the students to watch. Also prepare a blackline master with the questions listed in Explore, so that students can focus their viewing.

WARM UP   Review the performance that the students have seen together. Ask students for three qualities of the performance that they liked—perhaps the enthusiasm of the characters, or the mood created by the music, or colorful costumes. Also ask for particular events in the performance that were enjoyable. List these features on the board and compare the answers. Come to some consensus of what the students liked.

EXPLORE   Lead students to be more specific in evaluating the performance. Ask such questions as, "Did the actors wear costumes? If so, did the costumes relate to the actors' roles? Were any kinds of stage props (for example, a record player, or vase of flowers) used? How did the set and stage props convey the mood? Was music used? How? Did the actors move or talk in any specific ways to convey different characters?"

DEVELOP   Briefly review again the story of the viewed performance. Divide the class into small groups. Have each group choose a scene from the performance to replay. Ask each group to consider carefully anything they might change about the scene. (Could the costumes be made more suitable for the characters? Could the sets and props be different? Could the actors have portrayed their characters more believably?)

Plan and rehearse the scenes, then have students play them sequentially, with the teacher filling in narrative as necessary. Allow students to use their own words. Before each performance, let each group describe costumes and settings that they would use, and tell the class what changes they made and why. After the performance, give each group the opportunity to hear comments from their classmates. Ask the observing students to analyze each performance in terms of the visual aids that would best enhance that dramatic presentation.

EVALUATE

Student evaluation: Ask each small group to continue discussing the observations made by the class concerning their improvisations. Does the group agree with what the other students said? Have they changed their minds about sets, costumes, and props needed after hearing other students' observations?

Teacher observation: Did the analysis of visual aids used in performance help students see certain aspects of their performance that they would not have otherwise observed? Could the students be objective about their improvisations as they commented about their own work?

CONNECTIONS

Language Arts: Help students develop a rating scale for evaluating TV shows that they see. Ask students what criteria are important to them: interesting dialogue? attractive or appropriate sets? realistic costumes for the story? use of music in creating the mood? Make a list with check boxes, so that students can check Good, Fair, or Poor for each item. Make copies of the rating scale so that each student can use it at home. Discuss and compare students' evaluations on a regular basis.

SPECIAL NEEDS

Rather than asking visually impaired students to watch a performance, read aloud a play that contains detailed descriptions of props, sets, and costumes. There are also descriptive audiotapes available of such performances from local agencies for the visually impaired.

Analyzing Intent and Structure in Drama

COMPONENT	Aesthetic Valuing
SUBJECT	Evaluation
OBJECTIVE	Students learn and use established vocabulary to evaluate a theatrical work.
MATERIALS	None required

Note: Use a recent school play as a basis for this lesson, or assign a specific TV performance (different from the one used in Lesson 20) to be watched by all the students ahead of time.

WARM UP   Review Lesson 20, in which students responded to a theatrical piece by recalling qualities and events they liked in that work. Briefly discuss students' overall impression and evaluation of the work.

EXPLORE   Introduce two formal words of evaluation used in drama/theatre: *intent* and *structure*. Write these terms on the board and discuss each one.

Tell students that *intent* means what the play was about—the main idea, message, or theme being communicated. Refer to the assigned performance, and ask, "What was the play about? I don't mean what happened, but what was the idea of the story—honesty, doing good, sharing?" When the students have identified the idea, write it on the board under "intent."

Ask students how intent was shown in the viewed performance. Identify *structure* as how the theme or message was developed and carried out in the performance. Was the story believable? Did the events in the story follow one another logically? Were the characters true to life? Ask students to identify the problem of the story and how the characters solved it, and write "beginning: problem"; "middle: what happens"; and "end: solution" on the board under "structure."

DEVELOP   Divide the class into small groups. Review the story of the viewed performance and allow each group to select a scene that demonstrates in some way the intent of the story. Give students time to plan and rehearse the scene in their own words.

In order to demonstrate structure, have students present their chosen scenes sequentially. If no group presents a particular scene, briefly narrate the missing events. If some scenes are duplicated, allow them all to be played, one following another. Point out to the students that putting events into logical sequence is a form of structure. Narrating the omitted events helps to make transitions, or changes from one scene to another, which is also part of the structure.

After presenting the entire sequence of scenes, ask the students to recall the intent, or message of the performance. How was it demonstrated? Have students briefly analyze their own performance in terms of the intent and structure.

EVALUATE

Student evaluation: In smaller groups, have students discuss the class analysis of the play. Ask, "If you were going to talk with the performers and director of the play or scene or TV program, what would you tell them about the experience of seeing their production? Could you offer suggestions on what changes could be made to make the intent and structure of the work clearer?"

Teacher observation: Were students able to analyze their own reactions to the performance? Were they able to organize their opinions to evaluate the performance in terms of intent (theme or message) and structure (the way the theme or message was carried out in the performance)?

CONNECTIONS

Language Arts: Discuss with the class *intent* and *structure* in stories as well as in plays. Bring to class some examples of reviews of children's books from newspapers or magazines. Have students note whether reviewers discussed intent or structure (or used other terms with the same meaning) in the books they reviewed. If possible, ask the person who reviews books for the local newspaper to speak to the class about evaluating them. Then have each student write a review of a recently read book in terms of intent and structure.

Dramatizing "What If...?" Stories

COMPONENT	Creative Expression
SUBJECT	Improvisation
OBJECTIVE	Students analyze a previously written "What If...?" story in terms of drama/theatre, and then dramatize it.
MATERIALS	"What if...?" stories from Lesson 16

Note: Keep a brief record of students' dramatizations to help them develop a performance in Lesson 30.

WARM UP

Remind the students of an earlier lesson (Lesson 16), in which they wrote narratives using the "Magic If"—the idea that through the imagination anything is possible. Tell students that in that lesson the "Magic If" was used with fantasy, but it can also apply to real situations. Quite often authors ask themselves "What if...?" when they begin to write a play or story. Ask the students to reread the "What if...?" situations they wrote so as to reacquaint themselves with their stories.

EXPLORE

Choose one of the narratives and discuss with the class the possible ways to proceed if a group of students were to dramatize the narrative. Ask students to think about such questions as, "What should the audience see first if we were to act out the narrative? Who are the characters in our presentation? Where would the story take place? What would be the main action, and how could that action be shown? Would there be dialogue between the characters, or would we pantomime the action?"

DEVELOP

Return to the small groups in which the "What If...?" narratives were created. Using the narrative and information gained from the discussion period, have each group plan an improvisation, giving each member of the group a role in the story. (As an alternative, you may wish to select only one of the narratives to dramatize. In this case, plan with the entire class, then select the appropriate number of students for the characters in the dramatization.)

Ask students to consider different possibilities for presenting the narra-tive. Ask them to think, for instance, whether the action will be pantomimed, or accompanied by dialogue. Will they have a storyteller, or will each character develop her or his own dialogue for the story? After planning, have groups rehearse and share the stories with the entire class.

EVALUATE   *Student evaluation:* Ask students whether dramatizing their "What if...?" stories helped them understand the concept of the "Magic If" any better. What challenges did dramatizing the story pose?

Teacher observation: Do you feel that the students built on what they had learned previously about the "Magic If" to develop their dramatization in this lesson? Did you see evidence in the improvisations that the students understood the concept of "What if...?" and were able to translate that concept into a dramatization?

CONNECTIONS   *Science:* Ask students, "What if you were a coyote (or dragonfly, or whale, or other animal)?" Let students imagine being an animal and tell what they think it would be like. Make a list on the board of different kinds of animals. Then have each child choose an animal, research some basic facts about it, and write a story starting with "If I were a _____...." Students may choose an animal from the list or think of their own. Have them include in the story the reason they chose that particular animal.

Creating a Dramatization Through Playmaking

COMPONENT	Creative Expression
SUBJECT	Playmaking
OBJECTIVE	Students use the five W's and simple story analysis to create a dramatization.
MATERIALS	*Why the Tides Ebb and Flow,* by Joan Bowden

Note: Keep a brief record of students' dramatizations in this lesson to help them develop a performance in Lesson 30.

WARM UP

Review the following elements of story structure—the beginning, middle, and end (see Lesson 14). Review the five W's: *Who, What, Where, When,* and *Why* (Lessons 8, 9, and 10). Ask students to think about the story structure and the five W's as you read them a simple story such as *Why the Tides Ebb and Flow,* so that they can create a drama from it.

EXPLORE

Have the students identify the five W's and the beginning, middle, and end of *Why the Tides Ebb and Flow.* Ask such questions as, "Who are the characters? Which one did we meet first in the story? Which one did we meet next? What were the characters doing when we met them? What is the basic motivation or emotion of each? (What does that person want?) What is the sequence of action? What happens in the beginning of our story? What happens in the middle? How does the story end? What are the various environments or settings in which the action takes place?"

DEVELOP

Read the story again, and ask students to listen with the idea of developing the dialogue between characters and communicating to an audience the conditions in which the story takes place.

If possible, divide the class into groups of seven so that there are enough students in each group to play the following roles in the story:

1. Old Woman

2. Great Spirit

3. A bird

4. A fish

5. Great Dog

6. Beautiful Maiden

7. Strong Young Man

Should there be an uneven number for the groups, other animals could be added, or there could be two Great Dogs or Beautiful Maidens.

Group members should each select a character that they would like to play, then plan and rehearse the story from beginning to end. Tell students to look for places to develop dialogue in the story, and to find ways to convey the different environmental settings. (The environment can be identified through dialogue, or movement, as was done in Lesson 10.)

Following the planning, casting, and rehearsing, have each group share its dramatization with the class.

EVALUATE   *Student evaluation:* Lead a class discussion of each presentation, asking the following questions: "Which part of the story was the most difficult to dramatize, and why? If you were to repeat the dramatization, what would you change? How would these changes make the story or character clearer? Did you have to add to or leave out anything in the story? What was it? Did it make the dramatization easier to perform or clearer to the audience?" After evaluating all the presentations, ask, "What elements were the same in each group's presentation? What parts were different?"

Teacher observation: How were students able to use what they heard in the story to develop characterizations and convey a sense of the setting? Did the students use movement and voice variation? Were they imaginative in the development of the dramatizations? How effectively were students able to work together?

CONNECTIONS   *Science: Why the Tides Ebb and Flow* is a "How and Why" story that shows how people used their imagination to provide an answer for what was one of science's mysteries. Ask students if they know what really causes the tide. You may have to provide the answer that it is the pull of gravity from the moon acting upon the ocean. Working in small groups, have students think of creative ways to demonstrate this property of gravity. Have reference materials available so that students can do further research.

RESOURCES   Bowden, Joan. *Why the Tides Ebb and Flow.* Houghton Mifflin Co., 1979.

Parts of the Whole

COMPONENT Aesthetic Perception

SUBJECT Perception

OBJECTIVE Students analyze the parts of visual art and dramatic art in terms of a story in order to understand the whole presentation.

MATERIALS Prints of several paintings of flowers by Georgia O'Keeffe; "The Blind Ones and the Matter of the Elephant," from the anthology *World Tales,* by Idries Shah

WARM UP Frame a small portion of a painting of a large object, such as the flowers in one of Georgia O'Keeffe's paintings. Show the framed portion to the students. Ask students if they can identify the object. List their responses on the board. Ask, "How do you know? What makes you think it is _____?"

Now show the students the entire picture. Discuss the difficulty of identifying the flowers after seeing only a small portion of the painting. Tell the students that viewing a dramatic production is the same way. If students concentrate on one element by itself—for instance, the scenery—they may not understand what the dramatic work is trying to convey; the production must be considered as a whole. The actors, the story, the costumes, the props, the scenery, the lights, and the music and dance are all elements in the production.

EXPLORE Tell students that there is a famous story about some blind men who each became familiar with only a small part of a very large object, and decided what the whole thing was like from knowing about the small part. Read the story, "The Blind Ones and the Matter of the Elephant," by Idries Shah. After the reading ask the students what they think was the intent of the story and how that intent was related to viewing a small part of a painting. How is the message of the story related to all the jobs necessary for a whole theatre production? (The production needs to be seen as a whole, not just one of the parts.)

DEVELOP Write *collaboration* on the board and define the term as working together, cooperating on a project. Ask the students to name some of the people in the theatre who collaborate (see Lesson 11). Make a list on the board. The list should include: the actors, the director, the scene or set designer, the costume designer, and the property manager. Enlarge the list by asking, "Where does the play come from?" (the playwright writes it) "Who helps actors with their makeup?" (the makeup designer) "Who lights the stage?" (the lighting designer) "Who helps move the sets?" (the stage crew)

Assign to selected students the various job titles that are listed on the board. Have each of those students take on the assigned role and address the class, telling what her or his job is in the theatre and how that person collaborates with the others. For example, the actor's job is made easier by having someone provide the different costumes to wear, or by being given a prop that he or she needs in the play. Ask each student, "What would happen to a play if you didn't do your job?" Allow other students to ask questions about or comment on the jobs the collaborators perform.

EVALUATE   *Student evaluation:* Ask students, "Can any of the tasks in the theatre be performed without collaborating with others? If so, what might they be? If not, tell why not. In what other activities is collaboration important?" Have students compare the importance of collaborating in those activities with collaborating in the theatre.

Teacher observation: Do students understand the concept of collaboration and the necessity of seeing the whole in making educated judgments? Can they apply the concept of collaboration to other areas besides drama/theatre, such as home and school? Have they increased their awareness of the importance of all personnel involved in drama/theatre?

CONNECTIONS   *Social Studies:* Discuss the need for collaboration in the classroom, and the need to respect differences, especially when students are working together. Discuss the variety of nationalities and races within the classroom. Relate the small classroom group to the larger groups of people in the town, the country, and the world. Ask students for ideas on how to solve problems in the class, the town, the country, and the world when the people in each group are not in agreement.

RESOURCES   Georgia O'Keeffe Fine Arts Posters "Red Poppy" and "Black Iris" available from Dale Seymour Publications.

Shah, Idries. *World Tales*. Johnson Reprint Corp., 1979.

Exploring the Art Disciplines: Drama and the Visual Arts

COMPONENT	Aesthetic Perception
SUBJECT	Drama and the Visual Arts
OBJECTIVE	Students identify and describe the basic qualities of drama and visual arts, and participate in a activity from each discipline.
MATERIALS	Prints of various paintings; drawing materials; construction paper; scissors, tape; a videotape or audiotape of a dramatization; a book of poems such as *A New Treasury of Children's Poetry*, by Joanna Cole; *Arts Abound, The Painter* and *The Sculptor*, by GPN; *Art for Children Series*, by Ernest Raboff

Note: Performing artists could also be invited to the classroom as guests in addition to, or in place of, the videotapes.

WARM UP Show students some examples of visual arts—drawing, painting, and sculpture—and ask them to give examples of drama (theatre productions, TV). Ask students how drama and visual arts are similar and how they are different. Both are arts to be looked at, observed, and enjoyed by the participants and the viewers. They both use color, line, space, and texture. Drama, however, happens in time, so that it ends when the performance ends. Visual arts remain after they are created.

EXPLORE Show a video such as *Arts Abound, The Painter*, in which an artist talks about his artistic growth and development, or share prints of paintings, such as the ones from the *Art for Children Series* by Ernest Raboff. Examples include paintings by Remington, Chagall, Klee, Gauguin, Rembrandt, and Van Gogh.

For drama, show a video such as *Arts Abound, The Actor*, in which a young actor is followed through rehearsal to final production, and/or *Arts*

GRADE 3

Abound, The Playwright, in which an experienced playwright and an inexperienced one share their sources of inspiration and the creative process.

DEVELOP   Actively involve the students in an experience from each art discipline. For drama, choose a few short poems from a poetry anthology such as *The New Treasury of Children's Poetry,* and have selected students each read a poem to the class. Remind them to use voice inflection and to convey emotions as they read. Let other students offer suggestions for movements that might enhance the readings. If some students know poetry or other dramatic material by memory, give them the opportunity to recite their work in front of the class.

For visual arts, choose a setting such as a forest or outer space, and have the students draw a picture that describes that location, or have them create a three-dimensional sculpture such as a futuristic house or an animal in the zoo from construction paper and other materials.

EVALUATE   *Student evaluation:* Ask students to identify some similarities and differences between drama and the visual arts. How could the visual arts and drama be used to complement each other in a theatrical performance?

Teacher observation: Do students have a basic understanding of the differences and similarities between visual and dramatic arts? Could you identify students who showed a particular interest in either of the art forms? Did viewing the tape of an actor or an artist seem to stimulate interest in participating in an activity?

CONNECTIONS   *Visual Arts, Music:* Play Vivaldi's *The Four Seasons* to stimulate students' imagination. Point out how Vivaldi used his imagery of spring, summer, fall, and winter to help him compose the musical work. Ask students to think in terms of color, line, and texture as they listen to the four parts of the selection. Students may respond verbally, by drawing, or by making a collage with a variety of textured materials so that they can draw upon their imagery of the tactile sensations of each season. Ask students to think of what colors come to mind as they listen to the music.

SPECIAL NEEDS   Allow time to describe to severely visually impaired students the visual aspects of this lesson and have them create something sculptural, rather than drawing.

RESOURCES

Arts Abound (The Painter, The Actor, The Playwright). (videotape) GPN, affiliated with the University of Nebraska, Lincoln, Nebraska, 1990.

Cole, Joanna. *A New Treasury of Children's Poetry*. Doubleday, 1984.

Raboff, Ernest. *Art for Children Series*. Harper & Row Junior Books, 1988.

Vivaldi, Antonio. *The Four Seasons*. Academy of Ancient Music, Christopher Hogwood. Decca Records, 1984.

Exploring the Art Disciplines: Dance and Music

COMPONENT	Aesthetic Perception
SUBJECT	Dance and Music as Art Disciplines
OBJECTIVE	Students identify and describe the basic qualities of dance and music, and participate in an activity from each discipline.
MATERIALS	Videotape, *Arts Abound, The Dancer* and *The Musician,* by GPN; recordings of *Graceland,* by Paul Simon, and other musical selections; cassette recorder or record player; VCR

WARM UP

Tell the students that the art disciplines of music and dance have many similarities. They both use rhythm and tempo, and take practice to perform. Neither leaves anything to be viewed when the performance is over.

Ask the students, "What is dance?" The answers should indicate some perception of the beauty of bodily movement to express something; an emotion, an idea, a story.

Ask, "What is music?" The answers should indicate some awareness of melody, tonal quality, rhythm, and tempo.

EXPLORE

Share an example from each art form, music and dance. View a music videotape such as *Arts Abound, The Musician,* in which the Metropolitan Brass Quintet shows the fun and beauty of music-making. Share parts of videotapes or audiotapes featuring other styles of music such as jazz, popular, and folk music.

View a dance video such as *Arts Abound, The Dancer,* in which a dance company demonstrates the power, inventiveness, and humor of modern dance. If possible, also view excerpts from other dance videotapes that your district resource center might have on file.

Ask the students, "How would you describe the different styles of dance and music in the videotapes? How are they alike? How are they different?"

DEVELOP　　Actively involve the students in an experience from each art discipline. For dance, play an upbeat recording such as Paul Simon's *Graceland,* and have students move in an open space, responding to the rhythm and tempo of the music. Encourage students to use the different levels and explore the different shapes the body can make while moving. Have students experiment with the use of space and time. Play several different musical selections to which students can respond with movement.

For music, have the class sing together a song that all are familiar with, then sing other songs suggested by the students. Have any students who are experienced with an instrument play them for the class. After each selection, ask for a volunteer to hum the melody, and/or clap the rhythm.

Ask the students, "What is the relationship of dance and music?" Students will probably offer the comment that most dancing is done to music. Discuss how each of the disciplines is a separate art, but they each enhance the other.

EVALUATE　　*Student evaluation:* Ask students to recall some similarities and differences between dance and music. Can they recall some of the terms used in dance and music? Ask them to describe areas of their own lives in which music and dance are important, and why.

Teacher observation: Do students have a basic understanding of the qualities of music and dance? Did they seem to increase their awareness of the relationship of music and dance?

CONNECTIONS　　*Social Studies:* Dance has historically been used as a natural expression of united feeling and action. Many primitive dances have survived in the folk dances of modern time. American Indian dances were usually of a ritualistic or ceremonial nature, and illustrate some of the primitive purposes of dance. Invite students to think about what some of these primitive purposes might be. List students' ideas on the board and have them work in small groups to develop some form of dance or movement to mark an occasion. The occasion might be harvest, marriage, birth, death, or the new year. Have each group share its movement with the class.

RESOURCES　　*Arts Abound, The Musician* and *The Dancer,* (videotape) by GPN, affiliated with the University of Nebraska, Lincoln, Nebraska, 1990.

Simon, Paul. *Graceland.* Warner Brothers Records, Inc.

GRADE 3

Historical Traditions in Storytelling

COMPONENT   Historical and Cultural

SUBJECT   Theatre History

OBJECTIVE   Students investigate the oral traditions of ways stories have been passed on.

MATERIALS   None required

WARM UP   Discuss the oral tradition of storytelling—how stories are preserved from one generation to another by being told rather than written down. Tell the students that most countries have used the oral tradition of storytelling.

Ask students if they know of a story that was told to them by a parent or other adult. Do they know whether the story had been passed on to that adult by his or her parents or grandparents? What was the story about? Was it something that really happened or was it a folk tale, fairy tale, or something partly make-believe?

Ask, "What do you think happens to a story as it gets passed on from one person to another? Do you think the details in the story change slightly, or do you think they remain the same as each person retells the story?"

Move the students into a circle and play the Telephone Game as follows: Whisper a sentence to the first student. Tell the student to whisper that exact sentence to the person sitting next to him or her. Have students continue until everyone has heard the sentence. The last person in the circle to hear the sentence tells the group what he or she heard. Compare that sentence to the original sentence you told the first student.

EXPLORE   Explain to the class that in many cultures stories are acted out, and passed on in that way from parents to children.

Divide the class into four or five equal groups. Have the first group decide upon the beginning of a simple story, such as, "A group of children are walking home from school when one of them spots a treasure map in the grass. The children grab the map, read it, and start to follow the directions written on the map to find the treasure." Have students in this group act out a simple set of actions for their story.

At a given point say, "freeze." Have the first group of students return to their seats and give another group a few minutes to discuss what the first group did. Tell the second group to try to repeat exactly the dialogue that the first group used. Challenge the students even further to reenact the exact movements used by the first group.

Continue the activity until all the groups have had a turn attempting to duplicate what the preceding group did, and thus what the original group of students performed. Compare the differences in each presentation.

DEVELOP

Talk about whether students were able to retain the original story that was not written down but acted out. Also discuss why it is important to receive and give correct information (so that the story will keep its original content).

Tell the students that early theatre stories were not written down. Performers needed to remember not only the dialogue, but the movements important in telling a story.

Many stories that were told and/or performed focused around basic needs of people such as planting and harvesting crops; the need for rain, for sun, for snow; chores that needed to be done such as building, hunting, fishing, and caring for animals.

If time allows, or for another lesson (perhaps related to the current social studies focus), have the students choose one of these topics, and create a scene that focuses on the chosen theme. Stress the importance of passing on the correct information in both words and movements, so that younger people in the culture will know what to do and how to do it.

Give students ample time for planning and rehearsal. Have each group share its improvisation with the entire class.

EVALUATE

Student evaluation: As a class, discuss how well each group succeeded in repeating the preceding group's dialogue and movements. Ask students, "How do you suppose the story got changed? What does this tell you about the oral tradition of storytelling and the oral tradition of theatre?"

Teacher observation: Did students understand oral tradition any better following the Telephone Game? How close did the final sentence come to the original sentence? Could students copy the story drama closely, or were the actions and dialogue changed? Did the students concentrate and use careful observational and listening skills in order to complete the required tasks?

CONNECTIONS   *Language Arts:* Relate listening and observational skills in repeating a story to listening skills in following directions. Point out to students that the ability to follow directions depends on the ability to think sequentially and clearly. Start with a sequence of three directions involving physical movement. Terms could be any with which students are familiar: *right, left, backwards, parallel, in a circle,* and so on. Increase the number of directions given as students seem able to carry them out. Allow student volunteers to give directions to the group as well.

African Stories

COMPONENT	Historical and Cultural
SUBJECT	Theatre History
OBJECTIVE	Students increase their knowledge of African traditions by listening to African stories and hearing about African customs.
MATERIALS	*Ashanti to Zulu: African Traditions,* by Margaret Musgrove

Note: If possible, arrange for an African storyteller or mask maker to visit the class. Your school or town librarian may know of a local person who would be willing to come to the school.

WARM UP

If possible, show students a mask, or pictures of masks. Ask the students if they know of any groups of people who use masks for ceremonial purposes. Many cultures use them, including Native Americans and Amazonian Indians.

In early African drama, masks were used to represent different religious and nonreligious characters in ceremonies. Review Lesson 27, which focused on stories that were created from the experiences of the people. As with many other cultures, topics included life and death issues, such as amount of sunshine and rainfall, preparing for a hunt, and celebrating a harvest.

EXPLORE

Read from literature about Africa, such as *Ashanti to Zulu: African Traditions,* by Margaret Musgrove, which illustrates a few of the many nations that make up Africa.

Discuss the customs of the different nations and ask students to think about a possible dramatization of a scene using a particular custom as a theme. For example, students might choose a scene in which the Kung (koohng) people of Africa find and store water in ostrich shells in the desert, or how the Baule (BAH-oo-lay) people were saved by the crocodiles. (What other story do students know in which the queen's first child had to be given up?)

DEVELOP   If possible, invite an African mask maker and/or storyteller into the class to share a variety of traditions with the students. Discuss ahead of time with the visitor what will be the focus of the lesson, and how much time is available. Activities could include the showing and/or making of masks, telling a variety of traditional stories to the students, and assisting the students in dramatizing their own stories built on themes that are important to a particular culture.

If it is not possible to bring a guest into the classroom, divide the class into groups of four or five and let each group choose an African custom from the book read and plan a way to dramatize it (see Lesson 23). Have each group rehearse and then share the dramatization with the class. Comment after each dramatization on how the custom or tradition was demonstrated.

EVALUATE   *Student evaluation:* Ask students, "Are any of the customs, traditions, or stories in today's lesson familiar to you? Are they similar to some custom or tradition or story you know already? If masks were shown or made, can you tell the specific purpose of the mask?"

Teacher observation: Were students able to understand the concept of dramatic literature being motivated by the lives of the people? If there was a visiting artist, did that person seem to generate thoughtful and perceptive questions from the students? In their own dramatizations, did the students focus on the motivations of the African people?

CONNECTIONS   *Art Appreciation:* Explore further some African traditions through art. Bring into class some examples and pictures of African art. The ornamentation of textiles and the decoration of everyday tools were vital arts in nearly all African cultures. Discuss how art was used for religious ceremonies. After the discussion, invite students to create art that follows some of the African traditions. Have several media available for students to choose from: cloth, paper, clay, wood, shells, and so on.

RESOURCES   Allen, Judy, et al. *Cultural Awareness for Children.* Addison-Wesley Publishing Company, 1992.

Musgrove, Margaret. *Ashanti to Zulu: African Traditions.* Dial Books for Young Readers, 1976.

Sivin, Carole. *Maskmaking.* Davis Publications, 1987.

Mask Prints. (Portfolio of 12 Mask Prints 16 x 12 in.) Crystal Productions, 1991.

American Traditions and Customs

COMPONENT   Historical and Cultural

SUBJECT   American Culture

OBJECTIVE   Students become more aware of the diversity of American culture by hearing stories about particular events in United States history and dramatizing them.

MATERIALS   *The Courage of Sarah Noble,* by Alice Dalgliesh; *The Drinking Gourd,* by F.N. Monjo; *Corn is Maize: The Gift of the Indians,* by Aliki; *Wagon Wheels,* by Barbara Brenner

WARM UP   Divide the class into small groups. Tell students that they are to create a still "photograph," using everyone in the group as part of that still photograph.

Give the students topics for the photographs. Start out with topics that do not include people. For example, say, "In the Great Plains of America there are many wheat fields. Show me a photograph of a wheat field. The Rocky Mountains are high and pointed. Show me a photograph of the mountains." Then say, "The next photograph will have people in it. Show me a photograph of Americans in a shopping mall." Choose topics from American culture.

EXPLORE   Show students photographs from books such as the *Coming to America Series,* which documents experiences of American immigrants. Explain to students that photographs tell us many things: in these cases, they tell us something about the people, the place where they live, and what their life is like. Write "culture" on the board. Tell students that means all the traditions, customs, and history of the people in one particular place. People in the United States have brought their own cultures from many different lands; all of these make up American culture.

Continue the still photo exercise by challenging groups of students to create still photographs of historical or cultural scenes that they have studied or know about. Have the groups decide on a scene to illustrate,

GRADE 3

how they saw it in their mind's eye, and how they decided to use their bodies to show the photograph.

Give each group time to plan its photo in detail. Examples of events students might choose to portray could be pioneer families crossing the plains in covered wagons, Native Americans tracking deer, Chinese railroad workers in California, the first Thanksgiving, or other cultural experiences that students know about from their social studies lessons.

If time allows, invite students to create other still photographs that demonstrate American cultural history.

DEVELOP   Read several incidents from stories in children's literature that describe a variety of fictional and nonfictional characters and events focusing on American culture. Some such stories are: *The Courage of Sarah Noble,* in which a young girl finds courage to stay in the wilderness of the Old West; *Wagon Wheels,* in which a black family travels to Kansas during the Homestead Act; *Corn is Maize: The Gift of the Indians,* which tells about the discovery of corn by the Indians and how it came to be an important food throughout the world; and *The Drinking Gourd,* the story of the underground railroad. Identify for students the cultural group described in each story and the time the story took place.

In small groups, give students an opportunity to improvise scenes from the various stories. Have them develop possible dialogue, movement, and settings; then plan, rehearse, and share the improvisations with the rest of the class.

EVALUATE   *Student evaluation:* Ask the students to describe briefly what American culture is. Can they identify the group in American culture that they portrayed in their dramatization? What are some possibilities for other scenes from American culture?

Teacher observation: Were students able to work together effectively in creating group photographs of various scenes? How effectively were students able to use information from the stories to create a scene? Did students' awareness of groups in American culture different from their own seem to increase?

CONNECTIONS   *Social Studies:* Discuss with students the idea of a "melting pot" as it might apply to people. It used to mean that in becoming Americans, those people who came from another country ceased to be identified with the old country. Today the idea of diversity and pluralism are more widely accepted, and people are encouraged to maintain their cultural identity even as they become Americans.

Ask students to find out from their families whether they could bring to school examples of artifacts from their particular family culture, so that students can begin to appreciate the diversity that exists even within their own classroom. Have students share and tell the purpose of the artifacts they bring in.

RESOURCES

Aliki. *Corn Is Maize: The Gift of the Indians.* Crowell Junior Books, 1976.

Brenner, Barbara. *Wagon Wheels.* HarperCollins Children's Books, 1978.

Coming to America Series: Immigrants from Southern Europe (also *Northern Europe, Eastern Europe, the Far East, and the British Isles*). Delacorte Press, 1981.

Coming to North America Series: from Mexico, Cuba, and Puerto Rico. Delacorte Press, 1981.

Dalgliesh, Alice. *The Courage of Sarah Noble.* Macmillan, 1986.

De Saint-Beauquet, Henri. *The First Settlements.* Silver Burdett, 1987.

Monjo, F.N. *The Drinking Gourd.* HarperCollins Children's Books, 1983.

Celebration: Giving a Performance

COMPONENT	Aesthetic Perception
SUBJECT	Performance
OBJECTIVE	Students share with another class the results of playmaking, and develop the understanding that drama/theatre is a shared experience.
MATERIALS	Dramatizations from Lesson 22 or Lesson 23, or any other dramatization lesson with which students were satisfied

NOW PRESENTING
Why the Tides Ebb and Flow

DATE May 26

TIME 2:00

PLACE Cafetorium

Note: This lesson must be done in two time periods—one for Warm Up and Explore, and the other for Develop and Evaluate. Schedule the second part with the teacher of the other class.

WARM UP

Tell the students that drama/theatre is a sharing experience, as is all art. (Even though some art can be created by oneself, the ultimate value of art is sharing what has been done with others.) Because drama/theatre is a sharing experience (we say we "give" a performance!), it must be done to the best of one's ability in order to give the greatest amount of enjoyment to the observers and to the players themselves. Ask students for examples of times when they or someone else gave their best in a performance.

EXPLORE

Tell students that they will have the chance to give a performance for an audience. Ask students to select one or two of the dramatizations they have created during the year—ones that have given the greatest enjoyment and have exemplified the knowledge gained in drama/theatre. Review the dramatization(s) carefully, summarizing with the class the plot, characters, and settings that they created before. Use whatever materials are easily available for settings and costume pieces. Rehearse several times until the participating students are confident in their performances. Assign supporting roles (property manager, stage manager, prompters, artists to create pieces of simple costumes, and so on) to students who are not actors. Make a poster with the name of the performance and place it in a prominent spot.

DEVELOP   Invite another class (a second grade or another third grade) to view the dramatization(s). The performance can be in either the players' or the audience's classroom. Confer with the other teacher ahead of time so that she or he can brief the other class on the concepts your class has been working on and positive evaluation techniques. Briefly explain to the visiting students that what they are going to see is not a full play, but a sharing of the work your class has been doing in their drama/theatre activities.

After the demonstration, invite the visitors to ask questions of the students about their dramatizations and the performance.

EVALUATE   *Student evaluation:* Ask students, when they are in their own classroom again, "Did you find enjoyment in the sharing and giving of your work? Was it easier to share your work with your own classmates or with a different audience?"

Teacher observation: Are the students aware of the sharing qualities of drama/theatre? Were they comfortable in presenting their dramatizations to a different audience, perhaps in a different locale? Did they concentrate on their dramatization, or were they distracted by the audience?

CONNECTIONS   *Language Arts:* Divide the class into small groups. Assign each group a section of the drama the class is performing and have them write down a script for that part of the performance. Combine each group's efforts to create a complete script. Make copies so that each student can have one to keep and use. This can also be the start of a collection of dramas for future classes to perform.

RESOURCES   *Center Stage: Creative Dramatics Supplement.* (contains "Now Presenting" poster) Available from Dale Seymour Publications.

GRADE 3

Scope and Sequence

Subject	Grades K–1	Grade 2	Grade 3
	Students will		
Sensory Awareness	Identify and describe objects with the senses; Create a scene about sensory qualities	Imagine and identify sensory experiences	Imagine, describe, and dramatize sensory experiences
Emotional Awareness	Identify, respond to, and communicate emotions	Transform ideas, feelings, and values into artistic forms through improvisation	Identify and modify the emotional content of a story
Sound/ Voice/ Language/ Communication	Identify and create sounds with voice and/or movement	Create and record radio drama	Transform single word into idea for dramatic action; Express a single word in several ways
Discipline			Work with others to create a "body machine"; Recognize the value of collaboration in theatre

Subject	Grade 4	Grade 5	Grade 6
	Students will		
Sensory Awareness	Use sensory experiences to identify objects; Notice how sounds convey images; Strengthen observation skills with sensory experiences; Use sensory recall to improvise a scene	Use sensory recall to develop a pantomime; Imagine performing an activity without one of the senses; Depend on another for the sense of sight	Visualize objects, scenes, and activities to increase sensory awareness; Recognize how point of view affects observations
Emotional Awareness	Experience how color affects moods; Identify emotions expressed in poetry	Identify, visualize, and respond to emotions; Use emotional recall to act out an emotional situation; Analyze emotions of characters in a play or story	Recognize how emotions affect observations; Analyze thoughts and words to understand and express a character's emotions
Sound/ Voice/ Language/ Communication	Imitate the voice inflections of others; Use gibberish to give directions; Use sounds to convey images; Create sound effects to bring to mind a scene	Give directions to someone who cannot see; Portray emotions through speech; Use vocal exercises to increase the ability to convey meaning	Learn vocal techniques for drama; Use imagery to motivate dialogue; Learn technical terms related to the voice; Play a verbal communication game
Discipline	Practice concentration by focusing on reading aloud while being distracted; Work in a group to do improvisation, choral reading	Work with a group to create a story within a limited time; Concentrate on verbal direction; Recognize the need for collaboration in theatre	Practice concentration to visualize a scene; Recognize interdependence of theatrical personnel; Assume responsibility in theatrical production

Subject	Grades K–1	Grade 2	Grade 3
	Students will		
Rhythm and Movement	Respond physically to rhythmic patterns and moods in music; Use movement to solve problems; Use movement and music to explore characters; Use poetry to improvise movement	Respond in diverse ways to rhythmic patterns; Use movement to express feelings and explore characterization; Use movement to interpret poetry	Respond in diverse ways to rhythmic patterns; Dramatize stories from interpretive response to musical selections
Body Awareness	Use "living statues" to create a story	Practice body movement in response to rhythm and with imaginary objects; Mirror another's body movements; Use movement to convey meaning	Practice body movement in response to rhythm; Create a "machine" with others, using their bodies; Use movement to convey meaning
Pantomime	Use the body to express ideas, emotions, and characters	Imagine objects and stimuli in acting out a scene; Create a story by pantomiming specific actions; Solve problems through pantomime	Develop a pantomime from one word; Pantomime using an imaginary object; Pantomime as part of dramatic action in a story

Subject	Grade 4	Grade 5	Grade 6
	Students will		
Rhythm and Movement	Move like animals; Move in slow motion; Portray emotions and moods with movements; Observe and imitate body movements and gestures	Use body language to portray emotions; Move in the manner of a described character; Create movements suggested by haiku images; Move in open space; Use mental pictures to motivate movement	Use a script to motivate movement; Learn terms for stage movement; Use body control to portray characters and refine stage movements; Use movement to interpret a poem; Study the controlled movements of Noh Theatre
Body Awareness	Move in the manner of a particular animal; Use slow, controlled motions; Notice how body language shows emotions	Use body movements to portray an inanimate object; Use body movements to show emotions; Analyze body movements of characters	Practice good breathing and posture for body control; Recognize how physical condition affects observations; Practice controlled movements of Noh Theatre
Pantomime	Develop a pantomime using sensory recall; Pantomime using sensory details of an experience; Pantomime a character doing an activity in slow motion	Develop a pantomime using sensory recall; Pantomime an activity using only four of the five senses; Pantomime a weather condition; Pantomime an inanimate object; Pantomime a scene from *The Hobbit*	Use pantomime to develop an idea in the manner of a Noh play; Pantomime using Method acting; Play Imaginary Rooms to practice nonverbal communication

Subject	Grades K–1	Grade 2	Grade 3
	Students will		
Storytelling	Discover similarities and differences in stories; Identify the moral in a story; Learn about historical role of storyteller	Study oral and written traditions of American folklore	Investigate oral traditions of ways stories have been passed on; Listen to African stories
Story Elements	Recognize the *What* in a story; Portray more than one character in a story; Identify and act out the five W's in a story	Identify the *What, When, Who, Why,* and *Where* as basic story elements	Create and dramatize stories using the five W's
Improvisation	Use imagined objects to create a scene; Act out parts of a folk tale; Use poetry to improvise movement activities	Improvise facial expressions and postures; Improvise a scene with specific characters	With others, create with their bodies an imaginary machine; Create drama with imaginary objects; Improvise a scene with an object as a prop; Analyze a "What if...?" story and dramatize it

Subject	Grade 4	Grade 5	Grade 6
	Students will		
Storytelling	Create a story based on a sequence of events; Explore storytelling through shadow plays; Explore common themes in folklore	Create dialogue for a story; Choose dramatic presentation for a story from another culture; Invent characters and conflicts to create and develop a story	Dramatize a Mexican folk tale; Dramatize a familiar story reversing protagonist and antagonist; Use readers theatre for telling stories
Story Elements	Recognize beginning, middle and end to a story; Use the five W's to create a story and then add events to the story; Create an outline for a story	Create a story using five W's and three given objects; Identify characters, theme, plot, conflict, and resolution in a story; Use opposites to develop conflict in a story	Understand roles of protagonist and antagonist in story; Analyze a current topic and create a dramatization that fits one of the classifications of Chinese Theatre
Improvisation	Use emotional theme of a poem for improvisation; Improvise imagined characters; Do improvisations in different types of playing areas; Use sound effects as motivation for an improvisation	Develop improvisation based on a given *who, what,* and *where*; Create TV commercials; Become aware of creative choices in developing an improvisation; Improvise using an actual incident for a theme or plot; Improvise using a folk tale as a basis	Develop protagonist and antagonist characters; Improvise a scene in the commedia dell'arte style; Improvise a scene in the style of Shakespeare; Improvise a scene based on a Mexican folk tale; Improvise using the controlled movement of Noh theatre; Play *Freeze Tag* to practice verbal communication

Subject	Grades K–1	Grade 2	Grade 3
	Students will		
Folklore/ Cultural Awareness	Compare stories from different cultures with similar themes; Dramatize a Native American story; Participate in drama activities from various cultural celebrations	Recognize common themes from diverse cultures; Investigate fables, folk tales, myths, legends, and fairy tales; Read and dramatize a Native American myth; Create a legendary story; Dramatize a story from another culture	Compare "How and Why" stories; Investigate African stories; Become more aware of the diversity of American culture; Listen to and dramatize particular events in American history
Perception/ Art Appreciation	Use visual arts pieces and physical selves to create designs; Compare different moods and settings used in children's literature	Imagine objects or animals in specific environments; Interpret images in poetry	Analyze parts of visual and dramatic art to understand the whole; Identify, describe, and participate in drama, visual arts, dance, and music activities

Subject	Grade 4	Grade 5	Grade 6
	Students will		
Folklore/ Cultural Awareness	Study historical and cultural themes of good and evil; Study shadow puppetry and its origins in Asia; Use choral speaking to learn about the Greek theatre	Study and compare folklore from different cultures; Use a folk tale as a basis for an improvisation; Study and write haiku; Study how puppets are used around the world	Study history, vocabulary, and structure of commedia dell'arte; Study Elizabethan times and Shakespearean theatre; Learn the different types of Mexican folk tales; Learn about theatre in China during the Ming Dynasty; Study Japanese Noh Theatre; Learn about Stanislavsky and the Moscow Art Theater
Perception/ Art Appreciation	Use poetry to understand emotions; Use Lewis Carroll's "Jabberwocky" as a basis for characterization; Identify themes in literature by studying well-known stories	Use literature for establishing character images; Use *The Hobbit* by J.R.R. Tolkien as motivation for a pantomime	Study pattern and rhythm in poetry to create an improvisation; Study harmony of dance, poetry, music, mime, and acting in Noh Theatre

Subject	Grades K–1	Grade 2	Grade 3
	Students will		
Evaluation	Learn meaning of evaluation and its relationship to a story and to an audience	Use objective criteria in evaluating story performance	Analyze a performance in terms of props, sets, and costumes; Use *intent* and *structure* to evaluate a theatrical work
Problem Solving	Enact stories requiring problem solving	Explore real and imagined situations that require problem solving	Analyze the parts of a story and create different endings; Use "What if...?" situation to create stories
Characterization	Interpret meaning and movement qualities of story characters; Portray more than one character in a story	Improvise a scene with specific characters; Create characters and stories using costumes and props	Dramatize actions, ideas, and emotions by creating specific characters

Subject	Grade 4	Grade 5	Grade 6
	Students will		
Evaluation	Evaluate characterizations, movements, emotional validity, voice quality, and adaptability of stories for themes or plays; Use drama/theatre vocabulary and ethical standards to analyze a dramatic performance	Evaluate characterizations, movements, emotional validity, voice quality, and adaptability of stories for themes or plays; Evaluate drama/theatre elements in an actual performance	Evaluate characterizations, movements, emotional validity, voice quality and adaptability of stories for themes or plays; Evaluate and modify the aesthetic and technical elements in a production in process
Problem Solving	Sequence events for developing scripts; Plan a celebration day; Dramatize a current news story	Decide how to convince someone to buy a product; Analyze the qualities of creativity; Dramatize a theme or issue from current news	Dramatize a current topic that relates to the classifications of Chinese theatre in the Ming Dynasty; Plan rehearsal schedules; Produce a play for an audience
Characterization	Develop characters based on traits of animals; Use color as a motivation for character development	Analyze behavior to learn about characterization; Elaborate on given characters; Use emotional and sensory recall to develop characters	Practice making a character "real"; Use relaxation, breathing, and visualization to create characters; Use vocal tension and body tension for characterization; Recognize importance of make-up in developing a character; Act in a formal production

Subject	Grades K–1	Grade 2	Grade 3
	Students will		
Playmaking		Develop a beginning, middle, and end to a story and dramatize it; Create a simple sequence in a story; Investigate characteristics of theatre, TV, film, and radio and create and record a radio drama	Learn the structural differences between stories and plays, and create a play from a narrative; Create a "How and Why" story; Use five W's and simple story analysis to create a dramatization; Present a dramatic performance for another class
Technical Elements		Create characters and stories using costumes and props; Visualize and draw pictures of settings; Work with a visiting theatre artist	Learn the difference between *drama* and *theatre*; Learn about puppetry used in other cultures; Build simple puppets

Subject	Grade 4	Grade 5	Grade 6
	Students will		
Playmaking	Analyze a story in terms of plot, conflict, climax and resolution; Study criteria for changing a story into a play; Develop a play from a story; Develop a scene based on a story theme; Learn the vocabulary of stage directions; Develop a script; Make and use a shadow puppet	Create a detailed scene using developed settings and characters; Recognize the importance of creativity in playmaking; Analyze the suitability of elements in a story for play development; Write a two-character scene; Act out a scene using props; Act out a scene using a costume; Make and use a hand puppet	Analyze a script for stage movement; Understand the roles of protagonist and antagonist in a play; Study Stanislavsky's Method acting; Understand the purpose of, and practice auditioning; Develop a rehearsal schedule; Put on a formal performance for an audience
Technical Elements	Use sound effects to create a setting; Identify playing areas; Design a set and make a rendering; Use technical elements—lighting, sets, props, sound, make-up, and costumes—in developing a play; Use sound effects in dramatizing a story	Recognize the importance of creativity in developing technical elements; Create a drama vocabulary list and definitions for a notebook; Decide what props are needed for a scene; Develop a costume for a specific character in a play	Use make-up; Practice the role of director; Practice the skills needed by technical theatre personnel; Analyze a script for technical elements needed and develop a technical plan; Understand purpose of and conduct a technical rehearsal, a dress rehearsal, and a touch-up rehearsal; Use all the technical elements to produce a formal performance for an audience

Grade One List of Lessons by Component

AESTHETIC PERCEPTION

Lesson 1   Exploring the Sense of Touch
Students increase their sensory awareness and perception by touching objects and defining their qualities.

Lesson 2   Exploring the Sense of Sight
Students increase their awareness of the importance of the sense of sight in identifying objects.

Lesson 3   Exploring the Sense of Smell
Students increase their sensory awareness by identifying different odors.

Lesson 4   Exploring the Sense of Taste
Students increase sensory awareness by using the sense of taste to identify various foods.

Lesson 5   Exploring the Sense of Hearing
Students increase sensory awareness by identifying sounds in the environment.

Lesson 6   Exploring Mood: How Do You Feel?
Students identify, respond to, and communicate different emotions in stories.

Lesson 7   Using the Voice and Body to Create Sounds
Students identify and then create sounds using the voice and/or movement in a story.

Lesson 8   Exploring Rhythm and Movement
Students develop flexible and diversified physical movement in response to rhythmic patterns and moods in music.

Lesson 12   Using "Statues" to Create a Story
Students use "living statues" to create a story.

Lesson 15   Exploring Story Action: What Are You Doing?
Students learn to recognize the What *in a story as one of the basic elements of drama/theatre and its vocabulary.*

Lesson 19   Exploring Character: Who Are You?
Students create drama by portraying more than one character in a story.

Lesson 21   Exploring Design
Students create different designs within an established space using visual art pieces and their bodies.

Lesson 27   Revisiting the Five Senses
Students explore and communicate ways in which the senses are used in creating stories.

CREATIVE EXPRESSION

Lesson 9   Exploring Movement as a Group
As a group, students engage in purposeful movement that involves problem solving.

Lesson 10   Exploring Different Environments Through Movement
Students create a scene about the sensory qualities in an imagined environment.

Lesson 11   Exploring Characters Through Movement
Students use movement and music to be different characters in different environments.

Lesson 13   Exploring Movement: Pantomime
Students become aware of the body as a tool for expressing ideas, emotions, and characters, and recognize pantomime as one of the basic elements of drama/theatre and its vocabulary.

Lesson 16   Creating a Scene from Imagined Objects
Students create and communicate a scene through various imagined objects.

AESTHETIC VALUING

Lesson 20   Exploring Color: The Rainbow
Students use different colors as motivation to interpret meaning and movement qualities of characters in a story.

Lesson 22   Creating Mood with Pictures and Movement
Students use physical movement to compare the different moods and settings used in children's literature.

Lesson 23   Evaluating Performances
Students learn the meaning of evaluation and its relationship to the basic components of a story and to an audience.

Grade Two List of Lessons By Component

AESTHETIC PERCEPTION

Lesson 1   Sense Abilities: Touch and Smell
Students increase their perception and sensory awareness by imagining smells and textures in the environment.

Lesson 2   Sense Abilities: Taste and Sight
Students become aware of the relation of the senses of sight and taste by picturing objects "in the mind's eye" and by recalling specific foods seen and tasted.

Lesson 3   Sense Abilities: Sound and Hearing
Students develop categorizing skills by identifying specific sounds in the environment.

Lesson 4   Exploring Specific Environments
Students increase their perception and sensory awareness by imagining objects or animals that exist in specific environments.

Lesson 5   Exploring Rhythm and Movement
Students develop flexible and diversified physical movement in response to rhythmic patterns.

Lesson 7   Movement with Imaginary Objects
Students work in pairs, using perceptual skills to imagine objects and stimuli in acting out a scene.

Lesson 8   The Five W's: What and When
Students identify the What *and* When *as two of the basic elements and principles of drama/theatre and its vocabulary.*

Lesson 9   Nonverbal Communication: Pantomime
Students create a story by pantomiming specific actions.

Lesson 10   The Five W's: Exploring the *Who* in Stories
Students identify the Who *in a story as one of the basic elements and principles of drama/theatre and its vocabulary.*

Lesson 12   The Five W's: Exploring the *Why* in Stories
Students identify the Why *in a story as one of the basic elements and principles of drama/theatre and its vocabulary, and develop an understanding of the effect of the* Why *on the* What.

Lesson 13   The Five W's: Identifying the *Where*
Students identify the Where *in a story as one of the basic elements and principles of drama/theatre and its vocabulary.*

Lesson 17   Developing Stories Through Movement Activities
Students become aware of drama/theatre as a means of communication, and use movement to express feelings and explore characterization.

CREATIVE EXPRESSION

Lesson 6   Expressing Emotions
Students communicate feeling through drama by improvising facial expressions and postures that convey different emotions.

Lesson 11   Character Development
Students transform ideas, feelings, and values into artistic forms by improvising a scene with specific characters.

Lesson 14   Exploring Sequence in Stories
Students develop a beginning, middle, and end to a story and dramatize it.

Lesson 15   Creating a Story
Students develop personal insight and satisfaction by creating a simple sequence in a story.

APPENDIX

AESTHETIC VALUING

Lesson 18   Poetry and Nature
Students investigate the relationship of nature and the fine arts by using movement to interpret poetry.

Lesson 19   The Role of Evaluation in Drama/Theatre
Students discuss and evaluate a story that has been performed to help them learn to use objective criteria when analyzing drama/theatre.

Lesson 27   Using Costumes and Props
Students create characters and stories using costumes and props.

Lesson 28   Designing a Set
Students visualize and draw pictures of different story settings to help them understand one of the specific arts integral to drama/theatre.

Lesson 29   Comparing Dramatic Media
Students investigate the characteristics of theatre, TV, film, and radio, and create and record a radio drama.

Grade Three List of Lessons by Component

AESTHETIC PERCEPTION

Lesson 1   Settings and Senses: Sight, Touch, and Hearing
Students imagine and describe the visual, tactile, and auditory qualities of different settings.

Lesson 2   Settings and Senses: Taste and Smell
Students imagine and describe various tastes and smells and dramatize those experiences.

Lesson 3   Expressing Emotions
Students identify the emotional content of a story—what the characters are feeling—and experiment with changing it.

Lesson 4   Patterns in Rhythm and Movement
Students develop flexible and diversified movements in response to rhythmic patterns.

Lesson 10   Dramatizing Original *Who, What,* and *Where* Stories
Students use appropriate vocabulary to describe the basic elements of drama/theatre and to create stories using Who, What, and Where.

Lesson 11   Understanding Theatre Terminology
Students use appropriate vocabulary to understand the difference between drama and theatre.

Lesson 13   Creating a Play from a Story
Students become aware of the structural differences between stories and plays, and create a play from a narrative.

Lesson 15   Communicating Meaning Through Spoken Words
Students become aware of the communicative potential of drama/theatre by exploring the various ways to express a single word.

Lesson 24 Parts of the Whole
Students analyze the parts of visual art and dramatic art in terms of a story in order to understand the whole presentation.

Lesson 25 Exploring the Art Disciplines: Drama and the Visual Arts
Students identify and describe the basic qualities of drama and visual arts, and participate in an activity from each discipline.

Lesson 26 Exploring the Art Disciplines: Dance and Music
Students identify and describe the basic qualities of dance and music, and participate in an activity from each discipline.

Lesson 30 Celebration: Giving a Performance
Students share with another class the results of playmaking, and develop the understanding that drama/theatre is a shared experience.

CREATIVE EXPRESSION

Lesson 5 Inventing Body Machines
Students work together as a group to create with their bodies an imaginary machine.

Lesson 6 Developing Pantomime from a Word
Students explore verbal and nonverbal communication by transforming a single word into an idea for action and dramatic form.

Lesson 7 Imagining with a "Magic Box"
Visualizing their own remembered experiences, students create drama with imaginary objects.

Lesson 12 Creating Specific Characters
Students dramatize actions, ideas, and emotions by creating specific characters.

Lesson 14 Creating New Endings for Literature Selections
Students analyze the parts of a story and create different endings.

Lesson 16 Creating Stories from "What If...?" Questions
Students use fantasy situations to create stories.

AESTHETIC VALUING

Lesson 19   Music and Dramatic Action
Students create and dramatize stories from their own interpretive response to various musical selections.

Lesson 20   Elements of Evaluation
Students analyze a performance in terms of drama/theatre to determine what props, sets, and costumes would best suit a performance.

Lesson 21   Analyzing Intent and Structure in Drama
Students learn and use established vocabulary to evaluate a theatrical work.

Story Scripts

The Stonecutter

Once upon a time a stonecutter lived in a small wooden hut beside a tall mountain. He made his living by cutting stones out of the side of the mountain. People bought the stones from him and used them to mark graves and build houses.

The stonecutter understood stones very well. He was a careful worker, and he always had plenty of customers. For a long time he was happy and satisfied with his life. He never asked for anything more than his small hut and his hard bed.

Some people said that a magic spirit lived in the mountain. They claimed that the spirit could speak to people and help them become rich. But the stonecutter had never seen or heard the spirit, and he just shook his head when anyone asked him about it.

One day the stonecutter carried a gravestone to a rich man's house. When he entered the house, he gazed at the rich man's fine tables and chairs, and at his large soft bed with silk pillows.

Suddenly, the stonecutter's work seemed hard and heavy. He said to himself, "If I were a rich man, I could sleep in a soft bed with silk pillows. Oh, if only I were a rich man, how happy I would be!"

From out of nowhere a voice said, "I have heard your wish. A rich man you shall be!" It was the voice of the mountain spirit.

The stonecutter looked all around, but he couldn't see anybody. He began to wonder if he had really heard the voice. At last he picked up his tools and went home, for he did not feel like doing any more work that day.

When the stonecutter reached his home, he could not believe his eyes. Instead of his wooden hut there was a beautiful stone house filled with fine tables and chairs. Finest of all was a large soft bed with silk pillows, just like the bed in the rich man's house.

The stonecutter was happy beyond his wildest dreams. He was now a rich man, and he no longer had to work for a living. He soon forgot all about his old life.

Summer came, and each day the sun grew hotter and hotter. One morning it was so hot that the stonecutter decided to stay in bed. He tried to stay cool by fanning his face, but it was no use.

Just then, the stonecutter heard a noise in the street. He looked out and saw a little cart rolling by. Servants in blue and silver clothes ran along, pulling the cart by hand.

A prince sat inside the cart under a golden umbrella that protected him from the sun's rays. He was enjoying a nice shady ride on this hot summer day.

The stonecutter said to himself, "If I were a prince, I could ride in a cart and sit under a golden umbrella. Oh, if only I were a prince, how happy I would be!"

And the mountain spirit answered, "I have heard your wish. A prince you shall be!" And a prince he was. Servants in blue and silver clothes pulled his cart, and he sat under a golden umbrella. Everything he wanted was his. Yet it was not enough.

Even though his servants watered the grass, it still turned brown in the sun's rays. And even though he sat under the umbrella, he still felt the sun's heat. At last he cried out in anger, "The sun is more powerful than a prince! Oh, if only I were the sun, how happy I would be!"

And the mountain spirit answered, "I have heard your wish. The sun you shall be!" And the sun he was, and he was proud of his power. He shot his rays down to the earth and up to the sky. He burned up the grass in the fields and scorched the faces of princes and poor people.

But when a cloud covered his face and hid the earth from him, he cried out in anger, "The cloud is more powerful than the sun! Oh, if only I were a cloud, how happy I would be!"

And the mountain spirit answered, "I have heard your wish. A cloud you shall be!" And a cloud he was, and he floated between the sun and the earth. He caught the sun's rays and held them, and to his joy the earth grew green again and flowers bloomed. But that was not enough.

For days and weeks he poured down rain until the rivers flooded their banks and the rice fields stood in water. Towns and villages were destroyed by the force of the rain, but the tall mountain did not move.

The cloud cried out in anger, "The mountain is more powerful than the cloud! Oh, if only I were the mountain, how happy I would be!"

And the mountain spirit answered, "I have heard your wish. The mountain you shall be!"

And the mountain he was, and he rose proudly out of the ground. Nothing could move him. "This is the best of all!" he said to himself.

But one day the mountain heard a strange noise at his side, and when he looked down he saw a stonecutter at work. Suddenly a trembling feeling ran all through him, and a large stone fell out of his side. Then the mountain cried out in anger, "The stonecutter is more powerful than the mountain! Oh, if only I were a stonecutter, how happy I would be!"

And a stonecutter he was, and he worked again at his trade. His hut was small and his bed was hard, but he had learned to be satisfied with them. And because the stonecutter no longer wanted to be something or somebody else, he was happy at last.

The Bremen Town Musicians

Once upon a time, a donkey worked for a farmer. The donkey's job was to carry heavy sacks on his back, and he did this every day for many years. But at last he became old and weak and unable to work.

The donkey knew that the farmer would soon get rid of him, so he decided to run away. He set out on the road to Bremen Town, where he planned to make his living as a street musician.

After the donkey had walked along for a while, he found a dog panting by the side of the road.

"Why are you panting?" asked the donkey.

"Oh," answered the dog, "because I have just run away from my master. I am old and weak, and I can no longer hunt. My master decided to get rid of me, so I ran away."

"Why don't you join me?" said the donkey. "I am going to Bremen Town to become a street musician. I can bray and you can howl."

The dog liked this plan, so he decided to join the donkey. Then the two new friends set out on the road to Bremen Town.

They soon came upon a cat sitting in the road. The cat's face was as long as three rainy days.

"Why are you so unhappy?" asked the donkey.

"Who can be happy when life is so hard?" sighed the cat. ""I am old, and my teeth are dull, and I can no longer catch mice. My owner decided to get rid of me, so I ran away. Now I need a new way to make my living."

"Why don't you join us?" said the donkey. "We are going to Bremen Town to become street musicians. We could use your sweet meowing."

The cat liked this plan, so she decided to join the donkey and the dog. Then the three friends set out on the road to Bremen Town.

Soon they came to a farm. A rooster was standing on a fence and crowing with all his might.

"Kee-ka-ree-kee! Kee-ka-ree-kee!" he cried out.

"Why are you crowing so loudly?" asked the donkey.

"Tomorrow is a feast day," replied the rooster, "and the farmer's wife plans to put me in the soup. She told the cook to cut off my head, so I am using my voice as long as I can."

"Why don't you join us?" said the donkey. "We are going to Bremen Town to become street musicians. We could use your loud crowing."

The rooster liked this plan, so he joined the donkey, the dog, and the cat. Then the four friends set out on the road to Bremen Town.

They walked together all day long. At night they came to a forest and decided to spend the night there. The donkey and the dog lay down under a tall tree, and the cat stretched out on a branch. The rooster flew all the way to the top of the tree.

Before going to sleep, the rooster looked all around, and he saw candles shining in the distance. He called down to his friends, "We must be near a house, for I can see candles shining."

The cat said, "Let's go there. This tree isn't a very good bed."

And the dog added, "I could use some bones and a nice piece of meat."

So the four friends set off towards the light. It was dim at first, but it became brighter and brighter.

At last they came to a brightly lit house. The donkey, who was the biggest, sneaked up to a window and looked inside.

"What do you see?" asked the rooster.

"I see a table covered with food and drink," answered the donkey. "Robbers are sitting around the table and having a good time."

"We could be eating that food," said the rooster.

"Yes we could, if only we were inside!" answered the donkey.

So the four friends put their heads together and came up with a plan for chasing away the robbers. The donkey put his front paws on the window sill. The dog jumped onto the donkey's back. The cat climbed on top of the dog, and the rooster stood on the cat's head.

When the animals were all set, they began to make music together. The donkey brayed, the dog howled, the cat meowed, and the rooster crowed. Then they crashed through the window and landed in the house.

The robbers were terrified by the loud noise. They thought that a ghost was after them, and they ran from the house in fear for their lives. Then the four animals sat down at the table and had a wonderful feast.

When the animals finished eating, they blew out the candles and looked for places to sleep. The donkey lay in the yard on some hay. The dog curled up by the back door. The cat stretched out near the fire, and the rooster flew up to the roof. They were all tired from their long day, and soon they were fast asleep.

Meanwhile, the robbers got together in the forest. They saw the candles go out. The chief robber thought that the ghost might have left, so he ordered one of the other robbers to go back.

The robber sneaked up to the dark and quiet house. Then he went into the kitchen to light a candle. When he saw the cat's bright eyes, he thought they were bits of fire. So he held a candle up to them in order to light it.

The cat did not like this, and she sprang into the robber's face, scratching him with her sharp claws.

The robber was terrified and tried to run out the back door. But the dog, who was lying there, jumped up and bit him in the leg.

Then the robber ran into the yard, where the donkey gave him a mighty kick with his back legs. All the noise woke up the rooster, who began crowing, "Kee-ka-ree-kee! Kee-ka-ree-kee!"

The robber ran back to his chief as fast as he could. "Oh," he said, "inside the house is a frightening witch, who scratched my face with her long fingers. By the door stands a man with a knife, who stabbed me in the leg. In the yard lies a huge monster, who hit me with a wooden club. And on the roof sits a judge, who cried out, 'Bring him to me! Bring him to me!' So I ran for my life."

From then on the robbers did not dare to go back to the house. So the four animals lived there happily ever after.

The Deer and the Tortoise

Once upon a time a tall forest stood next to a wide, grassy plain. Thousands of slow tortoises crawled along under the shady trees and bushes of the forest. Thousands of fast deer ran back and forth across the wide, grassy plain.

One day a tortoise met a deer at the edge of the forest.

"What are you doing here?" asked the tortoise.

"I am taking a walk," answered the deer. "I am looking for leaves to eat. And what are you doing here?"

"I also am taking a walk," answered the tortoise. "I am looking for water to drink."

"And when will you reach the water?" asked the deer.

"Why do you ask that question?" answered the tortoise.

"Because your legs are so short," answered the deer, laughing.

"My legs may be short," said the tortoise, "but I can run faster than you."

"Then let's run a race!" said the deer.

"Perhaps," said the tortoise. "And when do you want to run?"

"Tomorrow morning," answered the deer.

"And where do you want to start?" asked the tortoise.

"Right here," came the reply.

"Fine," said the tortoise. So the two animals parted. The deer laughed to himself as he walked away on the wide, grassy plain. He was sure he would beat the slow tortoise in the race.

But the tortoise had a plan. She walked back to the forest and called together all her cousins. She had hundreds and hundreds of cousins, and they all looked and sounded alike.

This is what the tortoise told her cousins: "I am supposed to run a race with the deer tomorrow morning. But we are going to trick him."

Then the tortoise explained her plan. "I want all of you to line up in a row along the edge of the forest. Space yourselves far apart to make the row very, very long. Then hide under the bushes and keep perfectly still. When you hear the deer calling from behind you, answer him."

The cousins agreed to the plan. The next morning they all lined up in a long, long row along the edge of the forest. But the deer couldn't see them, for the cousins were hiding under the bushes.

Then the tortoise walked out of the forest and met the deer on the wide, grassy plain.

"Are you ready to race?" asked the deer.

"Yes," answered the tortoise, "but I have an idea. You live on the plain, so why don't you run on the plain? I live in the forest, so I'll run in the forest."

The deer laughed again. He knew it was easier to run on the plain, because there were no trees or bushes in the way. So he agreed with the tortoise's plan.

"Just run along the edge of the forest," said the tortoise, "so we can talk to each other during the race."

"All right," answered the deer, laughing some more. "When do we start?"

"As soon as I say Go!" answered the tortoise. Then she walked back to the forest and called out in a loud voice, "Go!"

The deer walked along slowly. After a little while he called out, "Are you still there, tortoise?"

"Oh yes, I'm here in front of you," answered the cousin who was hiding in the forest just ahead of the deer.

"Well," thought the deer, "the tortoise does run fast."
So the deer started walking faster. After a little while he called out again, "Are you still there, tortoise?"

"Oh yes, I'm here in front of you," answered another cousin who was hiding in the forest just ahead of the deer.

"That's strange," said the deer to himself. "The tortoise is still ahead of me."
So the deer began running.

When he felt sure that he had passed the tortoise, he called out again, "Are you still there, tortoise?"

"Oh yes, I'm here in front of you," answered still another cousin who was hiding in the forest just ahead of the deer.

Then the deer got worried. He started running faster and then called out again. But the answer was the same.

So the deer ran as fast as he could until he couldn't run any more. As he lay down to rest, he called out, ""Are you still there, tortoise?"

"Oh yes, I'm here in front of you," came the answer.

So the deer said, "I give up. You have won the race. You can run faster than I thought."

Then the cousins walked back to the tortoise and told her the good news. And to this day, the deer thinks that the tortoise can run fast.

The Poor Turkey Girl

Once upon a time a very poor girl lived at the edge of a small village. She was quite pretty, but her clothes were old and ragged.

All the people in the village owned turkeys—all except the girl. She herded the turkeys for the other people, and they paid her with food and old clothing.

The girl's life was hard, yet she was always kind to the turkeys. Every morning she opened the gate to their pen. Then she herded them to the plains below Thunder Mountain, not far from the village. They came at the sound of her voice and went wherever she wished. One day, as she walked behind the gobbling turkeys, the girl came near the town of Zuni. Inside the town a man stood on top of a house and cried out, "The Dance of the Bird will begin in four days."

The Dance of the Bird! Oh, how the girl longed to take part in that dance! But she was too poor and too ragged to join in the fun. And so she just walked past the town, herding the turkeys before her. She told the birds all about her troubles, but they only gobbled in reply.

For the next three days the girl watched the people of her village getting ready for the Dance of the Bird. They cleaned their beautiful clothes and cooked tasty food, laughing merrily all the time.

On the fourth day all the village people left for Zuni—all except the girl. She wandered through the empty village, herding the turkeys. Suddenly, the biggest turkey strutted up to her and began to speak!

"Dear girl," he said, "we know why you are sad, and we feel sorry for you. If you will do as we tell you, you can join the others at the Dance of the Bird."

At first the girl was too surprised to say anything. But at last she answered, "My dear turkeys, how glad I am that we can speak to each other. What do you want me to do?"

"Lead us back to our pen," said the turkey, "and you will see."

So the girl led them back to their pen and opened the gate. The turkeys walked in and the girl followed. Then the biggest turkey said, "Please sit down and give me your coat."

The girl took off her ragged old coat and laid it before the big turkey. He grabbed it in his beak, and spread it out, and picked and picked at it. Then he walked on it and brushed it with his wings.

At last he laid the coat at the girl's feet. It was now a beautiful white coat of the finest cloth.

One by one, the turkeys changed all the girl's old rags into new and beautiful clothes. Then they circled around her, gobbling and gobbling.

They brushed her with their wings until her skin was clear and smooth and bright. Her hair was now soft instead of hard. Her cheeks were round, and her eyes danced with smiles.

But that was not all. Over the years, the turkeys had found many jewels lying on the ground. From these jewels, they gave the girl a necklace, a pair of earrings, and a bracelet. The girl put them on, thanking the turkeys over and over again.

Then the biggest turkey came up to her and said, "Go to the dance in Zuni. But remember to come back to us before the sun sets."

The girl thanked the turkeys again and promised to return before sunset. As she was leaving the pen, the biggest turkey said, "Please leave the gate open. If you do not return, we will have to take care of ourselves."

The girl did as she was asked and then hurried toward Zuni. She went straight to the dance in the middle of town. Everyone looked at her, but no one knew who she was. All the people asked each other, "Where did that beautiful girl come from?"

The young men ran up to the girl and invited her to join in the dance. With a nod and a smile and a toss of her hair, the girl stepped into the dance circle.

Her heart became light and her feet merry. She danced and danced as the sun crossed the sky and began to sink in the west.

Time raced on, and the girl kept dancing. She forgot all about the turkeys. Then the sunlight left the sky. Suddenly the girl remembered her promise! She broke away from the dance and ran out of town before anyone could catch her.

Meanwhile, the turkeys wondered what had happened to the girl. They watched sadly as the sun set in the west. At last the biggest turkey said, "The girl has forgotten her promise. Let us go through the open gate and run toward Thunder Mountain."

A short while later the girl ran up to the pen and looked inside. The turkeys were gone! She ran after them as fast as she could. But they were already far ahead, on the plains below Thunder Mountain.

Still the girl kept running. At last she heard the turkeys gobbling. She called and called to them, but they only ran faster. And then they began to spread their wings. They rose into the air and flew up the side of the mountain.

The poor girl waved her arms in the air, but the turkeys did not come back. Then she looked down at her clothes. They had changed back into rags. She felt her hair, and it was hard again. She looked for her jewels, but they had all fallen off. The girl was just the same as she was before—ragged and poor.

Tired and crying, the girl returned to her village. And ever since that day, turkeys have run wild all up and down Thunder Mountain.

The Rainbow Goblins

Once there was a land that lived in fear of seven goblins. They were called the Rainbow Goblins, and each had his own color, which was also his name: Red, Orange, Yellow, Green, Blue, Indigo, and Violet. Yellow, being the craftiest, was their chief. The goblins lived on color—they prowled the valleys and climbed the highest mountains looking for rainbows, and when they found one, they caught it in their lassoes, sucked the colors out of it, and filled their bellies with its bright liquid.

Only one place in the land had never known goblin-fear—the hidden valley called the Valley of the Rainbow, where the great arches of color were born. There the animals still lived in paradise.

But the Rainbow Goblins had heard tales of this Valley, and their mouths watered whenever they thought of the feast that awaited them there; and so they gathered up their lassoes and their pails and set off.

With great effort, the goblins made their way over the jagged piles of rock that guarded the entrance. When the climbing became difficult, Yellow roared: "Don't lose heart, comrades! Think of the delicious colors ahead!"

The sun had almost set by the time they reached their goal—the very meadow where the Rainbow sprang to life. Immediately beneath the meadow they found a cave. "We'll spend the night here," the Yellow Goblin commanded.

When the moon rose and saw them warming themselves around the fire they had lit, it shouted out in alarm: "The Rainbow Goblins are in the Valley!" The trees and the bushes took up the cry, and the flowers and the grasses and the animals and the waters passed it on, and by midnight the evil tidings had spread throughout the Valley.

The goblins could hardly contain their excitement. "Soon all the colors of the Rainbow will be ours," Yellow gloated. "We'll snatch it as it rises," said Green, "when the colors are still fresh and creamy." The Blue Goblin cackled, "Look at the roots dangling from the walls. They're straining to hear our plans. A lot of good it will do them, or their friend the Rainbow."

Finally, exhausted by their scheming, the goblins fell asleep. Outside, the moon shone on the mirror-like surface of the water, and its magical light was reflected into the cave.

Then all seven goblins had a wonderful dream—the same wonderful dream about the paradise of Rainbowland, where all you had to do was lie on your back and open your mouth and the most succulent colors dripped down your throat.

The dream went on and on, the greedy goblins drank and drank, and at dawn, just as their bellies were about to burst, they were awakened by a distant clap of thunder.

The goblins sprang to their feet and rushed to the mouth of the cave. "A storm, a storm!" Red shouted. "Look how the wind is driving it toward us!" Orange cried.

And all the goblins danced and pranced about in glee, for they knew that after the wildest morning thunderstorm comes the most beautiful rainbow.

Yellow was so proud of his plan of attack that he went over it again, while each goblin tested his lasso. "Red, don't forget that you must seize the left flank." "And I move in on the right," the Violet Goblin burst out excitedly. Before the last roll of thunder had faded from the Valley the goblins took up their pails and lassoes and marched single file out of the cave.

The sight that greeted them when they reached the meadow took their breath away. The rising arch of the Rainbow, so rich with color and promise, almost blinded them. Trembling with excitement, Yellow finally managed to give the signal to attack.

The goblins swung their lassoes around and around, and hurled them into the sky. But in that same instant the Rainbow vanished, as if it had been swallowed up by the earth. The goblins were dumbfounded. Nothing like this had ever happened to them before. They stared up at their empty out-stretched lassoes . . . which a second later snapped back at them. Indigo wept, Blue cursed, Yellow stumbled, Orange cried out, "Treachery!" Violet tumbled to the grass, Red raged; but the more they thrashed about, the more tangled up they became in their own lassoes, until they had snarled them-selves into a grunting, groaning mass of goblins on the ground.

As they lay there helplessly, a flood of color poured forth from all the flow-ers of the meadow. "The flowers," screamed the Blue Goblin, "the flowers!" He had suddenly remembered the dangling roots he had made fun of in the cave. Through their roots the flowers had heard the goblins' plans, and they had devised a counterplan to save the Rainbow. The moment the attack was launched, the flowers had drained the colors of the Rainbow into their petals, and as soon as the goblins became ensnared in their own lassoes, the petals had let loose the deluge.

So the goblins drowned in the colors they had come to steal, and no one in the Valley wept for them.

The Rainbow itself was reborn more magnificently than ever. Out of grati-tude, it lifted up the flowers that had saved it and transformed them into glittering dragonflies and butterflies and splendidly plumed birds.

But since that time the Rainbow has become more cautious. Now when it arches across the sky it is careful not to touch the earth anywhere. No matter how you try to sneak up on it, you can never come to the place where it begins or ends.

Glossary

Abstraction   A quality expressed separately from the actual person or thing that possesses it.

Acting   Playing a part in a drama. Acting is a cumulative and culminating experience involving sensory awareness, rhythm and movement, pantomime, oral communication, improvisation, and playmaking. Acting is usually geared towards an audience.

Actor   A person who plays a role in a drama.

Art disciplines   Music, Drama/Theatre, Dance, and the Visual Arts.

Audience   At least one person, perhaps thousands, who observe a player or players as they engage in an action that imitates life.

Ceremony   An act or series of acts performed in some regular order.

Character   A person, animal, or entity in a story, scene, or play with specific distinguishing physical, mental, and attitudinal attributes. Character portrayal is likely to be more complex and unpredictable than role portrayal.

Collaboration   Interrelation of different elements of drama/theatre discipline in creating an artwork.

Color   Visual sensation dependent on the reflection or absorption of light from a given surface.

Common   Shared by all or many.

Communication   The process of interacting verbally or nonverbally with another person or persons to share meaning.

Contrast   To set in opposition for the purpose of comparing.

Costume   Clothes that performers wear in a presentation.

Creative dramatics   Drama as a learning tool, with the emphasis on the development of the individual through a problem-solving process. Creative dramatics can be extended to include formal performance.

Culture   All the traditions, customs, and history of a particular group of people.

Dance   An all-inclusive term referring to aesthetics of movement; physical movement with expressive intent, using rhythm and tempo.

Dialogue   The words spoken by the actors in a drama.

Director   In a theatrical presentation, the person who is responsible for bringing all the elements of the production together.

Drama   A term used broadly to mean the reenactment of life situations. Drama does not require an audience.

Dynamics   The comparative loudness and softness in music or speech.

Evaluation   Appraising personal efforts as well as reflecting on and making judgments about efforts of others.

Fable   A story that teaches a lesson, especially one in which animals act like people.

Fairy tale   A story about supernatural beings.

Fantasy   The use of imagination to create strange, unusual, or nonrealistic characters or settings.

Film   The photographed performance usually shown in a movie theater (or from videotapes on the home VCR). It involves no audience/performer interaction.

Five senses   Any of the bodily faculties of perception or feeling (sight, sound, touch, smell, taste).

Five W's   *Who* refers to roles and characterizations. *What* refers to dramatic action. *Where* refers to setting, locale, environment. *When* refers to time in history, time of year, and time of day. *Why* refers to motivation.

Folklore   Customs, beliefs, stories, and sayings of a people handed down from generation to generation.

Folk tale   Any story about a culture passed on from generation to generation. Myths, fairy tales, fables, and legends can also be folk tales.

Hearing   The sensation of receiving information through the ears.

"How and why" story   A story created by a particular culture to explain the cause of a natural phenomenon.

Human machine   Moving and connecting bodies in such a way that the shapes create a living machine with moving parts and sounds.

Imagery   Something perceived naturally and spontaneously by the senses.

Imagination   The power of forming mental pictures of things not present to the senses. A mental image; a creation of the mind.

Imitate   To follow, as a pattern, model, or example; to copy.

Improvise   To act out without previous study or preparation. To act out without a script.

Intent   The theme or message of a play.

Legend   A greatly exaggerated story relating to the history of a culture, usually about people who really lived. Legends have usually been embellished by the teller.

Line   In dramatic arts, the words spoken by one of the characters in a dramatic presentation; in visual arts, an identifiable path of a point moving in space that can vary in width, direction, and length.

Magic box   A device to stimulate imagination, of pretending to have in front of one an imaginary box, from which anything—an object, an idea, or a character to "put on"—may be taken.

Magic If   Drama/theatre term referring to "What would happen if...?"; releasing the imagination to create a story with limitless possibilities.

Marionette   Puppet worked by strings.

Mechanical sound All those sounds made in the environment by manufactured objects.

Mind's eye Imagination.

Moral   (adj.) Relating to the distinction between right and wrong. (n.) The lesson taught by a particular story.

Motivations   Those reasons or occurrences in a scene, story, or play that prompt a character to act and react in a certain way.

Music   The art discipline using voice and/or instruments for listening and performing pleasure that incorporates melody, tonal quality, rhythm, and tempo.

Myth   A story used to explain the unknown.

Natural sound   All those sounds in the environment made by things that exist in nature.

Nonverbal   Without words.

Pantomime   Acting without words; using the body to express an idea, an emotion, or a character.

Perception   The process, act, or faculty of using the senses (sight, sound, touch, smell, taste, and kinesthesia) to gain information from the physical environment.

Pitch   Referring to the range of sound in music (high or low); sounds that can be repeated.

Play   A story written in dramatic form; that is, scripted, with dialogue and stage directions written out for the actors.

Playmaking   A term used to describe dramatic activities that lead to improvised drama with a beginning, middle, and end, employing the general form and some of the elements of theatre. The product may or may not be shared with others.

Plot   The "what happens" in a story: the beginning, which involves the setting, the characters, and the problem they are facing; the middle, which tells how the characters work to solve the problem; and the ending, in which the problem is resolved.

Prop, or property   Any object used on the stage (excluding scenery, lights, and costumes) such as furniture, utensils, ornaments, and personal possessions. Personal props are those objects used by the actors on stage, and stage props are those items on stage that help create the setting.

Puppetry   The animation of artificial figures (not always, but often, doll-like figures), often jointed, by means of the hand, by a rod or rods, by strings, or by a combination of means.

Radio   A public broadcasting medium that is an auditory experience only. There is no audience interaction with the performers.

Repetitive   Reoccurring.

Role playing   Improvising movement and dialogue by putting oneself in another's place in a particular situation.

Rhythm   A regular pattern of sound, as in music and poetry, or of action as in dancing, measured by units of time. These pulses or beats can be organized in sets (meter) which move in twos or threes or multiples and combinations thereof.

Scene   A small part of a play or dramatized story. *Scene* often refers to the location of the story or play.

Scenery Set pieces and backdrops that help the audience visualize the location of a dramatic performance.

Script The written form of a dramatic performance; the lines and movements written out for the actors in a stage, film, radio, or television show.

Seeing The sensations perceived with the eyes.

Sensory awareness Heightened perception of the physical sensations of touch, sight, hearing, taste, and smell; and of emotional states.

Sensory recall To be able to recall various stimuli associated with persons, places, or things.

Sequence The order in which events happen or tasks are performed.

Shadow play A drama produced by placing a light source behind actors or puppets, so that the audience sees only their shadows on a screen.

Shape A two-dimensional area or plane that may be organic or inorganic, free-form or geometric, open or closed, natural or manufactured. In dance and drama, *shape* can refer to the configuration of the body or the space in which the actors move.

Smell Sensations perceived by the nose that distinguish odor.

Sound Vibrations in the air that stimulate the auditory nerves and produce the sensation of hearing.

Story The narrative form of a series of events with an identifiable beginning, middle, and end; or plot.

Storyteller A person who uses the oral tradition to pass on information.

Structure The way the theme or message of a play is carried out in performance.

Symbol That which stands for and represents something else.

Taste The sensations perceived by the tongue that distinguish flavor.

Technique The physical skills essential to the performer; the integral training of the body.

Television (TV) The electronic public broadcast medium with live or prerecorded shows that is both an auditory and a visual experience. There is no audience/performer interaction.

Tempo The rate of speed of a composition or section of music.

Texture   The surface quality of materials, either actual (tactile) or visual.

Theater   The place where a performance or show is held for an audience to see. It can be an outdoor setting as well as an enclosed building.

Theatre   All the collaborative activities needed to present a dramatic work to an audience.

Theme   The central thought, idea, or significance of action with which a play or story deals.

Time   Measurement of sound or movement involving breathing time, emotional time, and metric time (beat, pulse, accent, tempo, duration).

Universal   Including all; present everywhere.

Values   The social principles or standards held by an individual, class, or culture.

Visual arts   Those creations that may still be viewed when the artist's work is finished.

Visualization   The formation of a mental image or picture; something in the mind's eye.

Resources

CHILDREN'S LITERATURE

Aardema, Verna. *Bringing the Rain to Kapiti Plain*. Dial Books for Young Readers, 1981.
A story with a cumulative rhythm relating how Ki-Pat brought rain to the drought-stricken Kapiti Plain.

Addison-Wesley Big Book Program. *The Three Little Pigs* and *The Little Red Hen*. Addison-Wesley Publishing Company, Inc., 1988, 1989.
Big Book versions of the two traditional classics have attractive illustrations and predictable text.

Alexander, Martha. *When the New Baby Comes I'm Moving Out*. Dial Books for Young Readers, 1979.
Oliver is going to be a big brother, and doesn't like the idea one bit.

Aliki. *Corn Is Maize: The Gift of the Indians*. Crowell Junior Books, 1976.
The history and life cycle of the plant are described.

_____. *Feelings*. Greenwillow Books, 1984.
Brightly colored cartoons show children experiencing different feelings in everyday settings. Good for parent/child interaction or classroom use.

_____. *My Five Senses*. Crowell Junior Books, 1989.
The facts about the five senses are simply presented and humorously illustrated.

Andersen, Hans Christian. *The Princess and the Pea*. Clarion (Houghton Mifflin Company), 1979.
In this well-loved fairy tale, the princess is tested to find out if she is a real princess. The test is to see whether she feels the pea that has been placed under the twenty mattresses she sleeps on at night.

Anderson, Joan. *Christmas on the Prairie*. Clarion (Ticknor & Fields), 1985.
This book recreates Christmas eve and Christmas morning in 1836 in the fictional village of Prairietown, Indiana, to show how the holiday was celebrated at that time.

Anderson, Joy. *Juma and the Magic Jinn*. Lothrop, Lee & Shepard Books, 1986.
Juma likes to sing and draw, but dislikes school until the Jinn of the Jar teaches him to do better.

Aruego, Jose, and Ariane Dewey. *We Hide, You Seek*. Greenwillow Books, 1979.
Readers are invited to find animals hidden in their natural habitats.

Asbjornsen, Peter Christen, and Jorgen Moe. *Norwegian Folk Tales*. Pantheon Books, 1982.
This collection of Norwegian folktales contains an undertone of realism and folk humor.

Baylor, Byrd. *Hawk, I'm Your Brother*. Macmillan Publishing Company, 1976.
Determined to learn to fly, Rudy adopts a hawk, hoping that their kinship will bring him closer to his goal.

Bowden, Joan. *Why the Tides Ebb and Flow*. Houghton Mifflin Company, 1979.
In this folktale, explaining why the sea has tides, an old woman threatens to pull the rock that holds the water in the sea.

Brenner, Barbara. *Wagon Wheels*. HarperCollins Children's Books, 1978.
A black family moves from Kentucky to Kansas in the 1870s, experiencing both hardships and family support. This book is based on historical fact.

Briggs, Raymond. Virginia Haviland, ed. *The Fairy Tale Treasury*. Dell Publishing Company, 1986.
This is a collection of 32 of the world's best-loved fairy tales, including the *Emperor's New Clothes, The Frog Prince, Gone is Gone,* and *The Sun and the Wind.*

Broekel, Ray. *Your Five Senses*. Children's Press, 1984.
The importance of the five senses and the structure of the sense organs and how they work are discussed.

Brown, Marcia (illus.), and Charles Perrault. *Cinderella*. Scribner (Macmillan), 1981.
This is a free translation from the French of the classic tale.

Brown, Marcia. *Stone Soup*. Scribner (Macmillan), 1979.
Townspeople reluctantly cooperate when three traveling soldiers trick them into providing their best ingredients "to make soup from a stone."

Browne, Anthony. *Bear Hunt*. Doubleday & Company, Inc., 1990.
This book invites the listener to participate in the story telling through movement and sound effects.

Caduto, Michael J., and Joseph Bruchac. *Keepers of the Earth: Native American Stories*. Fulcrum Publishing, 1988.
This collection of stories presents the first Americans as observers of the natural world. It also contains imaginative exercises to teach children how to be observers themselves (includes "Loo-Wit, The Fire Keeper" and "How Grandmother Spider Stole the Sun").

Carpenter, Frances. *Tales of a Korean Grandmother*. C.E. Tuttle, 1972.

Cauley, Lorinda Bryan, retold and illustrated by. *Goldilocks and the Three Bears*. Putnam Publishing Group, 1981.

Chase, Richard, ed. *The Jack Tales*. Houghton Mifflin Company, 1943.
These Anglo-American folktales are told in the dialect and style of the mountain country of North Carolina.

Cheney, Alan Glenn. *The Amazon*. Franklin Watts, Inc. 1984.
The author describes the geography of the Amazon region, its history, its economy, and its people.

Chocolate, Deborah M. *Kwanzaa*. Children's Press, 1990.
The story of the African-American celebration that lasts seven days from Christmas to New Year.

Coatsworth, Elizabeth. *Away Goes Sally*. Macmillan Publishing Company, 1934, Elizabeth Coatsworth Beston, 1962.
This book contains the poem, "Swift Things Are Beautiful." The images in the poem are of occurrences in nature.

Cohen, Miriam. Lillian Hoban, illus. *Will I Have a Friend?* Macmillan, 1967.
A little boy worries that he will not find a friend on his first day at nursery school.

Cole, Joanna, ed. *New Treasury of Children's Poetry*. Doubleday, 1984.
Over 200 poems are arranged from very simple poems to more complex for older readers. The emphasis is on 19th and 20th Century American poets.

Crump, Fred, Jr. *Cinderella: A Retold Story*. Winston-Derek, 1990.
This newly translated story of the classic tale of Cinderella is excellent for reading aloud.

Dalgliesh, Alice. *The Courage of Sarah Noble*. Macmillan, 1986.
A young girl finds the courage to go alone with her father to build a new home in the wilderness.

Dayrell, Elphinstone. *Why the Sun and Moon Live in the Sky*. Houghton Mifflin Company, 1990.
In this old African folktale, the storyteller explains how the Sun, the Moon and the Water came to be where they are.

de Paola, Tomie. *Nana Upstairs and Nana Downstairs*. Putnam Publishing Group, 1973.
A small boy enjoys his relationship with his grandmother and his great-grandmother, and he learns to face their inevitable death.

De Rico, Ul. *The Rainbow Goblins*. Thames Hudson, Inc., 1978.
Seven goblins have adventures looking for a rainbow. (This book is out of print, but the story may be found in the Appendix of *Center Stage*.)

Ernst, Lisa Campbell. *Sam Johnson and the Blue Ribbon Quilt*. Lothrop, Lee & Shepard, 1983.
While mending the awning over the pig pen, Sam discovers that he enjoys sewing the various patches together, but he meets with scorn and ridicule when he asks to join a quilting club.

Fox, Mem. *Hattie and the Fox*. Bradbury Press (Macmillan), 1988.
Hattie, a big black hen, discovers a fox in the bushes, which creates varying reactions in the other barnyard animals.

Frank, Josette, ed. Dagmar Wilson, illus. *Poems to Read to the Very Young*. Random House, Inc., 1988.
The poetry in this book is particularly suitable for reading aloud.

Freeman, Don. *Corduroy*. Viking, 1968.

This story is about a teddy bear's search through a department store for a button. His search ends when he finds a friend—Lisa, a little black girl.

_____. *A Pocket for Corduroy*. Viking, 1978.

The teddy bear Corduroy goes in search of a pocket and has some adventures in a laundromat.

Gackenbach, Dick. *Harry and the Terrible Whatzit*. Clarion (Ticknor & Fields), 1984.

Harry's mother goes to the cellar and does not return right away. Harry goes down to search for her and confronts the terrible two-headed whatzit.

_____. *Hattie Be Quiet, Hattie Be Good*. HarperCollins Children's Books, 1977.

Galdone, Paul. *Jack and the Beanstalk*. Clarion (Ticknor & Fields), 1982.

This is the familiar tale of Jack and the adventures he has while trying to regain his possessions from the giant.

_____. *The Little Red Hen*. Clarion (Ticknor & Fields), 1985.

A little hen works for her lazy housemates, but has the last laugh.

_____. *Rumpelstiltskin*. Houghton Mifflin Company, 1985.

A funny little man offers to spin straw into gold for a young girl. When she becomes a princess, he comes to take away her child.

_____. *The Three Bears*. Clarion (Ticknor & Fields), 1985.

The illustrations for this familiar story of the three bears and their visitor are colorful and humorous.

_____. *The Three Billy Goats Gruff*. Clarion (Ticknor & Fields), 1981.

The author retells and illustrates the classic Norwegian folk tale.

_____. *The Turtle and the Monkey*. Clarion (Houghton Mifflin Company), 1983.

This Philippine folk tale is the story of a turtle who fools a greedy monkey.

Goble, Paul. *Buffalo Woman*. Bradbury (Macmillan), 1984.

A young hunter marries a female buffalo who has taken the form of a beautiful maiden. When his people reject her, he must pass several tests before being allowed to join the buffalo nation.

_____, retold and illustrated by. *Iktomi and the Boulder: A Plains Indian Story*. Orchard Books (Franklin Watts, Inc.), 1988.
The author/artist's distinctive style and bright colors enhance this story of the Sioux Indian trickster, Iktomi.

Grimm, Jacob, and Wilhelm K. Grimm. *Snow-White and the Seven Dwarfs*. Farrar, Straus, & Giroux, Inc., 1987.
The beautiful princess escapes her wicked stepmother by hiding in the forest cottage of seven dwarfs.

Hamilton, Virginia. *In the Beginning: Creation Stories from Around the World* (contains "The God Brings Fire to Man"). Harcourt Brace Jovanovich, 1988.
Twenty-five creation myths are retold in language true to the original. Contains 42 full-page illustrations and a commentary on each story's origin.

Hausherr, Rosemarie. *The One-Room School at Squabble Hollow*. Four Winds Press (Macmillan), 1988.

Haviland, Virginia. *North American Legends*. Philomel Books (Putnam Publishing Group), 1979.
The author tells some of the stories of legendary American characters.

Hazen, Barbara Shook. *Even If I Did Something Awful?* Atheneum (Macmillan), 1981.
A mother declares she will always love her child, no matter what happens.

Heine, Helme. *Friends*. McElderry (Macmillan), 1982.
Good friends always stick together. Charlie Rooster, Johnny Mouse, and Fat Percy the Pig examine the idea.

Heyer, Marilee. *The Weaving of a Dream: A Chinese Folktale*. Viking, 1986.
When the beautiful tapestry woven by a poor woman is stolen by fairies, her three sons set out on a magical journey to retrieve it.

Hodges, Margaret. *The Wave*. Houghton Mifflin Company, 1964.
A wise old Japanese farmer burns his rice fields to warn the people in the village of an approaching tidal wave.

Hugue, Michael. *Aesop's Fables*. Henry Holt & Company, 1985.
A collection of animal stories with morals for humans by the Greek writer, Aesop.

Kaufman, Joe. *Joe Kaufman's Big Book About the Human Body*. Golden Books (Western Publishing Company), 1987.

Keats, Ezra Jack. *John Henry: An American Legend*. Alfred A. Knopf, Inc., 1987.
Strong illustrations enhance the adventures of the famous African-American folk hero, John Henry.

_____. *The Snowy Day*. Viking Children's Books, 1962.
A small boy's delight and enjoyment of snow in the city is shown in vibrant illustrations.

Kellogg, Steven. *Johnny Appleseed*. William Morrow Junior Books, 1988.
Johnny Appleseed planted apple trees all over the country, and became an American legend.

Kipling, Rudyard. *How the Camel Got His Hump*. Frederick Warne & Company, Inc., 1988.
This is one of the famous *Just So* stories of Rudyard Kipling.

Kraus, Robert. *Leo the Late Bloomer*. Crowell (HarperCollins Children's Books), 1971.
Leo, a young tiger, finally blooms under the anxious eyes of his parents.

La Fontaine, Jean de. *The Lion and the Rat*. Oxford University Press (reprinted in paperback), 1987.
The moral of this story is that small creatures can be useful friends to large creatures.

_____. *The North Wind and the Sun*. Oxford University Press, 1987.
Though her father seeks to protect her from all unpleasant things, this young princess begins to listen to the wind outside of the castle calling her to new adventures.

Lasker, Joe. Kathleen Tucker, ed. *Nick Joins In*. Albert Whitman & Company, 1980.

When Nick, confined to a wheelchair, enters a regular classroom for the first time, he and his classmates must resolve their initial reactions.

Levinson, Riki. *Touch! Touch!* Dutton, 1987.
Grandma tells about her mama's journey to America years ago by boat.

Lionni, Leo. *A Color of His Own*. Pantheon, 1976.
A sad little chameleon wants to have his own color like other animals.

_____. *It's Mine*. Knopf, 1986.
Three selfish frogs quarrel over who owns their pond and island until a storm makes them value the benefits of sharing.

Lobel, Arnold. *Frog and Toad Are Friends*. HarperCollins Children's Books, 1970.
Five tales—Spring, The Story, A Lost Button, A Swim, and The Letter—recount the adventures of two best friends, Frog and Toad.

Louie, Ai-Lang. *Yeh Shen: A Cinderella Story from China*. Philomel Books (Putnam Publishing Company), 1990.
A young Chinese girl overcomes the wickedness of her stepsister and step-mother to become the bride of a prince.

Marshall, James. *George and Martha One Fine Day*. Houghton Mifflin Company, 1982.
Here are five new episodes about the friendship of two hippopotamuses.

Martin, Jr., Bill, and John Archambault. *Knots on a Counting Rope*. Henry Holt & Company, 1987.
A grandfather and his blind grandson, Boy-Strength-Of-Blue-Horse, reminisce about the young boy's birth, his first horse, and an exciting horse race.

Matsuno, Masako. *A Pair of Red Clogs*. World Publishing Company, 1960.
A little Japanese girl tries to hide the fact that she has cracked her new red clogs. (This book is out of print, but is worth looking for in the library.)

McDermott, Gerald, retold and illustrated by. *Anansi the Spider: A Tale from the Ashanti*. Henry Holt & Company, 1972.
An African tale about the travels of Anansi the Spider and how he is saved by his six sons from a terrible fate.

_____. *Arrow to the Sun: A Pueblo Indian Tale*. Viking Penguin, 1974.
An adaptation of the Pueblo Indian myth explains how the spirit of the lord of the sun was brought to the world of men.

McPhail, David. *First Flight*. Joy Street Books/Little, Brown & Company, 1987.
A naughty teddy bear, in contrast with his well-behaved owner, ignores all the rules and disrupts their first airplane trip.

Monjo, F.N. *The Drinking Gourd*. HarperCollins Children's Books, 1983.
A little boy discovers that his family's farm is a stop on the Underground Railway.

Musgrove, Margaret. *Ashanti to Zulu: African Traditions*. Dial Books for Young Readers, 1976.
A collection of vignettes introduces 26 African peoples.

Ness, Evaline. *Sam, Bangs, and Moonshine*. Henry Holt & Company, 1966.
This story relates the experience of a little girl as she learns to tell the difference between make believe and real life.

Osborn, Steve. *Story Chest: Treasured Tales from Many Lands*. Addison-Wesley Publishing Company, Inc., 1992.
   "The Bremen Town Musicians": A folk tale from Germany about four animals who frighten away robbers in an attempt to become musicians.
   "The Deer and the Tortoise": In this folk tale from Brazil about a race between a deer and a tortoise, the tortoise outsmarts the deer.
   "The Poor Turkey Girl": In this Zuni version of the Cinderella story, the girl who tends the turkeys forgets the promise she has made them.
   "The Stonecutter": The main character in this Japanese folk tale is granted his wishes several times to be more powerful, until at last he is satisfied to be a stonecutter again.

Parramón, J.M., et al. *Five Senses*. Barron's Educational Series, Inc., 1985.
These are five 32-page booklets that give information on each sense (sight, hearing, smell, taste, touch), including activities.

Politi, Leo. *The Nicest Gift*. Scribner (Macmillan), 1973.
A little boy loses and then find his dog at Christmas mass. (This book is out of print, but may be in the local library.)

Pryor, Bonnie. *The House on Maple Street.* William Morrow Junior Books, 1987.
During the course of 300 years, many people have passed by or lived on the spot now occupied by a house numbered 107 Maple Street.

Rackham, Arthur (illus.). *Aesop's Fables.* Outlet Book Company.

Ringgold, Faith. *Tar Beach.* Crown Publishers, Inc., 1991.
Cassie, the narrator of *Tar Beach,* flies over Harlem and the George Washington Bridge, dreaming of what she can give her father. The page borders are reproduced from the author/artist's story quilt.

Ross, Tony. *I'm Coming to Get You!* Dial Books for Young Readers, 1984.
After eating all the planets in outerspace, a horrible monster gets a big surprise when it comes to earth and tries to capture a little boy.

Rossetti, Christina Georgina. *Sing Song: A Nursery Rhyme Book.* Macmillan, 1924.
The author's poems include "Who Has Seen the Wind?"

Scarry, Richard. *Richard Scarry's Best Story Book Ever.* Golden Press (Western Publishing Company), 1980.
This book has action illustrations.

Sendak, Maurice. *Where the Wild Things Are.* HarperCollins Children's Books, 1988.
The Caldecott medal winner tells a perceptive story in very few words as Max imagines himself king of the wild things.

Shah, Idries. *World Tales,* Johnson Reprint Corp., 1979.
These tales demonstrate extraordinary similarities among stories that have been told throughout history, all over the world (includes the story "The Blind Ones and the Matter of the Elephant").

Shute, Linda. *Momotaro the Peach Boy.* Lothrop, Lee & Shepard Books, 1986.
An old man and an old woman find a boy in a peach one day. He becomes their loving son, who eventually sets off to fight the terrible *oni.*

Silverstein, Shel. *Giving Tree.* HarperCollins Children's Books, 1964.
A warm story tells how a little boy grows older with his favorite tree.

Spier, Peter. *Gobble, Growl, Grunt.* Doubleday, 1988.
Over 600 animals are identified by name, sound, and illustration.

Steig, William. *Amos and Boris.* Farrar, Straus, & Giroux, Inc., 1971.
Amos the mouse and Boris the whale have little in common except that they are both mammals and save each other's lives.

Steptoe, John. *Mufaro's Beautiful Daughters: An African Tale.* Lothrop, Lee & Shepard Books, 1987.
Mufaro's beautiful daughters, one bad-tempered, one kind and sweet, go before the king, who is choosing a wife.

_____. *Stevie.* HarperCollins Children's Books, 1969.
Robert wishes Stevie, a houseguest, would go away. When he does, Robert realizes how much fun they had together.

Stevenson, James. *When I Was Nine.* Greenwillow Books, 1986.
James remembers taking a trip through several states in the West with his family during his ninth year.

Stories Series. *William Tell.* Raintree Publications, 1989.
William Tell defies the cruel tyrant by shooting an apple off his son's head with his bow and arrow.

Suzuki, David, with Barbara Hehner. *Looking at Senses.* John Wiley & Sons, Inc., 1991.
How the sense organs work is simply explained, with projects for experimenting with each one. Activities that need adult supervision are marked with a special logo.

Szilagyi, Mary. *The Adventures of Charlie and His Wheat-Straw Hat.* Putnam Publishing Group, 1986.
Money is short in seven-year-old Charlie's Appalachian home during the Civil War. There is not enough to buy the straw hat that Charlie wants to wear to school, so he and his grandmother make one.

Turkle, Brinton. *Thy Friend, Obadiah.* Puffin Books, 1982.
A seagull befriends a Quaker boy, much to the boy's embarrassment. It is not until the boy has helped the bird that he can accept the bird's friendship.

Viorst, Judith. *Alexander and the Terrible, Horrible, No Good, Very Bad Day.* Atheneum (Macmillan), 1972.

From the time Alexander gets out of bed and trips on his skateboard till the moment he goes to bed in the pajamas he doesn't like, and the cat doesn't even want to sleep with him, nothing good happens.

_____. *Alexander Who Used to Be Rich Last Sunday.* Aladdin (Macmillan), 1987.

Although Alexander and his money are quickly parted, he comes to realize all the things that can be done with a dollar.

Wear, Jean Simmons. *Jean Rides a Tiger to Washington.* Regina Books, 1990.

The true story of a young girl who accompanies her mother and senator father to Washington, and in one incident, sees President Coolidge award Charles Lindbergh the Congressional Medal of Honor.

Williams, Vera B. *A Chair for My Mother.* Greenwillow Books, 1982.

A child, her waitress mother, and her grandmother save dimes to buy a comfortable armchair after all their furniture is lost in a fire.

Wood, Audrey. *The Napping House.* Harcourt Brace Jovanovich, 1984.

In this cumulative tale, a wakeful flea atop a number of sleeping creatures causes a commotion with just one bite.

Yarbrough, Camille. *Cornrows.* Coward (Putnam Publishing Group), 1981.

This book explains how the hairstyle of cornrows, a symbol in Africa since ancient times, can today in this country symbolize the courage of outstanding African Americans.

Yashima, Taro. *Umbrella.* Puffin Books 1977.

A little Japanese girl living in New York City is given an umbrella and a pair of red rubber boots. When rain falls, beautiful colored pictures capture the child's joy and excitement.

Yolen, Jane. *The Girl Who Loved the Wind.* Crowell Junior Books (HarperCollins Children's Books), 1972.

Though her father seeks to protect her from all unpleasant things, a young princess is intrigued by the voice of the wind that tells her of the world beyond the palace walls.

Zemach, Harve. *A Penny a Look: An Old Story*. Farrar, Straus & Giroux, Inc., 1971.
Two brothers set out to capture a one-eyed man in order to display him in the marketplace.

Zion, Gene. *Harry the Dirty Dog*. HarperCollins Children's Books, 1956.
A white dog with black spots hates baths and runs away. He returns in such a sad condition that even the family members do not recognize him.

ADULT REFERENCES

Aesop. Joseph Jacobs, ed. *Fables of Aesop*. B. Franklin, 1970.
These adaptations of 82 of Aesop's best-known fables include a brief history of the fables.

Allen, Judy, Earldene McNeill, and Velma Schmidt. *Cultural Awareness for Children*. Addison-Wesley Publishing Company, 1992.
Activities from eight cultures for preschoolers through primary age children are described in this resource book for teachers. Units include African and African-American Cultures, American Indian Cultures, Chinese and Chinese-American Cultures, Japanese and Japanese-American Cultures, Korean and Korean-American Cultures, Mexican and Mexican-American Cultures, Thai Cultures, and Southeast Asian Cultures.

Ancona, George. *Dancing Is*. Dutton Children's Books, 1981.
These are illustrations and historical perspectives of dances from the world community.

Banks, James and Cherry, eds. *Multicultural Education: Issues and Perspectives*. Allyn & Bacon, 1989.

Barth, Edna. *Turkeys, Pilgrims and Indian Corn: The Story of the Thanksgiving Symbols*. Clarion (Ticknor & Fields), 1981.

Behrens, June. *Fiesta! Ethnic Traditional Holidays*. Children's Press, 1978.

Bettelheim, Bruno. *The Uses of Enchantment: The Meaning and Importance of Fairy Tales*. Random House, Inc., 1989.
A distinguished researcher analyzes fairy tales and their meanings and explores their role in children's psychological development.

Bierhorst, John. *Doctor Coyote: A Native American Aesop's Fables.* Macmillan, 1987.

The coyote is featured in each of these Aztec interpretations of Aesop's fables.

Brooks, Charles V.W. *Sensory Awareness: Rediscovery of Experiencing Through the Workshops and Classes of Charlotte Selver.* William Morrow, 1986.

Brown, Tricia. *Chinese New Year.* Henry Holt & Company, 1987.

Text and photographs depict the celebration of Chinese New Year by Chinese Americans living in San Francisco.

California State Department of Education. *Drama/Theatre Framework for the California Public Schools.* 1974.

Center Stage: Creative Dramatics Supplement, © 1993.

Planned to complement *Center Stage* lessons, the kit contains 2 audiotape cassettes of 4 folk tales each and scripts for the folk tales, a book of playscripts of some of Aesop's fables, and 4 posters. Available from Dale Seymour Publications.

Cook, Marcy. *Cooperative Learning Seminars and Materials.* California Elementary Education Association, 3420 Kashiwa St., Ste. 3000, P.O. Box 3168, Torrance, CA 90510

Currell, David. *The Complete Book of Puppet Theatre.* B & N Imports, 1986.

This superbly comprehensive book is invaluable for anyone interested in making and performing with puppets.

de Paola, Tomie. *Mother Goose Story Streamers.* Putnam Publishing Group, 1984.

De Regniers, Beatrice, et al, eds. *Sing a Song of Popcorn: Every Child's Book of Poems.* Scholastic Inc., 1988.

This collection includes 115 poems by a variety of well-known authors.

Dodson, Fitzhugh. *I Wish I Had a Computer That Makes Waffles: Teaching Your Child with Modern Nursery Rhymes.* Oak Tree Publications, 1978.

This is a collection of contemporary nursery rhymes with tips for writing original rhymes and a note to parents.

Dudley, Louise, et al. *The Humanities.* McGraw-Hill, Inc., 1978.
An overview of the humanities shows how aesthetics relate to a humanities program.

D'Zamko, Mary Elizabeth, and Hedges, William D. *Helping Exceptional Students Succeed in the Regular Classroom.* Parker, 1985.

Espy, William R. *A Children's Almanac of Words at Play.* Potter (Crown), 1988.

Faber, Doris, and Harold Faber. *Great Lives: American Government.* Scribners (Macmillan), 1988.
This excellent resource is also suitable for children.

Frank, Josette, ed. Dagmar Wilson, illus. *Poems to Read to the Very Young.* Random House, 1988.

Glazer, Tom. *Tom Glazer's Treasury of Songs for Children.* Doubleday, 1988.

Gottschalk, Bernice, Lola Kearns, Mary Taylor. *Art in Special Education Project of Pennsylvania.*

Graham, Alma. *Discovering Maps: A Young Person's World Atlas.* Hammond, Inc., 1991.

Grater, Michael. *The Complete Book of Paper Maskmaking.* Dover Publications, 1967.
A do-it-yourself guide gives detailed instructions with photos and diagrams for making masks of animals and people.

Greene, Carol. *Holidays Around the World.* Children's Press, 1982.
The different holidays that are celebrated around the world are explored in this volume. It includes activities and historical perspectives.

Gregor, Josef. *Masks of the World.* Ayer Company Publishers, Inc., 1968.
This is a complete historical and pictorial survey of many kinds of masks from around the world.

Haley, Gail E. *A Story, A Story.* Atheneum (Macmillan), 1970.
This book recounts how most African folktales came to be called "Spider Stories."

Hamilton, Edith. *Mythology*. Little, 1942.
This collection of stories about gods and heroes in mythology is a handy reference.

Hammill, Donald D., and Nettie R. Bartel. *Teaching Children with Learning and Behavior Problems*. Allyn & Bacon, Inc., 1975.

Hann, Judith. *How Science Works: One Hundred Ways Parents and Kids Can Share the Secrets of Science*. RD Associates, 1991.

Hansen, Merrily P. *Now Presenting: Classic Tales for Readers Theatre*. Addison-Wesley Publishing Company, Inc., 1992.
Illustrated scripts for six plays are accompanied by teaching suggestions, simple costume patterns, and ideas for props.

Haring, Norris G. *Behavior of Exceptional Children*. Charles E. Merrill Publishing Company, 1978.

Hazen and Smith. *Cut and Make North American Indian Masks*. Dover Publications.
Patterns and assembly instructions for eight full-color masks based on authentic North American Indian designs.

Head, Sydney, and Christopher Sterling. *Broadcasting in America, Brief*. Houghton Mifflin Company, 1991.

International Wildlife magazine

Ireland, Norma Olin, compiled by. *Index to Fairy Tales, 1949 to 1972: Including Folklore, Legends and Myths in Collections*. Scarecrow, 1973.
This collection analyzes over 400 stories.

Jaffe, Roberta. *The Growing Classroom*. Addison-Wesley Publishing Company, Inc., 1991.
Science is taught through hands-on gardening in this resource book for elementary teachers.

Janson, H.W., and Anthony F. Janson. *History of Art for Young People*. Harry N. Abrams, Inc., 1987.
This book contains illustrations, pictures of "The Thinker," "David," and "Bird in Space," an index to artworks, and art history.

Kipnis, Claude. Neil Kleinman, ed. *The Mime Book*. Meriwether Publishing Ltd., 1988.
Mime techniques, history, and activities are outlined for students.

Locker, Thomas. *The Young Artist*. Dial Books for Young Readers, 1989.

Madhubuti, Haki R. *Kwanzaa: A Progressive and Uplifting African-American Holiday*. Third World Press (revised), 1987.

Mask Prints.
Portfolio of twelve 16-by-12-inch fine art reproductions of masks from all regions of the world. Crystal Productions, Box 2159, Glenview, IL 60025.

McCaslin, Nellie. *Creative Drama in the Classroom*. Longman, 1990.
Practical activities involve young students' creative dramatics.

McNamara, Barry E. *The Resource Room: A Guide for Special Educators*. State University of New York Press, 1989.

Mettler, Barbara. *Creative Dance in Kindergarten*. Mettler Studios, 1976.
Explanations and activities involve students in creative movement.

Moores, Donald F. *Educating the Deaf: Psychology, Principles, and Practices*. Houghton Mifflin Company, 1987.

Nash, Grace C. *Creative Approaches to Child Development with Music, Language and Movement*. Alfred Publishing, Inc., 1974.
This book incorporates the philosophies and techniques of Orff, Kodaly, and Laban.

National Arts Education Research Center. *A Framework for Multicultural Arts Education*. National Arts Education Research Center at New York University, 1989.
This 57-page booklet for educators outlines approaches and organization of content for multicultural education in the arts, and lists extensive references.

National Geographic. All the World's Animals. Torstar Books, 1985.

National Wildlife magazine

Nature Conservancy magazine

Paasche, Carol, et al. *Children with Special Needs in Early Childhood Settings.* Addison-Wesley Publishing Company, 1990.
For mainstream educators who teach special needs children, this resource book helps identify and provide for children with different special needs in the regular classroom, from birth through age 7.

Parker, W. Oren. *Stage Lighting: Practice and Design.* Holt, Rinehart and Winston, Inc., 1987.
The author explains techniques for making scenery for the theater and proper lighting techniques used in the theater.

Raboff, Ernest. *Art for Children Series.* Harper & Row Junior Books, 1988.
Look for information on individual artists under book titles by their names.

Russell, Joan. *Creative Dance in the Primary School.* (3rd ed.) Northcase House (Princeton Book Company).
The author suggests many creative movement activities for young children.

Scholl, Geraldine T. *Foundations of Education for Blind and Visually Handicapped Children and Youth: Theory and Practice.* American Foundation for the Blind, 1986.

Seeger, Ruth. *American Folk Songs for Children.* Doubleday, 1980.

Simmens, Rene. *The World of Puppets.* Elsevier Phaidon, 1975. (This book is out of print, but the many clear illustrations and photographs make it worth looking for in the library.)

Simon, Seymour. *Oceans.* William Morrow Junior Books, 1990.

Sivin, Carole. *Maskmaking.* Davis Publications, 1987.
The history of masks is followed by detailed instructions of how to make both easy and complex masks.

Spolin, Viola. *Improvisation for the Theater: A Handbook of Teaching and Directing Techniques.* Northwestern University Press, 1983.
This sophisticated publication by a renowned author contains theater games, improvisational exercises, and sensory awareness activities geared for all ages.

Sullivan, Charles. *Imaginary Gardens: American Poetry and Art for Young People.* Harry Abrams, 1989.
This is an excellent resource that combines poetry with historic photographs.

Thesaurus and Dictionary for Children. Thorndike-Barnhart, HarperCollins, 1991.

Townsend, Lucy, and Jane B. Moncure. *Creative Dramatics for Young Children.* The Child's World, Inc., 1986.
This book has many age-appropriate activities that give the teacher a working knowledge of how to use creative dramas with young children.

Van Cleave, Janice Pratt. *Biology for Every Kid: One Hundred and One Easy Experiments That Really Work.* John Wiley & Sons, Inc., 1989.
This book has easy experiments that work.

Von Boehn, Max (Josephine Nicoll, tr.). *Dolls and Puppets.* Cooper Square, 1966.
The history of puppets is presented with over 500 illustrations of puppets.

Simon & Schuster Staff. *Why Things Are: A Guide to Understanding the World Around Us.* Simon & Schuster Trade, 1988.

MUSIC

Coltrane, Alice. *Alice Coltrane with Strings.* Impulse ABC Records.

Environments/3. Atlantic Records.
This cassette has psychoacoustic sounds and dusk. It was recorded at New Hope, Pennsylvania.

Flamenco, Cameo Classics. Moss Music Group.

Grusin, David, and Lee Ritenour. *Harlequin.*

Harris Eddie. *The Electrifying Eddie Harris.* Atlantic.

Hodgson, John. *Improvisation.* Methune & Company, Ltd.

Ivanovici, J. *Waves of the Danube.*

Ives, Burl. *Burl Ives for Boys & Girls,* MCAC.

Jazz Crusaders. *Jazz Crusaders 1.* Chisa Records.
The up-beat instrumental jazz music on this record is very effective for movement activities. The selection, "Put It Where You Want It" is especially good.

Jones, Quincy. *Sounds*. A & M Records.

Kellaway, Roger. *Creation*. Van Gelder Studios.
This record of instrumental songs has a very up-beat tempo. It would be good for warm-up movement activities.

Kubrick, Stanley. *2001 (A Space Odyssey)*. MGM Records.
This movie soundtrack can be used as background for environments to stimulate story development. A selection especially good for dramatizations is "Also Sprach Zarathustra."

Lawrence, Esther. *Songs of the Jewish People*. T-KUME Records.

Living Sound Effects. Vol. 1. Bainbridge Entertainment Company.
This cassette includes the sounds of a rainstorm, a waterfall, and noises in a restaurant and a bowling alley.

Living Sound Effects. Vol. 3. Bainbridge Entertainment Company.
This cassette includes the sounds of water, a jig saw, an air conditioner, and a shower.

Living Sound Effects. Vol. 7. Bainbridge Entertainment Company.
This cassette includes the sounds of a city street, an indoor pool, barking dogs, a door slamming, and train whistles.

Metheny, Pat. *Pat Metheny Group (Offramp)*. ECM Records.
These moody jazz selections are good for movement activities and for creating different settings for dramatizations.

Miscellaneous Sound Effects. Vol. 10. Total Records.
This cassette includes the sounds of clocks, doors, horns, bells, and Halloween night.

Simon, Paul. *Graceland*. Warner Brothers Records, Inc.
This is a popular recording combining Simon's European style of music with South African indigenous music.

Sousa, John Phillip. *The Stars and Stripes Forever*.

Strauss, Richard. *First Waltz Sequence*. Moss Music Group.

Stravinsky, Igor. *The Rite of Spring*.

Vangelis. *Chariots of Fire*. PolyGram Records.
This movie soundtrack offers many selections suitable for movement activities and creating different environments for story dramatizations.

Vivaldi, Antonio. *Four Seasons*. Academy of Ancient Music, Christopher Hogwood. Decca Records, 1984.

Williams, John. *Close Encounters of the Third Kind*. Arista Records.
This movie soundtrack offers a wonderful variety of music for creating environments that stimulate the writing of imaginative stories.

VIDEOTAPES

Arts Abound Series. Great Plains National: Affiliated with the University of Nebraska-Lincoln, 1985. Sixteen 15-minute programs on the arts.

The Playwright. Two playwrights—one established, the other a 14-year-old girl—talk about their source of inspiration and creative process.

The Musician. The Metropolitan Brass Quintet shows the fun and beauty of their music making.

The Actor. A young actor is followed through rehearsal to final production, showing the effort that goes into characterization and character development.

The Painter. An artist talks about his artistic growth and development from early figurative drawing to his current highly colorful abstract work.

The Sculptor. A sculptor is concerned with the way her sculpture fits into a park, sidewalk, or college campus. The program examines the stages that a sculpture goes through before it is finished.

The Dancer. A dance company demonstrates the power, inventiveness, and humor of modern dance. The company choreographer shows how ideas and feelings are translated into dance/movement.